TAKE ME WITH YOU

TAKE ME WITH YOU

a memoir

Carlos Frías

ATRIA BOOKS
New York London Toronto Sydney

ATRIA BOOKS

A Division of Simon & Schuster, Inc.
1230 Avenue of the Americas
New York, NY 10020

First Atria Books hardcover edition November 2008

ATRIA BOOKS and colophon are trademarks of Simon & Schuster, Inc.

For information about special discounts for bulk purchases,
please contact Simon & Schuster Special Sales at
1-800-456-6798 or business@simonandschuster.com.

Designed by Claudia Martinez

Manufactured in the United States of America

1 3 5 7 9 10 8 6 4 2

Library of Congress Cataloging-in-Publication Data

Frías, Carlos.
Take me with you : a memoir / Carlos Frías.—1st Atria Books hardcover ed.
p. cm.
Includes bibliographical references and index.
1. Frías, Carlos—Travel—Cuba. 2. Frías, Carlos—Family.
3. Cuba—Description and travel. 4. Cuba—Social conditions—21st century.
5. Cuban Americans—Cuba—Biography. I. Title.
F1765.3.F75 2008
972.9104'64—dc22
2008004412

ISBN-13: 978-1-4165-5951-1
ISBN-10:   1-4165-5951-5

Dedicated to all my girls, who soften my heart and hearten my spirit: Christy, Elise, Amelia, and Catalina. Thank Heaven for little girls.

The "Cast"

In the United States

Fernando Frías, my father

Iraida (Iris) Frías, my mother

Christine (Christy), my wife

Elise, my oldest daughter

Amelia, my middle daughter

Catalina, my youngest daughter

Rogerio, my brother

Abuelito Pepe and Abuelita Elisa, my next-door neighbors who
helped raise me

Abuela Teresa, my father's mother

Tío Ciro, my father's brother

Tío Felipe, my father's brother

Tía Teresita, Felipe's wife

Felipe, my cousin, Tío Felipe's son

Lily, my cousin, Tío Felipe's daughter

Tío Rafael, my father's brother

Tío Ramón, my father's brother

Ray, my cousin, Tío Ramón's oldest son

The "Cast"

Marcus, Ray's oldest son

Jesus, my cousin, Tío Ramón's middle son

Frank, my cousin, Tío Ramón's youngest son

Isabella, Frank's youngest daughter

Tía Teresa, my father's oldest sister

Amado, my cousin, Tía Teresa's son

Tía Dania, my father's sister

Danita, my cousin, Tía Dania's older daughter

Solange, my cousin, Tía Dania's younger daughter

Kristie, my *Quinces* cousin

In Havana

Abuelo Francisco (Pancho) Frías, my father's father

Ricardo, Tío Ramón's long-lost son in Marianao

Gisela, Ricardo's wife

Magaly, Ricardo's daughter

Julio, Ricardo's son

Ana Ester, my father's daughter

Maribel Sánchez, Ana Ester's mother

Mario, my father's cousin in Marianao

Lucía, Mario's younger daughter

Lídia, Mario's older daughter

María, Mario's wife

Alina, Tío Felipe's old girlfriend, a friend of the Frías family

The "Cast"

Manuela, Alina's sister

Magda, Alina's niece

Rosita, a waitress at Mi Buchito Oriental

Raúl, Rosita's husband

Maira, Rosita's daughter in Miami

Miguel, my father's close friend

Teresita, a waitress at Mi Buchito Oriental

Armando and Marina, Alina's close friends

Nelson and Antonia, a nurse and doctor/drivers

José, bellboy/driver/confidant

Martín, driver

In Cárdenas

Abuelo Bartolomé, my mother's father

Tía Sofía, my mother's sister

Pipo, Tía Sofía's husband

Jorge, my cousin, Sofía and Pipo's oldest son

Barbara, Jorge's youngest daughter in the United States

Luis, my cousin, Sofía and Pipo's middle son

Luisito, Luis' son

Ernesto, my cousin, Sofía and Pipo's youngest son

Elena and Tomás, Jorge's oldest daughter and her husband

Isabel, Tomás and Elena's daughter

Luisa, Elena's older daughter

The "Cast"

Andrea and Joaquín, Jorge's middle daughter and her husband

Tía Hortencia (Tata), my mother's late sister

Tío Julio, my mother's late brother

Juli, my cousin, Tío Julio's son in the United States

Diani, my cousin, Tío Julio's daughter in the United States

Maribel, my mother's friend from adolescence

Emma, my mother's friend/graduation godmother

Lolita, a close family friend

Santiago, driver of the Blue Bird

Silvio, Jorge's friend/backyard baker

Christy's family

Ileana, my mother-in-law, Christy's mother

Maria Laura, Ileana's cousin

Raciel, Maria Laura's husband

Pablo, Maria Laura's older son

Normita, Maria Laura's daughter

Enrique, Maria Laura's younger son

Ismael, Normita's boyfriend

Estela, Ileana's mother, Christy's grandmother

TAKE ME
WITH YOU

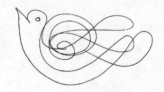

PROLOGUE

I dial and hang up. Dial and hang up, before I finally let it ring through.

There is no easy way to say it, so when I hear his voice, I just blurt it out:

'Papi,' I'm going to Cuba!

The first phone call I make when I learn I'm going to Cuba is to my father.

His silence comes as I knew it would. What is no more than a moment of quiet echoes between us. It resounds and rebounds through the void that separates a father and a son. To me, an empty chasm of the unknown. To him, a space treacherous with memories of a life that was. I can hear the white noise of the grocery store behind him clearly through his cell phone as he ponders my words. It is a moment, but it is enough for both of us to contemplate what this means.

I know how my father feels about returning to Cuba: As long as Fidel Castro is in power, he can never, will never go back.

"How can I go back? How can I go and spend my money there? How can I support a system that kicked me on the way out of my own country?"

The memory of his words rings in our silence like distant church bells.

I have never questioned his mind-set. It extends to most Cuban-Americans of my generation. To those of us born in the United

1

States, Cuban only through the anecdotes of our parents, the idea of visiting Cuba is like visiting Heaven—or Hell. We presume we will go there one day, but we never imagine actually doing so.

I have the chance to pass through the Pearly Gates. But my father is my St. Peter. He stands guard as he always has, and I know I cannot go on without his blessing. I can hear his thoughts, see them, really, swirling in the air between us as if he has cast a spell and is sending me the images telepathically, considering my worthiness, gauging my readiness to know what he knows:

He is looking out the window of the commuter plane on the morning of November 5, 1969—a day after his forty-second birthday—watching a world of lush green and red clay streak by in a blur as the wheels leave the ground and his connection to his home is severed forever. He leaves behind everything he knows, everything that defines him: His childhood on the family farm in the far eastern province of Oriente, where he grew up one of eleven children. His life as a businessman in the capital city of Havana, where he and his four brothers, the *guajiros* from the country, made a name for themselves—the Frías Brothers of Marianao— as café owners and entrepreneurs. His time in jail as a political prisoner for attempting to "abandon" a fledgling revolution. His slavery—digging latrines, burning sugarcane—in an agricultural camp for two years to earn his freedom, to earn the right to be called a *gusano*, a worm, and have to form a new life in exile, never to see his country again.

All of that, the good and the bad, it was his home. His *Patria*. His Fatherland. The images flow between us. And now, for the first time in thirty-seven years, someone from our family is asking his permission to visit this place.

His own son.

"Do you swear it—*me lo juras?*" he finally says.

'*Sí, Papi.*' I swear.

Another pause, another lifetime of memories washes over us in an instant.

"Well, then . . ." he says. "Take me with you."

A warm spot in the center of my chest, first the size of a pinpoint, grows, grows until I can feel the heat radiating from the tips of my fingers, the ends of my toes, and from the hairs that are standing on the back of my neck. St. Peter smiles, steps aside, and waves me through.

For the Cuban boy not from Cuba, growing up in Miramar and not Miami, Florida, felt a little like living in exile itself.

So when he visited his Miami family at his Abuela Teresa's, something came alive in the boy in a way that a child cannot articulate. It meant seeing the aunts and uncles and cousins who shared his history. It felt like going home. This ritual was religion, yet so much richer and truer to the boy than his rehearsed prayers and genuflections in Catholic school.

The drive south seemed to take hours. The boy would lie on the white leather seats in the back of his father's wine red Cadillac as orange streetlights passed overhead and someone read the news in Spanish over the AM radio. He nodded off, dreaming of the games he and his cousins would play, trying to remember all the stories from school he could share with them.

His father had a key to Abuela's house, and the boy never asked why. He only knew that when the lock tumbled and the door swung open, the smell of freshly brewed Cuban coffee, the murmur of Spanish being spoken, and the laughter of other children was like Christmas. The boy kissed all of the aunts and uncles and let Abuela squeeze him to her fill. His attention, though, was already on the laughter of the other children, their squeals and arguments erupting, and he would shoot out of her arms to join their games.

All of his cousins had their own siblings, and this was not lost on the boy, an only child who was the youngest of them all. Whether they knew it or not, he adopted them as his own. It was with them, not in school, that he learned to play the games of his youth, freeze tag and four corners, all the games parents cherish for their moments' peace. The cousins would talk and play and fight and joke until late, until the boy recognized the jangle of his father's key chain, signaling it was time to go back into exile.

But even in exile, the boy found a sanctuary for his culture. Spanish was all he spoke to his parents and to his Abuelita Elisa and Abuelito Pepe, the next-door neighbors who cared for him while his parents worked at the jewelry store they owned in Carol City. His Cuban *abuelitos* were not actually blood, but they helped raise the boy until he was a teenager. And whenever anyone asked him about his grandparents, they were the ones who always came to mind: The tall, blond, blue-eyed Gallego Pepe, who could fix a sprinkler or make an entire chair and table set out of PVC pipe; the soft, round Elisa with the kind smile and a cackle for a laugh who gave the boy the most soothing, rhythmic pats on the back when they hugged; the television always tuned to a *telenovela* or the Spanish evening news. The boy sat between his *abuelitos* with watered-down Cuban coffee, munching on crisp Cuban crackers, and he was exactly where he wanted to be.

About the time his parents were supposed to get home from the jewelry store, the boy and his Abuelito Pepe would sit on the porch overlooking the four-lane boulevard in front of their house and count how many Volkswagen Beetles sped by. They each picked a side, and usually one lane had hands down more Beetles. And the boy believed him when Abuelito joked that the exterminator, *el fumigador*, was chasing them away.

When the lights from his parents' car flashed onto the drive, the boy kissed Abuelito, ran inside to kiss Abuelita, and put away the folding chair where he had been sitting—a place for everything and everything in its place, Abuelito would urge.

At home, the boy would shower quickly, race to his parents' bedroom and cuddle next to his father, lying in the crook of his arm. Every night, his father had a new bedtime story in Spanish. Sometimes, they were ones his father's father used to tell him, like the one about the three dogs who save their master from a lion he stumbles across in the grasslands. (Were there lions in Cuba? The boy suspended his disbelief.) Other stories, his father made up that very night. Many nights, the boy would say, "*Papi*, tell me again the one about the parrot that goes on the long trip," and his father would look at him with total confusion. Once a fable left his mouth, it was gone, stored only in the boy's memory.

Most of the time, as they lay in the dark, the boy's father would just talk about growing up on the farm in Cuba with his ten brothers and sisters. There was the time when, as kids, he and his younger brother Ramón snuck out to the tobacco houses and made off with a foot-long stogie. They sat under a shady avocado tree and smoked the cigar until they were green and retching. Then, there was the time he was fourteen and took a cart loaded with tomatoes into the city to sell—alone. Told that the town was overloaded with tomatoes, he got back on the train and kept going to another town—all without telling his parents. He sold all the tomatoes in a day and stayed there the rest of the week with family. The boy lies very still when he hears his father sniffle as he recounts how his mother ran out to meet him, tears in her eyes, when he opened the door to the little farmhouse late the night he returned.

These are the nights that would shape the boy, the stories he remembers best. When his father would recount the arc of his life, from growing up on the farm to how each of the five brothers ended up in Havana, and how they became the Frías Brothers of Marianao. This was his father's favorite story. He would tell it not just at night but while he taught his boy to play chess, a game he learned in prison. They retraced the stories while they picked grapefruits or mangoes off the trees in their backyard. His father relived this story the boy's entire childhood. Still does. Still yearns.

The boy remembers watching the Olympic Games one day and seeing the Cubans prepare to box the Americans. In this match, the boy is torn between two undefeatable opponents. He knows them both as the red-white-and-blue. The boy is Cuban and he is American and he has no answers.

Who do I root for, 'Papi'?

"You always have to cheer for the United States. Cuba, that's our *Patria*. But this is the country that has given us everything," his father tells him. As the fight goes on, he listens to his father and uncles speak of Fidel Castro in epithets: *Fidelijueputa . . . Fideldesgraciado . . .* and the boy has his answer.

When the boy becomes a young man, he looks back and knows that his life, his experiences, were not like those of the other boys and girls at Fairway Elementary. And yet, not like those of his cousins or other Cuban-American kids down south, either. His cousins grew up under what he imagined were the bright lights of Little Havana. He felt, sometimes, that they were more Cuban than he. The young man watched those lights from a distance as a boy and felt the separation. Like his father, he, too, yearns.

In college, he learns about literature and theater and culture, about dorm life and outdoor concerts on the lawn. But at night, he swears he can still see the lights of Little Havana when he looks into the southern sky. There is a girl there, too, and in her is reflected his pull to family, to culture, *their* culture. And in every way, large and small, she is everything that is home.

The young man graduates and spends the formative years of a journalism career traveling the South as a sportswriter. This new life suits him and that girl in college who agreed to be his wife. The young man and young woman make a life for themselves far from home, in Atlanta, yet when they talk about visiting their families in South Florida, they speak of "going home." He longs for his culture.

On trips home, they soak it up. One day, they might be at the wedding of one of his cousins. The next, at the birthday party for a cousin's child. If they work it out just right, all the cousins might get together to play poker or go to the beach. He is still the "little one," still just happy to be part of this world. His wife's grandmother sends him back to Atlanta with a box of Cuban pastries, guava and cheese *pastelitos*, their aroma filling the airplane cabin. He and his wife are revived, and they cannot deny the pull of home.

That diffuse feeling crystallizes in the ice-blue eyes of their daughter Elise, their first child, whom they name after his late Abuelita Elisa, a journalist in her time, ahead of her time, and the first writer he ever met. When the young man looks into his daughter's eyes, he knows what is next for them all. Six months later, he is working out a deal to leave his job of nearly six years for a paper back home. Family calls.

For the young man is still the boy lying in his father's arms at night, dreaming of Cuba.

I am still that boy.

My cell phone rings just after 10:00 A.M., as I knew it would. It is who I think it will be: the office.

All night, my wife and I had been glued to the television. News anchors read and reread statements that came out of Havana the afternoon of Tuesday, August 1, 2006. Fidel Castro is gravely ill. He has had surgery. He has handed over control to his brother, Raúl. Experts pontificated on the future of Cuba as they awaited signs of the dictator's fate. The news stations aired clips of Castro stumbling and falling on his face after giving a speech a few years ago. Cuban exiles and their children filled the streets of Little Havana, waving Cuban flags and cheering as if the Marlins had won another World Series. Speculation fueled speculation. Day turned to night. My television barely rested.

And now, my phone is ringing. Although I'm a sportswriter, I know I am one of the few on staff at *The Palm Beach Post* who speaks fluent Spanish, and they know I am also Cuban. I know why the office is calling. Naturally, they would want me to write some kind of "reaction" story on Castro's illness, maybe go down to Calle Ocho and interview some old-timers.

I thought I'd be getting a call this morning, I tell my editor as I'm driving to the bank, running errands.

Let me guess, you want me to go down to Little Havana.

"We want to send you to Cuba," he says.

Silence. This time, from me.

"Hello?" he says.

Are you effing kidding me?

My boss has a good sense of humor, but he is not joking.

I am going to Cuba.

I have to race to the office, about sixty miles north of my home in Pembroke Pines, to be briefed, loaded with equipment, given a wad of cash to last me two weeks, paired with a photographer, and sent off to Cuba for twelve days, he says. And I leave *today*. I whip the car around and break every speed limit on the way home. I call my father, and his words echo in my mind, "Take me with you . . . Take me with you . . ." as I hang up and call my wife to give her the news. We laugh and scream, and our nervous energy could power this city.

"This is your book," Christy says, her voice becoming suddenly solemn.

I know.

I must have sounded like I wasn't paying attention.

"No, *Lind*"—she calls me *Lind*, short for *lindo*, pretty boy— "this . . . is . . . your . . . book."

This is my book. I say it out loud. The girl, my muse, her instincts never fail her. She knows what this means to me. To us. To all of us.

"I'm *so* jealous, but I'm *so* excited for you. I wish I could go with you. . . .

"This is your book, *Lind*."

This is my book.

DAY ONE

There is a shaking, a nervous vibration at my core.

I close my eyes in the taxi as it zips down Interstate 95 toward Miami International Airport. I try to rest after a night of endless shifting. But this involuntary shiver, this jumbling of my insides, shakes me into an uncomfortable wakened state. So I lean back and turn to watch traffic go by, the sky still in twilight, the road illuminated by red taillights and the orange glow of street-lamps. Most mornings, the interstate is a snarled mess, four lanes inching so terribly slowly as people make the commute toward downtown Miami. Today, we glide through and past traffic—Miami is a late-rising town—and I feel more and more like I am sitting in the cart of a roller coaster as it clack, clack, clacks its way up the steep incline toward an inevitable plunge. There are no brakes. No turning back. I close my eyes and breathe.

What exactly does a Cuban jail cell look like? When I shut my eyes, the image insists on forming. I have a cartoon image in my head. Dank walls, covered in a film of cold humidity, made of large stone blocks, as if part of a castle dungeon. There is a small window, about the width of a cinder block, high on the wall, so you can see only the cloudy gray sky outside between rusting iron bars. Inside, I'm dressed in khaki pants and a brown striped pullover, sitting on the cold, hard floor. For how long, there is no telling. I force my eyes open to keep the thoughts at bay. It's nonsense. I am a journalist and an American-born U.S. citizen at that. The Cuban government won't want to start an international incident—Elián in reverse—by holding a reporter against his will. I tell myself this, over and over. It is little comfort. There is no way to know how I will be received. Whether I will be discovered. Whether I will truly step on Cuban soil at all.

I try to ignore the shaking and focus on the doing. Walk up the concourse, check in at the ticket counter, head for the international gates. I do it all over again, but not as I did a week ago. I do it robotically, trying to detach myself from the conversation my mind is having with itself: *You are never going to get in. Not last time. Not this time.*

There is time to kill at the gate. I look around the rows of blue chairs with chrome arms as other passengers squirm to get comfortable enough to close their eyes and feign sleep, and I try to join them. But the lights and the chairs and the cold, cold air prod me to stay awake. To keep my mind busy, I examine the other passengers, these travelers who are not the regular, early-rising business crowd, commuting on a shuttle to work, carrying leather briefcases and wheeled computer bags. Most here are adults, dressed the way you might expect to see recently arrived refugees on the streets of Little Havana. Few children are on this flight, and the room is as quiet as a library. Two men and a woman traveling together catch my attention as I twist myself into a comfortable position.

From under half-closed eyes I peek at one of the men, who looks to be in his early forties. He is wearing a new pair of dark blue jeans, white sneakers, and a FUBU T-shirt tucked into his pants. He exudes the air of a relatively young man, but his complexion seems aged beyond his years. Wrinkles crisscross his forehead, and his skin appears weathered and tan. He is stocky, with wide shoulders and a round belly pushing up against his shirt. He is traveling with another man, who looks younger. He is wearing black Tommy Hilfiger jeans, also with crisp, white shoes and a black T-shirt. He has a gold bracelet and a gold chain with a medallion of the Virgin of Charity, *la Virgen de la Caridad,* hanging on the outside of his shirt. This apparition of Mary is the patron saint for Cubans, who still have a shrine to her in Santiago, on the island's southeastern coast. Cubans in Miami have re-created this grotto to her, also near the water, in Coral Gables. The woman traveling with these men wears a low-cut beige blouse with tight black pants. The many gold bangles on her arm jingle as she trans-fers items from a white plastic shopping bag to a Bloomingdale's Big Brown Bag. And I know why they are on this flight.

These are Cubans, most likely recent immigrants, going home to visit family. The concourse is full of them, and I wonder if their in-sides are shaking, too. Do they care that what they're doing is illegal, that the U.S. government could crack down on them for trying to get around the embargo by entering Cuba through a third country? I try to imagine my cousin Jorge on this flight, desperate because he is legally allowed to return to see his mother, my Tía Sofía, only once every three years. Should that be sufficient, that arbitrary determina-tion of how much contact is needed to satisfy a mother's love? That this gate is packed at such an early hour screams that it is not.

A gate agent calls out in Spanish that our flight is boarding, and I grunt as I extricate myself from my seat to grab my bags and get in line. All around me, others are picking up their bags, some of them large suitcases with their contents pushing against the nylon sides at odd angles. A crash and a tumbling sound make several of us turn around to see the woman I had been watching, whose shopping bag has torn open, its contents scattering out onto the carpet. A plastic, chrome-colored robot. Board games. A baseball glove. Several children's shirts folded over but still on hangers. The man with the weathered face drops the Big Brown Bag stuffed with T-shirts and jeans and helps her repack. The unofficial Flight of Charity—from Miami to Havana, via Cancún, Mexico—is now boarding, and my fellow passengers are loaded with relief pack-ages. Inside the plane, they push and tuck and force their carry-ons into the overhead compartments.

As I stow my neatly packed belongings, I wonder if they will make me stand out too much. These other visitors, who come loaded with dollars and supplies, are exactly what the Cuban gov-ernment wants. But what would it make of me, an unregistered foreign journalist floating unescorted throughout the island, es-pecially at a time like this, with Cuba on high alert after its leader of forty-seven years has given up control for the first time? A passenger heading to his seat finally forces me to move, and I realize I have been frozen in the aisle, lost again in the conversation my mind can't stop having with itself.

I settle in and stare out the window to a risen sun that is casting a warm red-orange glow. The flight attendant is reading her safety statement in Spanish, and then in heavily accented English, but I barely pay attention. I close my eyes and pray as we rumble down the runway, as I always do on takeoff. Pray that I have made at least one positive contribution to the world. Pray that my children will remember that I love them. Pray until the plane levels off and my mind stops spinning with crash scenarios. I start to pray, too, that God will let me set foot on Cuban soil, but I stop myself. The Almighty doesn't take requests, I know, because prayer didn't help the last time I was on this flight. A *ding* in the cabin says we've reached our cruising altitude, and I notice that the quivering inside of me has been replaced by a machinelike impassiveness.

I am not going to get my hopes up, not again.

As my mind tries to scold itself, louder and louder, I cannot help but hear it recount my last disappointment.

Less than a week ago, the day after Castro's announcement, I was on my way to Cuba, via Cancún, with three other journalists from *The Palm Beach Post*.

The same day I was told I was going to Cuba, I raced from Pembroke Pines to Palm Beach and back to make a 4:00 P.M. flight out of Miami International, a turnaround of about 150 miles. My wife started packing for me, knowing I was cutting things close, and when my parents called, I told them quickly what I needed: I asked my father to write down the names of all the people he still knew in Cuba and might have telephone numbers or addresses for. I also asked him to write the names and locations of the seven businesses he and my uncles had owned, because I planned to visit them. And I told my mother to write down the phone number for her sister, my Tía Sofía, my closest living relative in Cuba.

By the time I got home from the paper, two hours before my flight, my parents' blue Ford Escort was already parked in front of my home, a small, pale yellow ranch-style house with a brick front. The aroma of Cuban coffee filled the air, and my parents, sitting on the couch, started to stand as I came through the door. But I barely made eye contact as I rushed to finish packing.

Did you guys write down the information I asked you for? I yelled from the bedroom.

"We have it right here, *Papo*," my mother answered.

There was not much time to let this moment soak in. I tossed whatever clothing I thought I might need into my luggage. I know the people in Cuba go without all of the finer things, so I took mostly T-shirts and shorts and a pair of pullovers. I came wheeling out of the hall with my bags to find my parents and my wife standing next to one another, and for the first time, I allowed myself to feel my heart pound, pound as we looked at one another with knowing smiles.

My father and mother handed me three scraps of paper. On one piece, my father had written me instructions: Ask for Felipe's old girlfriend, Alina, who lives near La Plaza in Marianao, where three of the main businesses were. Tell her to take you to see our cousin Mario, my friend Miguel, and Rosita, who used to work for us.

Felipe's old girlfriend? 'Papi,' are you sure about that?

"She's like family," he said, "and she knows all the old names and places." There was no time to argue, no time to let insecurity set in. As I hugged my mother, I could feel her seizing up as she tried to hold back tears.

Don't worry, 'Mami,' I can take care of myself.

She nodded without speaking at first, then swallowed hard. She said she had already called my cousin Jorge, who, coincidentally, was visiting his mother, my Tía Sofía, in Cuba. She had already told him that I am his responsibility. And I could tell she would not rest until I returned.

"Enough, Iris, he knows how to take care of himself," my father told her in an effort to break the tension. We clapped a strong hug, kissed on the cheek, and shook hands, he continuing to hold my hand and look at me.

"*Coño, Papo*, you're going to visit my *Patria*," he said.

The look in his eyes, it was the same one he gave me the day he saw me off to college, like he knew something I didn't, that my life was about to change in a way I could not yet grasp.

I'll bring you back a bottle of rum, 'Viejo.'

I turned to Christy and held her close for a second, like it was just the two of us in the room.

That afternoon, I landed in Cancún, bought a ticket to Havana, and spent the night in a hotel waiting for my morning flight. From the room, I managed to make a long-distance call to Cuba to speak with my Tía Sofía. She sounded just as I had remembered: her voice high and a little squeaky, like a sonorous instrument slightly out of tune. And from her tone, I could tell she was smiling.

"Your mother already called here, and she is so nervous. But I told her not to worry. We're going to take great care of you," she said, and I hugged her with my voice.

I can't wait to see you, Tía. By tomorrow, we'll be that much closer.

In the morning, word came that Cuba had shut the door to incoming journalists. A team of our reporters was detained overnight before being sent back along with reporters from several other news organizations. We never saw them. Our bosses decided that two would try to go on, two would return to South Florida. Including me.

I called my Tía Sofía to break the news.

"God knows why He does things," she told me, and I am not at all sure of God's plans.

Soon, we were back at the Cancún airport, my colleagues going on to Havana, and I to Miami. I could have sworn, as the plane flew back over the Caribbean, that I saw the outline of an island in the distance. It might not have been Cuba, but it didn't matter. I pressed my hand to the window and rested my forehead against the glass, wondering if this really was as close as I would ever come.

Three *dings* release me from my mind's grip and bring me back to the cabin, where the hour-and-a-half flight is almost over as the plane approaches Mexican soil. Shortly, we will be landing in Cancún.

As I follow the signs toward Immigration, I make a wrong turn in the concourse and hear a voice call to me: *"Oye, mi sangre*—my brother—it's this way!"

I turn to see the man with the weathered face, smiling and waving me back the right way. He and his companions clearly have made this trip before. I follow them through the airport and to the ticket station, along a row of glass windows, where I buy my second ticket in a week bound for Havana. I pay for the nonrefundable twenty-five-dollar visa in cash that goes to the Cuban government.

I have about two hours to kill before I wait for the flight—giving me time to contemplate all the scenarios that might be. But I can barely focus, for of all my luggage, what weighs the most is the thin money belt strapped tight, tight to my waist. I lock myself in a bathroom stall so I can unclip the beige nylon belt, which has left red imprints on my hips and just below my belly button. I am carrying US$9,990 in tens, twenties, and fifties. American credit cards are not accepted in Cuba. Neither are traveler's checks, and hundred-dollar bills are looked at with suspicion. The only way to pay for things is in cold, hard cash. I wonder if this is what it feels like to drive an armored car. I break up the amount, keeping some in my backpack, some in my pocket, some in my wallet, and the rest in the money belt. No one else might notice the slightest bulge that to me feels as if it is radioactive, like everyone can see it glowing from beneath my pants. I have to get it out, *out* of my mind before I arrive in Cuba.

Several people told me it's good to have trinkets to give out to those I meet in Cuba; it's a kind gesture. But I am confused about what I should buy. A box of toy cars in the duty-free store catches my eye, and I can imagine giving it to a little boy. I grab a handful of souvenir pens with the word "Cancún" written on them, because they serve two purposes. Since I am not supposed to be a journalist, I haven't brought any pens or paper.

When the flight to Havana is called, my insides squirm back to life. I try to listen for voices within me, for the conversation looping endlessly in my head, but find that it has gone silent. *This,*

this is new. Instead, it is replaced by the sound of pounding, a gushing that I realize is the quickening of my heart. I don't want to let it break again. I might, after all, be stopped at Immigration in Havana. I might be turned right around, never having stood on Cuban soil. That may be the hardest frustration to bear. But it is too late. A sting tells me I have bitten one of my nails to the quick, and my hands are cold and clammy.

The forty-five-minute flight is a blur, and the plane climbs and descends before I have a chance to prepare myself.

I look out the window and I see it.

Cuba.

The deep blue ocean has become turquoise, a sea green blue. White sand quickly turns to lush vegetation as we fly east over the island. It looks like vast, empty farmland, and the earth is red, like the infield of a baseball diamond; it reminds me of hilly Georgia clay.

The landscape begins to change. The ground is now covered in houses and concrete. It looks like when I've flown into San José, Costa Rica, where the buildings are laid out with the natural flow of the land, not in a planned, organized grid. This is an old country, a colonial city. A place of history. And I know we have crossed into Havana.

The vegetation below opens up into a clearing, José Martí International Airport. The engines whine, the ground closes in, and I pray again as I anticipate the rumble of wheels touching down. We bounce, bounce onto the runway. We are in Cuba, I know, but the air in the cabin is still Mexican, and I wait to fill my lungs with their first breath of Cuba. The plane taxis toward a terminal, and the ground crew comes to meet us. They are dressed in olive drab fatigues. Cuban military. Immediately, I feel a stab in my stomach as the plane squeaks to a halt. We are led out of a Jetway toward Immigration, and I try to ignore the weakness in my legs, willing them forward. There are posters on a wall welcoming us to Cuba: a black-skinned girl with her hair in long pigtails jumping, a caramel-skinned young man with blue-green eyes playing the bongos. Most of the Cubans I have known in the United States are

European-looking, and I wonder what my countrymen will look like, an island full of Cubans, all of us sharing the same dialect of Spanish. It is then that I see the lines and the guards. Between me and Cuban soil are immigration agents in uniform.

The rest of the airport is walled off, and two agents stand in each of about ten cubicles. A soldier in a dress uniform waves me toward one of the posts, and I can feel my roll-aboard slip in my hands from the perspiration.

I come to a counter, which separates me from a man and a woman, who look to be in their late twenties, dressed in military attire. The woman is seated at a computer terminal, and a video camera is watching me from above. A constant red light says it's alive, examining me. I can feel my heart go from beating to pounding. I wipe my hand on my khaki pants to offer the man my passport, and I smile. *Try to smile,* I tell myself.

He is not smiling.

Nor is she.

When he sees the blue American passport, his eyes immediately flash up at me, and I can see him going over and over my name and place of birth: Miami, Florida.

"Carlos Frías," he says, rolling the *rs* exaggeratedly, enunciating every syllable. *"¿Hablas español?"*

His distrustful eyes jump from the passport to me. Passport to me. I have debated what to say at this moment for days, and even now I am not sure how to answer. My cousin Jorge said I should just feign being American. Talk to them in English the whole time. Separate myself as much as I can from being a Miami Cuban-American.

'Sí, hablo español,' I say finally, unable to play it any way but straight.

"Why have you come to Cuba?" he asks.

I've come to get to know the country.

"To know the country?" he says, screwing up his face as if I've just told him that two plus two equals five. He looks from the passport to me. Passport to me. I scramble to fill the silence.

Well, I, um, have some distant relatives here I'd like to meet. They're in Havana, I ad-lib.

"Well, then, you're not here to know the country. You're here to know *Havana*," he says tersely.

Um, right, 'claro,' well then, I guess I'm here to know Havana.

He looks from the passport to me. Passport to me. He whispers something to the blond woman seated next to him. She is punching information into her computer, her *café*-colored eyes going over a screen I cannot see, and I wonder if they can see the blood throbbing in my neck. Is my shirt visibly moving? My God, if they search me and find all this cash, what will they say? A Cuban-American, born in the United States, coming to Cuba after the recent illness of Fidel Castro, with ten grand on him? Oh God, they'll think I'm a spy! I look at the locked door to my left and wonder if I will make it to the other side. Or whether I even want to. A part of me just wants to get back on the plane.

"And what is your occupation in the United States?" he says, looking from the passport to me. Passport to me.

Busted, my mind comes to life to tell me.

I . . . comment on sports.

This is it. Rubber meets the road. If he thinks I'm here as a journalist, it all falls down. I decided I would say specifically that I opine on sports, not that I'm part of a newspaper or anything that would identify me as a reporter. But if they ask pointedly, I will not lie.

"Huh," he says, staring at the passport photo and squinting at me.

"For television?" he says. Passport to me. Passport to me.

No, not for television.

"Radio?" Passport to me. Passport to me.

No, not radio.

"Then what?" He's sounding impatient.

I write . . . for different publications about baseball, basketball, football. All sports, really.

It takes a moment for a smile to form on his lips.

"Sounds like a pretty fun job," he says.

He grabs a stamp and—*Bam-bam! Bam-bam! Bam-bam!*—marks the visa. He knows the drill: stamp the visa, not the passport. This way, there is no evidence that I have ever visited Cuba. The pounding startles me, and the door to my left begins to buzz.

"Proceed," he says, and the door unlocks.

I made it. Have I made it? I can't think, and I try not to rush, but my mind is spinning, spinning, spinning. And now, I have to wait at a stupid luggage carousel for my bag. I feel like, at any moment, someone will call to me from the other room and say there has been . . . a mistake. And instead of getting out of here, I am just waiting here, waiting for a bag that won't come, and there are agents dressed in drab all around me and I can't think straight and I try to stare only at the floor. *Come on, come on.* My bag is among the first ones out. I grab it quickly, too quickly. *Stay cool, stay cool,* I tell myself, as I slow my pace and head for the exit with my mind still jumbled.

It is warm in the lobby. If there is air-conditioning, it is not running. Lines of people are waiting along a chute at Immigration, and I hear excited cheers as family members receive their relatives. They are all smiling. And I find that I, too, am smiling, despite a still-exploding heart.

But I am still too close to the many Cubans dressed in military attire moving through the terminal. I hurry to find a booth to exchange $500, and I get back 410 Cuban Convertibles after Cuba's tax. At the airport curbside, a man in a blue uniform hails a cab for me. From a row of cars, a yellow-and-black, square-looking taxi pulls up. This Russian Lada looks like the kind of car a ten-year-old would draw in art class, a generic "car" as it were. I ask the driver to take me to the Hotel Plaza in Old Havana, one suggested by a colleague because it is both a historic, renovated building and central to the city.

The Lada winds up with a nasally hum and is off. Its windows are down, and I rest my right arm on the sill as the wind musses my hair. The driver and I are both quiet as the Lada stirs a gray-beige dust down a craggy, narrow road, and I find myself trying to recognize a land I feel I should know. Yet every detail is new, and I let them paint the image. The smell of diesel fumes in the air mixes with the metallic, rich country earth. An impossibly bright sun immediately heats my bare arm, reflects off a vastness of greenery that stretches in every direction. Air thick with humidity veils me in a thin layer of perspiration as the breeze envelopes me. I close my eyes and let it blow over and through me. And then I hear the driver pop in a cassette tape. I recognize the sappy soft rock: "How can we be lovers if we can't be friends? How can we start over when the fighting never ends? . . ."

Is this . . . Michael Bolton?

Yes, he says, turning around for a second to show me his excitement through arched eyebrows. Oh, how he loves American music, he says. This stuff is nice and soft, for long drives, he says. We have a twenty- to thirty-minute haul into the city. At home, though, he prefers the Police or Van Halen or Black Sabbath—he absolutely loves Ozzy Osbourne—something with a little more bite.

"You should see my collection of tapes at home," he says.

But recently his tapes are getting mixed in with his teenage son's pirated recordings of hip-hop, rap, and reggaeton. He just can't get into that stuff.

"He doesn't like Ozzy, can you believe that? I don't know what's wrong with that boy," he says, glancing back through his rearview mirror, shaking his head.

As we drive east and get closer to the city of Havana, we leave the lushness of the countryside behind.

Who lives here? I ask every few minutes, trying to get a sense of the neighborhoods as we drive through, whether these are working-class or upper-class.

"Just regular folks," he says every time. "Working folks."

We drive down tight streets, dust kicking into the air, between high-rises with rusting fire escapes hanging off their walls like twisted metal fingers. The walls of the buildings are cracked, chunks of concrete missing in parts. Fissures span the height of some buildings. There are stains, black like mold and others the color of rust, weeping down the sides. Laundered clothing waves in the breeze from the fire escapes and balconies. And I realize they are *all* working classes here.

Traffic builds, and more and more, I'm overwhelmed by the smell of diesel. As we reach the center of Old Havana, there is an anthill of activity. Buses and Ladas and American cars from the fifties. People filling the sidewalks, crossing the streets in the mid-afternoon sun. We circle a park where people are gathered, sitting on concrete benches and filing past a large, white statue of the father of Cuban independence, José Martí, *el poeta*, "the Poet," as Cubans call him. His right arm rises into the sun, huddled masses sculpted at the base of the monument beneath him. There are a pair of hotels facing this central park, and we stop at the Plaza at one corner.

The hotel where I am staying has been painted recently. It is not like one of those back-street buildings. New speckled peach tiles have been laid around the entrance. And inside, it reminds me of an ornate home of the Old South. Tiny, pastel, octagonal tiles form intricate patterns on the floor. Fluted columns lead to an array of plaster moldings on the ceiling. It is the kind of intense, detailed work you expect to see in the Old World.

I check in at the front, and they request my passport. They want to know how long I will be staying, because each day must be paid for up front, in cash, and I start with four nights. I ride up two floors on a squeaky elevator, and the doors clank and shimmy when they open to my floor. At the end of the hall is my simple room, about ten by ten, with a bed and a pair of black painted nightstands and a television on a table across from the bed. A floor-to-ceiling stained-glass window that has cracked in places and been repaired lets in a flood of natural light. The door slams shut behind me, and it is what's missing that finally lets me exhale: noise. I flop onto the bed, rustling the well-worn pink sheets, and stare up at the fifteen-foot ceiling. I feel a buzzing in my legs, as if they are still moving, and the sound of my only thought seems to echo in the cozy room:

I made it.

I pick up the phone on the nightstand, and it immediately begins to ring. An operator answers and says I must make all my calls from the lobby. Eventually I have to call the office, my wife, my parents, and my family here in Cuba, and I know I have to be on guard. We have all heard stories about lines being tapped, and even in my calls home, I can't let slip why I am really here.

Before it all starts, before I have to refer to Castro as the "Birthday Boy" with my bosses at the office, since he will be turning eighty in four days, I just want to rest here a few more moments and breathe. Breathe the air that is cool from the air conditioner in the window. Breathe, slowly, deeply, and I can't help but smile to be breathing the air in Cuba.

By the time I step outside, the sun is a sliver on the horizon.

Yet the streets are just as full as streetlamps begin to flicker their orange sodium lights. This city moves on, unhindered by nightfall. My stomach rumbles with hunger, and I decide to walk the streets to soak up the atmosphere and find a place to eat. I walk through the park with the Martí statue. Couples sit close on the benches in the near darkness. A pair of young men whistle at a pair of girls, who don't look to be older than sixteen, walking past me on the sidewalk in tight shorts, flip-flops, and mismatched, skimpy tops. The world is as alive at night as it is by day, its scenes illuminated by pockets where people are concentrated, like pointing a flashlight in the dark. I pass a line of people, a mass really, easily five hundred bodies waiting outside a movie theater. Some are sitting on the sidewalk, some leaning up against the theater, chatting in the dark. It is a locally produced movie about the life of the Cuban singer Beny Moré, and "it's terrible," one person I ask tells me, "but it's better than sitting at home."

I follow the lights, since there are few, and they lead me to Obispo Street, a corridor beautified for tourists. The cobblestone street and buildings on either side have been repaired, repainted, and stores reopened as magnets for dollars and euros. The long corridor leads to the famous seawall of El Malecón, and I am tempted to walk its length as salsa pours from the open windows and doors of a jazz club. But I am too tired, too dizzy from hunger and the infatuating swirl of Cuban Spanish being spoken from every corner. It is like a siren's song, and I feel drunk with my new surroundings, like a million beautiful voices are speaking at once, and I am powerless to make out the words.

When I find myself back at the mouth of Obispo, in front of a restaurant called El Floridita, I know this is where I must stay. A Cuban co-worker of mine at *The Post* who was stationed in a bureau in Havana asked me to do one thing for her, said that she could live Cuba through me if I would just have a daiquiri at El Floridita. This is where the drink was invented, and it was also a favorite haunt of the novelist Ernest Hemingway. I cannot resist the pull of a promise and prose.

Just inside the doors, a Cuban band is playing a jazzy, Afro-Cuban riff: *"Así me gusta que bailes, Marieta . . ."* the band sings as one plays the congas, one an upright bass, and another a trumpet. The lead vocalist, a thin but curvaceous Cuban woman of burnt coffee skin, sways with the beat, singing in a smoky, melodic voice. I sit at a table across from the bar so I can bathe in the music as I eat.

Tourists fill the restaurant, and I hear Argentine Spanish spoken at one end of the bar. A table of Europeans clink cocktails to my left, and the only Cubans in here are performing or serving drinks. Rich, velvety red drapes and tapestries cover the windows and walls, and a newly upholstered bench, where I sit, stretches along the back. A life-size bronze statue of Hemingway leans up against the bar in the corner, and I snap a photo for a pair of young Argentines.

My grumbling stomach directs me to the menu expectantly, but when I open it, there are none of the dishes I expect. There are, strangely, many different kinds of pizza. No Cuban food at all. None of the typical dishes, like *ropa vieja*, stewed shredded beef, or *arroz con pollo*, the dishes *Mami* made for me when I was a boy, food that defines a culture.

One item, though, stands out: a Cuban sandwich. My stomach seems to sigh with relief. As a boy, when I would go to my parents' jewelry store every day in the summer, I would always order a Cuban sandwich from the corner bakery. It is the quintessential Cuban meal: a delicious blend of sweet ham, roasted pork loin, Swiss cheese, pickles and mustard and mayo on soft, sweet bread, toasted in a press. But it stands out for another reason.

When a cousin of my wife's emigrated from Cuba eight years ago, they all went out that very night to a Cuban dive in Miami called Rio Crystal that makes great steak sandwiches. My brother-in-law joked that she should order a Cuban sandwich, figuring she would be sick of them. She looked at him quizzically.

"Cuban sandwich? *¿Qué es eso?* What's that?" she asked.

Her whole life in Cuba, she had never eaten one. Never heard of one. This part of Cuba doesn't exist here for a regular Cuban. Ham and roasted pork are luxuries, and having them put together in this way, unimaginable. Our food and our culture, I always thought them inextricable. It was the one thing I expected to be familiar. But I am learning that the culture I know may exist only on the other side of the Florida Straits.

I order the Cuban sandwich in defiance, and I sip my daiquiri slowly as the band plays into the night on this, my first night in the land of my parents.

DAY TWO

A warm breeze thick with the scent of the nearby ocean sweeps through the rooftop patio of the Hotel Plaza, blowing napkins off tables and tussling the hair of tourists enjoying their buffet breakfasts. The salty sea air heightens the anticipation in my palate as I prepare an experiment with a selection of fresh-cut tropical fruits I've set out on separate plates before me. Papaya, mango, mamey—by some measure exotic fruits, but not to the boy raised with them growing in his backyard, the proud crop of a Cuban farmer planting seeds of his childhood in American soil.

He devoured his fruits with such *gusto*, my father did, that I was always surprised to hear him pine for fruits born of his native earth. And I wonder if I will be able to tell the difference. I choose deliberately from the chunked fruits glistening with their juices, and I hold each bite in my mouth to compare it with my father's crop, softly sucking in air to let the flavors swirl as if considering a fine wine. The canary yellow mango is smooth and firm, tangy, and not stringy like some poorer varieties. The papaya, red-orange like a sunset, is sweet through and through and the flesh tender, not grainy. The mamey is red velvet and evaporates like cotton candy. My father was right: The fruits are more delicious in Cuba. I look out at the collage of faded buildings that await me below and wonder whether the sights on my first full day in Cuba can be as sweet as my first taste.

Downstairs in the lobby, hotel guests slathered with too much sunscreen sign up for bus tours around the city. I watch the lines form from the other end of the room as I buy a map of Old Havana that shows all the streets and back alleys I hope to know on foot. Before I head out, I pay to check my e-mail at an Internet café set up for tourists and see I have a message to call the office. Before I sign off, I send a brief e-mail to my wife to tell her I'm okay. I want to tell her that I wish she were here so we could hold hands walking down the streets of Old Havana. And that it is unbearable to have to do this alone. Instead, I just tell her I love her. And I ask her to call my parents so they will not worry.

The operator on the lobby phone connects me to *The Post*, and she does not know it because I call a cell phone number and not a landline. We speak in code, and I'm not sure if we understand each other, but I know they want me to report if I see any kind of buildup for Castro's eightieth birthday celebration, since he still has not been seen after his surgery. No one knows if he is alive or dead. I hear clicks and pops, and I am well aware of the operator in the hotel who monitors these calls. I know it is time to look for a better way to communicate, I tell them, and hang up.

I ask to make one more call, to my Tía Sofía's house, and when my cousin Jorge picks up the phone, a little bit of the weight begins to lift.

"¡*Primo! Coño*, what a coincidence!" he says. "Well, you've picked an exciting time to be here."

A lifelong Cuban now living in the States, he speaks our code and speaks it well. He will be here a little more than two weeks, visiting his mother and brothers, and we make plans for him to come pick me up later in the week. He wishes he could come right away to show me around Havana, to show me the beautiful sand of Varadero Beach, and to take me to my Tía Sofía's house in Cárdenas. But he knows why I am here, and he has one important piece of advice: Be careful not to confuse Cuban Convertibles with the Cuban national peso. Although the brightly colored currency I converted my dollars into reads "Un Peso," they are very different animals. Cubans, he tells me, are paid in national pesos. It takes 24 pesos to make just one Convertible. And you can imagine what a coup it would be for someone who makes 240 pesos a month— about $10, the average for Cubans—to walk away with 240 Convertibles, nearly $300. So if I need to convert money, I should always go to an official exchange station. Otherwise, someone on the street might try to give me the "poor" peso, *el pobre*, as Cubans secretly call it, instead of *el rojo*, the colorful red one.

'Coño, primo,' I'm glad you told me that. What I need is for you to show me the ropes. By the way, weren't you here last year? How did you get in?

He is quiet for a moment to let me realize I have slipped and broken our code.

"I'll tell you all about it when I see you," he says, recovering for the both of us, and we hang up.

On my way out of the hotel, I ask one of the bellboys, a twenty-eight-year-old named José, if he has any idea where I can rent a cell phone. He says the only place to do that is at an office on the other end of Old Havana, by the old train station, and I ask him to circle it on my map. He moves to hail me a taxi, but I tell him not to bother, that I plan on walking. He turns to look at me as if trying to decipher a riddle.

"In what year did you leave?" he asks, finally.

He thinks I am Cuban-born. And I cannot help smiling.

I tell him I was born in the United States, but my parents came from Cuba in the late sixties.

"Now it makes sense," he says, "but your Spanish, it sounds *criollo*, native."

I smile wider, and the image of my Abuelito Pepe, who taught me to roll my r's and stopped me when I didn't pronounce every syllable correctly, flashes with a knowing grin. When José asks why I'm here, I tell him just that I have come to Cuba for the first time to know the country of my parents, to retrace their footsteps, to learn about who they were and who I am. And I can't resist telling him a little about my father's cafés, the Frías Brothers of Marianao, and how they all left and became successful entrepreneurs in the U.S. He smiles back at me, nodding. Call it intuition, but I trust José immediately.

"And your *Papá*, he's never been back?" he asks.

No. Never. I'm the first one back in decades.

"You're going to have a lot of stories to tell your *viejo*, your old man," he says, shaking my hand firmly and wishing me luck on my walking tour.

The city is again noisy and alive, and I wonder if it ever sleeps. Ladas and old American cars grumble by, motorcycles zip through traffic, and pedestrians fill the sidewalks at an easy pace. No one seems in a rush. They move like figurines in a music box, dancing along at their preprogrammed pace. In El Parque Central, I sit on one of the benches and can already feel the heat of a late-morning sun as I peruse a copy of a newspaper someone has left behind. *Granma*, the tabloid-size organ of the state, reads like a historical novel, with a story again reliving the triumphs of Fidel Castro, saying how he is strong like a *caguairán*, a variety of hardwood tree that grows in Cuba. On another page, there is a story about the sentencing of five Cuban spies who were arrested, tried, and convicted in the United States. The mouthpiece calls them the Five Heroes of the Revolution and demands their return. In the Hotel Plaza, there are three poster-size diatribes telling guests how unjust the convictions were and bemoaning the corruption of the American justice system. Most of the boldface type seems to highlight stories about supposed American injustices around the world, from dealings in Latin America to the death toll in the Iraq war.

I crumple the paper and cross the park toward Obispo Street, which is already bustling with activity. The corridor is hopping with locals and tourists, turning to pass one another on the narrow sidewalks, some spilling out onto the cobblestone street. The buildings along either side climb three, four stories. Many have been freshly painted in pastels, with rich, detailed ironwork reminiscent of what might have been original to Old Havana's colonial period. The storefronts are a varied mix. There is a dog-grooming parlor next to a store that sells state-approved and communist literature. Farther down, a restaurant, open to the air, is playing a soft *danzón* as tourists sit at a long counter and quaint iron tables, enjoying Cuban coffee. Across the street, next to a shop that sells Dolce & Gabbana sunglasses, a store with long glass windows ornately framed in rich, dark wood displays all manner of designer clothing on wooden hangers. New hardwood floors span the store. The clothing, neatly folded or on display racks, gives the feeling of an Abercrombie & Fitch at a mall back home.

Obispo opens up into a lovely park, and I am reminded of the squares in Savannah, Georgia. Under a canopy of trees, the oasis of greenery and red flowering plants is separated from the walkways with a low iron fence. I sit on a small wooden bench to rest. In walking, I can feel the money belt chafing, the deep, red marks already forming around my waist. It is a burden and a constant reminder that I am carrying around enough cash to buy a brand-new Lada right off the lot and have enough left over for a year's worth of gas. But I have heard stories from other journalists who socked money away at their hotels, only to find it missing from the supposed safe boxes in their rooms. I have no choice but to carry it with me at all times. It also reminds me I am not here as just a visitor. So, I gather my supplies.

On Obispo, I find a store that sells everything from coffee-makers and rubber bands to school supplies. People are huddled around a glass counter with no semblance of order, and I ask who is last in line. A woman with her daughter raises her hand, and I stand by her. A second later, a Cuban woman comes to the counter and asks who is last. I raise my hand and expect her to stand by me. She doesn't and just says, "I'm the last one," and begins looking at other items. They are pros at waiting in line in Cuba, lines for supplies, lines for medicine, lines for rations. They make the best use of their time, and standing single file is not part of the plan.

More than thirty minutes later, a short wait by Cuban standards, I find myself at the counter. I ask the woman if they have any notebooks, and she shows me a stack of shiny blue school notebooks about eight inches long, with cartoon characters on the covers. I buy seven, some with motorcycle riders on the front, others with soccer players. As I pay, I see a little girl with jet-black hair and huge, light brown eyes standing next to me, eyeing my purchase with awe. She is here to buy school supplies with her mother—classes will start in less than a month. When she thinks I am not looking, she reaches her hand up and gently strokes a laminated cover, as if caressing a new baby. She turns back to her mother. As I leave, I give one to her, saying I bought one too many, and head out before her mother can object.

Outside, the street curves to the right and opens into a grand cobblestone plaza with a great sculpted fountain at its center, and clay planters with miniature palm trees are thoughtfully placed throughout. At one end of the square, gleaming new tour buses drop off and pick up tourists in groups. Pigeons move as in a choreographed dance, fluttering away from the plaza's visitors. Along one side of the square are stores, brightly painted, from little art galleries that sell local artists' paintings to a United Colors of Benetton. Tourists move lazily between them, posing for pictures, shopping bags in hand.

At the far end of the square is the church of St. Francis of Assisi, a long stone colonial building with a tower at its entrance. Beyond a pair of iron gates, candles are lit, and a mixture of tourists and local Cubans sit quietly in pews as the smell of incense graces the air. And to any visitor stopping off here, and only here, this must seem like a blessed paradise.

I take my map out of my bag and plot a course through a maze of city blocks where Cubans live. My route leads me back to Obispo, and when I find the right intersecting street, I leave the tailored path. Doing so is like stepping off the yellow brick road. As I move farther from the Obispo gateway, the paint on the buildings fades until nothing more than mottled, stained concrete makes up the towering buildings on either side. The sidewalks soon become impassable, narrow and cracked, and from above, cold water drips on my neck. A tapestry of laundry hangs from rusted iron balconies, the view unchanging as it stretches between blighted buildings to the horizon. I walk on the street to avoid the drips from above as other Cubans pass. We stay near the center of these narrow, potholed, pockmarked roads that are too small, and the views too unsightly, for any sparkling Chinese-made tour bus to ford.

Lining the sides of the street are pools of water, teeming with insects and swirling with indistinguishable green and brown. Sewage backs up from the centuries-old buildings and releases along the street in a fetid mix. I walk by marvelously detailed doorways of buildings that are constructed like brownstones. But the concrete is cracked, falling off in chunks. One archway is held up by a wooden two-by-four, which itself is black and rotting. The wooden doors to these apartments, when they are not missing, appear original to the buildings. They are splintered and eaten by rot and termites at the edges. Just inside one open doorway, a man lies on a piece of cardboard, which pads only half his body, his bare legs and feet resting against a cracked, speckled floor. One building front is nothing but rubble, a crumbled façade with exposed beams holding up the framework. A hand-painted sign reads: "Do not demolish. People live in here."

Block after block, building after building, more of the same. The acrid odor of sewage mixes with the ever-present diesel fumes and a musty smell of lives packed in storage boxes in a forgotten attic. The entire city smells ancient.

In what appears to be an alley between these buildings, there is an open-air market. Under corrugated metal roofs, vendors slump against wooden tables with all manner of perishables before them. There are heads of garlic and plantains, mangoes and beans, onions and calabaza squashes. Shoppers with bags in hand visit each station, their sandals and sneakers kicking up orange dust from the ground.

My map leads me past more than a mile of these buildings where some Cubans live their entire existence, these tenements that, were it not for the bravery of my parents, could easily have been my home.

It is midafternoon when I arrive at the circled spot on my map, where José said I could rent a cell phone. Just on the outer edges of the dilapidated buildings, this one looks modern with black glass doors. Inside, it feels like an office building, with freshly painted gray walls, tiled floors, and air-conditioning that cools the patches of sweat on my shirt. A half dozen people are meandering outside, and this time, I know the drill.

Who's last?

Inside, it is like a cell phone store for us in the United States. There is a glass case displaying several phones, people sitting with saleswomen paying bills. When it is my turn, I ask one woman about renting a cell phone and she makes a sucking sound. "It's expensive," she says, almost apologizing.

It costs 100 CUC to open a new line (with the exchange rate, that's about US$120), I have to put down another 100 as a security deposit, and it would cost me about 10 CUC a day to rent. Sometimes it is cheaper just to buy a phone outright, she says, but they are out of the cheapest phones—at about $40, they sell out the moment they come in. The ones in the glass case cost $250. She can't remember how long they have been sitting there, and I see a film of dust surrounding one.

Why even stock something like that?

She shrugs her shoulders. "Some foreigners buy them," she says.

For the average Cuban, even the $40 phone is a dream, she confides, leaning in and lowering her voice. She asks to see my passport.

"This," she says, tapping my passport picture, "is the reason you're allowed a phone."

Even if they had the money, Cubans are not allowed to just waltz in and buy a phone. They need special dispensation, she says. Other Cubans will ask a foreigner they make friends with to buy a phone and open a prepaid account in their name, even if it is illegal. With that, she hands me my rental, an old Nokia that is a blue brick, and sends me on my way.

As I follow a road that curves back toward the hotel, I cannot ignore the rumble in my stomach. I have been walking for more than five hours, and this exercise for my legs and my mind has left me starved. And then, the smell of fresh-baked bread. Along the sidewalk, a small storefront opens to the street with a sign that advertises fresh-made pizzas. I step inside but just barely. The room is no bigger than a walk-in closet. A large L-shaped counter leaves space for only about seven people to stand around. On the menu board, painted by hand in red, are listings of different kinds of pizzas. When the man behind the counter steps to me, I only glance at the menu board and ask for a simple cheese pizza.

"Have a mixed pizza instead," he says, wiping a glass with his stained white apron. "It's only two pesos more, and it's really good."

He writes up my order on a note the size of a raffle ticket and attaches it to an open paper clip tied to a string hanging from a hole in the ceiling. He gives the string a yank, and someone I cannot see pulls the note, up, up, and out of sight. While I wait, I review the rest of the menu board, looking for something to accompany my pie: There is *pizza napolitana,* cheese pizza; *pizza de cebolla,* onion pizza; *pizza de perro* . . . and my eyes can't read any further. I read it and reread it, letting the words roll around in my head: *pizza de perro.*

Dog pizza.

My cousin Jorge once told me the story of a neighbor of his in Cuba who took to catching and eating stray cats during the early nineties, and I wonder, *Dios,* have things gotten to the point where people in Cuba are eating dogs?

Excuse me.

The man in the stained apron turns to me.

What's in the mixed pizza?

He waves his hand over the entire menu. "Everything." I consider slowly slinking out of the restaurant, leaving my order wherever it is on the other side of the ceiling, when a young man walks in, quickly gets the man's attention, and asks for a *pan con perro,* a dog and bread. *Jesus, people are lining up for this!* I decide right there, if it's good enough for these folks, it's good enough for me. I try not to think of my Yorkshire terrier back home as the smell of cooked meat begins to waft from upstairs.

His order comes down first, and he and the owner both look at me when I breathe a heavy sigh of relief at the sight of a hot dog. *Pizza de perro* is pizza with hot dog slices. I greet my little eight-inch pie a few minutes later with delight. *That's a good pie, good pie.* There is very little sauce on the pizza, and the cheese is dark yellow, with the pungent scent of a goat's cheese, not the mild, creamy mozzarella we are used to back home. The man tells me it is eight pesos, and I get change back from one CUC. The pizza costs about thirty-four cents.

As I begin to eat, a woman comes in, wiping her sweat from the sun, and asks for a cup of water and a pizza. She is older, dark-skinned, her hair in short, soft black curls. The man points at mine. "That was our last piece of bread," he says, wiping the counter.

She looks at me, then slumps her head and asks for a cup of *refresco*, a soft drink. She hands him a single peso, and out of a Gatorade-style cooler, he pours a glowing, lime green concoction. I ask him for a knife, cut my pie into quarters, and give the woman a piece. A man standing between us scolds her when she begins to eat.

"She's not even embarrassed," he says.

Why should she be? I know exactly what it's like to come expecting one thing and finding another.

"*Gracias, muchacho,*" she says, quickly devouring the slice.

While eating my second piece, I bite down on something hard. I spit into my hand something the size of a marble that appears to be a round, pitted bone, like from the end of a rib. I look at the menu. Hot dog is the only meat on it. My stomach is still rumbling, and there is almost half a pie left. I drop the jawbreaker to the floor before anyone can notice and decide to keep eating, even if today I've eaten the dog and its bone.

On my way back toward the center of town, I sit under a tree along the main road to rest. Under the shade of its large, waxy leaves, I watch cars go by as I write in my children's notebook. People are waiting on a corner, and, shortly, a rig like a semi comes up the street. But instead of a trailer, it is towing people. The trailer has been converted into the body of a bus, and there are windows along the side. These *camellos,* so named because of a dip in the middle, have become a main form of public transportation in this part of the city. The camel squeaks, hisses, and groans to a stop, takes more passengers into its humps, and belches a cloud of black diesel waste as it lurches on.

As I pass new streets, glancing every so often at my map, I see one that I recognize, Lamparilla. I repeat the name several times to myself before I recognize where I've seen it before. I dig into my backpack and sift through the scraps of paper my parents gave me before I left. Fourth on the list of the businesses my father and his brothers had owned was a café on the corner of San Ignacio and Lamparilla in Old Havana. I am close to one of the cafés. I grab my map and find that Lamparilla intersects San Ignacio eight blocks in, and I begin to walk, my heart beginning to race.

I am on my way to find something I recognize from the anecdotes in my mind. How my father had talked about his life as a businessman in Cuba. I have seen him my entire life as that self-driven figure. Every day, he woke up with the sun to drive to downtown Miami to pick up repaired jewelry items, buy more inventory, and be at the store for a full day of work. Even on weekends, he was the first one up, toiling in the yard, fertilizing plants, picking fruit, cutting the grass, repairing sprinkler heads. He was restless if not working.

I am eager to put myself in his place, to stand in front of one of the cafés he owned and imagine him leaning against the counter, complimenting a woman on her dress and serving coffee to customers himself because, well, even though he's the boss, he loves interacting with people. He used to do it at the jewelry store all the time, buying coffee at the corner bakery and pouring for his clients as they studied the glittery things in the showcase.

As I approach an intersection, I see engraved in stone above a corner storefront the words SAN IGNACIO, and I know that this is it. On one corner of this intersection, a boarded-up building has chains on the door. On another, across the street from an empty lot of rubble where boys are playing soccer, is an apartment building. Finally, there is a *bodega*, a market, with a service counter at the edge of the sidewalk and another long counter inside where people are waiting to be helped. It looks to be the most likely candidate, and I walk up to it cautiously, passing under the corrugated metal rolling doors, which are pulled up only halfway and pockmarked with rust holes.

A man with a red cap leans against the counter chatting with friends from the neighborhood. He is older, looks to be in his late sixties, and the top few buttons of his plaid shirt, whose sleeves have been cut off, are undone to reveal tight naps of gray and black hair surrounding a simple golden crucifix that hangs from a delicately thin chain. He is smiling from behind his crooked glasses, a pen wedged behind his ear.

"*Hallo,*" he tries in English, looking at me curiously, nodding his head, his lips in an open grin.

Morning, chief—'buenos días, jefe.'

He's surprised to hear me speaking Spanish. I catch a glimpse of myself in a mirror behind the counter. I have sweat through my aqua T-shirt where the backpack straps come across my chest. I am freshly shaven and wearing a watch. Yes, I look like a tourist who has taken a wrong turn. I explain about my father, that I was born in the States—"*Mira, chico,* this kid is from Miami," he says to an older man at the counter, who nods his head—and that my father and uncles used to own a café at this intersection.

"A café?" he says. He rubs his chin.

He's not originally from Old Havana, but he has worked here, at this *bodega,* for more than fifteen years and has learned much of its history. I find out he is actually in his fifties. From his appearance, it is hard to imagine. His eyes are cloudy with what look like cataracts, and several dark moles dot his face. He rides his bicycle in every morning from the town of Marianao, he says, and the name burns in my ears.

Marianao? That's where my father's family used to live.

He says it is not more than a twenty-minute car ride.

This store where we are standing, he tells me, couldn't be the café. It has always been a *bodega.* It used to belong to Chinese-Cuban brothers who left for America in the late fifties, just as the grumblings of a revolution began. It continued to be a *bodega* when the government took it over and set it up as a rations station. The man pulls out a ration book from under the counter and explains it to me, showing me how each household has its own book, about the size of a notepad, and that each member of each household is listed in it. This one shows checks next to what that house has accepted this month, rations of rice, sugar, detergent. This family has a child at home, and the box for milk is checked. He holds up a clear bag of milk, which is dripping at one corner. He stands it up, so it will not drain out. He says that only families with children younger than seven can buy milk legally. If the children are older than that, the family must purchase yogurt for their calcium needs. Behind him, a black chalkboard shows the items available here, where this community must shop. Next to each rationed item, such as black beans, oil, *chícharos* or split peas, even cigarettes, is the date it is expected in. But not all of them have dates and not all of them come in, he says. People from bordering neighborhoods will barter items, cooking oil for coffee, black beans for rice.

On a little burner, he is brewing coffee in one of the aluminum Italian espresso makers I know from home. He rinses out his own espresso cup, wipes it, and fills it for me.

"Try this. This is the good stuff from Oriente. Not the *basura*, the garbage, you get around here," he says. It is hot and sweet with a rich aroma, and soon I can feel it give new life to my tired legs.

As we talk, he tries to remember what was on each corner. That one has always been an apartment building. And the other was a *carnicería*, a butcher shop, which was closed down in the late sixties. The man who owned it, before it was taken over by the government, an old Gallego, a Spaniard, ran it for years. He died recently of a heart attack in his apartment above the store, where he had lived for more than thirty years. That is the ease of retracing roots in Cuba. Because there is no personal property, people do not buy and sell their homes. Often, the homes they lived in before the revolution are the ones in which they will take their last breath.

A man who looks to be in his early forties comes into the *bodega* and raps on the counter. "*Qué pasó*, what's going on, old man?" he says to the man in the red cap.

He is carrying with him a transistor radio that looks to be at least twenty years old.

"*Coño*, just the guy I needed to see," the man in the red cap tells him, then turns to me. "This guy has lived in this neighborhood all his life."

He tells Radio Man my story, about my parents, my birth in Miami—"*Miami*, I don't believe it!" he exclaims—and that I am looking for a café that used to belong to my father.

"*Hombre*, how I would love to visit Miami just once," he says wistfully. "At least with this," he says, pointing to his ancient radio, "I can find out a little bit about what's going on."

The radio looks beyond repair, but he and the man in the red cap agree he has a knack for fixing things, and he has kept this one running through the years. If he places it just so, in one corner of his home, he can pick up the pirate Radio Martí signals that the U.S. broadcasts from C-130s just offshore.

"*Papo*," the man in the red cap says, "do you remember where the *cafetería* used to be?"

Well, that used to be the butcher shop, Radio Man says, pointing across the street. This has always been a *bodega*, and that has always been an apartment building. But on *that* corner . . . yeah, he says, on that corner he remembers there being a café.

He is pointing to the flat, leveled land where shirtless boys kick around a tattered soccer ball between piles of broken concrete and garbage.

I look at Radio Man. I look at the corner. And I wait for him to think better of his answer.

"*Sí*, I remember it. That was definitely it," he says, nodding.

I step off the curb and walk to the corner that was a café and now is a memory. Garbage is piled along the street. Rubble from the former building—chunks of concrete and twisted metal—is dammed from the sidewalk by a wall of corrugated metal sheets. Neighbors have dumped household garbage on it as well, and the flies swirl around it, around me and the smell of decay. The boys play on the lot. One, wearing nothing but a pair of swim trunks, tiptoes barefoot over the rocks and splintered wood. Radio Man and the man in the red cap appear next to me, and we are all lost in the wreckage.

"It's hard to visualize," the man in the red cap says.

I am trying very hard not to. The building was torn down so new homes could be built, and there is a sign saying this is the future site of forty-five new apartments. But he says the lot has been like this for more than twenty-five years, and construction never started. I think about navigating the rubble to walk on the land where the boys are playing, to at least say I set foot on the ground where my father once labored.

"We really picked that café up and made it into a seller," he told me once.

But my feet won't move. My father claimed this as his years ago, but I cannot do it now. Standing on it will mean that I accept what has become of the fairy tale I was told as a boy, and I am not willing to fully awake from that dream. Those dreams are my memories, and I won't give them up for piles of rocks. But I cannot deny that this, too, is part of my history now: shoeless boys chasing a soccer ball over the broken dreams of my father.

The afternoon is fading as I return to Obispo, stepping off the Trail of Tears and back to pastel buildings with smiling, happy tourists posing for each other's pictures, and I cannot bring myself to look any of them in the eye.

At the end of the street, I hear voices over a loudspeaker, and as I get closer, I see a gathering of children, easily forty, watching actors dressed as clowns dance and tell jokes and make sock puppets come to life as Cuban reggaeton plays on a boom box.

"And why are we here?" one of the young clowns asks the children before answering his own question.

"Because today we are celebrating the very happy birthday of our *comandante*, the president, Fidel Castro," he says, as other clowns give out balloon animals. "And we are very grateful for all of this to the government of Cuba."

Tourists clap and sway along with the music while the twenty-something actors fall to the ground to the children's delight as day-light fades. And I wonder whether the boys playing soccer on the flattened, empty lot have gone home for the night.

I walk past the clowns, past El Parque Central, and past the statue of the Poet sheltering the huddled masses. Night falls, and guests of another hotel sit outside along a veranda, listening to a live band play soft Cuban jazz as they dine on fine foods served on fine china over fine white linen tablecloths, and I cannot meet their eyes, either. I stop in long enough to use a computer at the Internet café, force myself to write a few lines about the clowns anticipating Castro's birthday and·send them to my bosses back at the paper. My legs throb as I walk back to my hotel in the full shroud of night, the streets alive again with locals meandering on their aimless courses.

It is José who opens the doors of the Hotel Plaza, and light from inside floods the darkened street and burns my tired eyes.

"*Coño, mi hermano,* you don't look like you've stopped today," he says.

I drop to the stoop, and he sits next to me. I can feel a humming in my legs, a numbness from total exhaustion, and I recap my day. The beautiful church and the crumbling Cuban homes. We laugh about the *pizza de perro,* and he shakes his head when I tell him about the café.

"*Chocaste*—you crashed into reality," he says. "I've seen people who come back, and they can't deal with all the things that have changed. And all the things that haven't."

He asks if I'm up for going to a jazz club, but really, all I want is to be alone. I ask him if he knows where Marianao is and whether he knows anyone who can spend the day as my driver and take me around to the places I need to see.

"Well . . ." he begins, before stopping to look around. He stands up, starts down the outside walkway, and beckons to me.

We walk along the sidewalk and past the hotel, and he says he passes Marianao every day on the way to work. He drives an old American car he has fixed up and clandestinely works as a driver to make extra money. This, of course, is illegal, because he is not licensed as a taxi driver. The police know it is going on, José says, but people take the risk anyway, even though it could mean a fine. José has never met anyone who has been prosecuted for giving another Cuban a ride for just a couple of pesos. Whenever he is stopped, he just says the person riding with him is a *socio*, a friend, to whom he's giving a ride. But if he's seen with a foreigner, the penalties are much greater. He could lose his car, and that would mean losing a significant portion of income. Still, he has a wife and a young daughter, and must take the risk.

"Besides, you look like you're from here. If we get stopped, I'll just say you're my cousin," he says.

Okay, 'primo,' we're on for tomorrow. And we make plans to meet up the street from the hotel at 10:00 A.M. We walk back to the hotel entrance, and I climb two flights of marble stairs to my room. Each step is like a mountain after a day on foot, but since a power outage froze the elevator between floors this morning, I decide I wouldn't mind the extra exercise.

I stand in the shower and watch the dust from the city streak off me and swirl down the drain. The dust from those alleys, from the open market, from the corner that was a building that was a café, a café with my father inside that is now a soccer pitch for barefoot children. I clean away soot that has gathered around my nostrils from the diesel fumes. I hold my breath and face the shower stream, trying to rinse away parts of this day. But the layer of dust washes away more easily than the memories.

Sitting on the hotel bed, I open my backpack and pull out the scraps of paper. There are two names on the list my father gave me: Rosita and Alina. Rosita was a waitress at one of my family's cafés in Marianao, the very first one my father opened. She has visited the United States several times, and the Frías Brothers always make a point of visiting her when she comes to town. I've grown up hearing about Alina, too. My cousins Lily and Felipe know all about their father's old girlfriend in Cuba. She is in all the stories of my Tío Felipe's life in Marianao. I am often surprised at how casually she comes up in conversation, considering that my uncle has been married to his wife, his only wife, since before I was born.

I set Alina's name aside and decide to make first contact with Rosita.

"*Ay, Dios santo*, my holy Lord," she says when I tell her who I am.

Her voice is light and airy and welcoming, and already I am looking forward to seeing her. What am I doing here? Where am I staying? It doesn't matter, come, come to see me, she says. I tell her I want to spend the whole day in Marianao, getting to know the city where the Frías Brothers made a name for themselves, and I can't wait to tell her why I am here so she can help fill in the holes of my family history. I ask if she can call Miguel, who was the Fríases' butcher and one of my father's few close friends, and she says she will, of course, of course. I tell her I am thinking of calling Alina, and she says, yes, yes, I must. But come early, she will be waiting for me. My heart is pumping when I hang up, and I can feel the smile on my tired face.

I begin to dial Alina's number several times before I get the nerve to finish and let it ring. I am calling the *other* woman. But my father gave me her name for a reason, and so I dial.

"*Ay, mi madre*, Fernando's son!" she yells. Her voice is scratchy and low, smoky, like the sound of a favorite record that has been played time and again. I tell her I have already spoken with Rosita, and I hope that she can spend some time with me, too. She says she lives right next to La Plaza de Marianao, and I know this is the place where my family had their most successful businesses, the ones my father speaks of as if they are old friends. Alina says she has not seen Rosita in a long while, and I say maybe I can stop by, see La Plaza with her, and we can go together to Rosita's. Perfect, she says. Perfect!

"*Ay*, Carlos, hearing your voice is like hearing Fernando. It gives me this . . . *feeling* inside," she says. "You don't know how much I think about your family."

There is a nostalgia in her voice that I can almost touch. It awakens a swelling of emotion that I know we both can feel. And the promise of tomorrow is like Christmas morning.

For the first time in thirty-seven years, a Frías is coming to Marianao.

DAY THREE

José is late.

I am where I should be, on the corner, one block up from the hotel. But I search the street and do not see him. Several old American cars go by, and I remember him telling me his was a '58 Ford. But all the dented sheet metal and massive chrome grilles look the same to me. My mother, on the other hand, could identify those old cars at a glance. One of her favorite things to do when I was a boy was to go to a car dealership at night, when the sales staff was away, and peacefully walk the parking lot under the bluish white lights looking at all the new models. But my DNA doesn't help with identifying these older cars. I peek inside as each goes by, looking for my *socio*, my friend, with no luck.

Rather than stand on the corner conspicuously with my backpack, I stroll along the street to pass the time, turning back every so often to check for José. The grand thoroughfare of El Prado is a wide boulevard with a great median for walking, period lanterns for light posts, and white concrete benches where people sit under shade trees in the late-morning sun.

In one direction, El Prado leads to the restored hotels of the old city and loops in front of El Capitolio, which was once the capital building. In the late 1920s, it was constructed as a replica of the U.S. Capitol, from the perfectly symmetrical sides to the recognizable dome that can be seen from miles away, to house the legislature in a democratic Cuba. The first constitution was signed there, a constitution usurped by dictators. That the building no longer serves a legislative function seems a fitting bit of respect.

To the east, El Prado leads to the sea, and the ocean breeze seems to carry me in that direction with a gentle hand. The buildings on either side remind me of a transitioning downtown neighborhood. One is a perfect pastel pink, with stone arches and a painstakingly detailed wrought-iron balcony. A pair of others just down from it, though, look like they have been firebombed. Concrete is missing in swaths, and great black streaks of mildew and neglect stream from the broken windows like running mascara, as if the buildings themselves are weeping at the attempt to conceal the decades of neglect and abandonment.

At the end of the boulevard, I come to a great seawall that twists and turns and stretches as far as the eye can see. A squeaky bike, tourists walking hand in hand, a Cuban girl raising her hand for a ride, they all share this great, wide boardwalk kissed by the crashing waves.

El Malecón.

How I've heard about this place, from my father and mother, who told their individual stories about sitting on the wall and listening to the sea break softly against it at night. I raise my face to the sun and breathe in the thick, salty air as the breeze cools my brow. The soft mist of the ocean kisses the flesh in spite of a relentless tropical sun.

On the other side of the Bay of Havana, a tall, domed tower rises to the sky under a fluttering Cuban flag.

El Morro. I have heard about this place, too, seen it depicted in Cuban paintings and photographed longingly in black and white. Beyond the tower, darker, colder, is what looks like a great stone castle, a fortress guarding the entrance to the bay, cannons like jagged nails threatening the sea traffic. I peek at my watch and realize I have become lost in the beauty and the breeze, and I hustle back toward my rendezvous point with José.

I am heading down an alley when I hear a distant whistle and see José waving his arms. He is standing by his car, and as I reach him, he waves his arm over it like a game show model.

"What do you think?" he asks.

It's incredible.

And it is. This car, forty-eight years old, should be in a museum. The turquoise paint looks like it has been slathered on with a broad brush and is chipping at the seams. The car's sheet metal is wavy from the many times it has been dinged, dented, crashed, and repaired over the span of its hard, hard life. The chrome is swirled with scratches but polished to a sheen that glistens brightly in the sun. The rims have come off a modern car, and the side-view mirrors have been adapted from an old Lada. And the engine, well, let's just say it's not original. José has transplanted it from an old Chevy, and the patient did not reject the conflicting but vital organ. This is Frankenstein's monster, and the good doctor is smiling, stroking his hand gently over its long, snub-nosed hood.

"The happiest day of my life, except for when my daughter was born, was the day I bought this car," he says.

He has been working on it for months and gets inspiration from the cars he sees on American and international satellite television at the hotel. He spends his lunch breaks flipping through channels that only tourists are given access to. CNN in Spanish. ESPN. HBO. More than thirty channels in all, including, of course, the five Cuban stations, one of which is dedicated to politics—and only the politics between Cuba and the United States. His favorite show is *Overhaulin'*, a cable series on which a crew remodels a beat-up car in a week. "Those guys are *artistas*," José says.

"*Bueno*, are you ready?"

Oh, yeah, I'm ready.

The door creaks open like a dungeon's, and José warns me to close it gently. As softly as I try, it clanks shut, and the insides of the door rattle for the next few seconds. When he turns over the engine, I am reminded of sitting in a stock car, the grumbling and shaking massaging my insides. The doctor is smiling at the throaty idle, nodding his head, seeking my approval.

Nice! I yell over the grumble.

He puts it in drive, and we are off with a mighty shimmy and a groan. As we drive down the street, people step off the curb and raise their hands, trying to hail our "cab."

"Where were you?" he asks. I tell him about my walk to the sea and ask about the domed tower. "Oh, you mean the monument, El Morro–La Cabaña."

The words are like a stiff punch to the gut.

Did you say La Cabaña?

That is the name of the prison where my father was held for nearly two years for attempting to flee the country on a boat in 1965. I had imagined the prison from the stories he had told me over the years, and I always pictured it far off, lost and forgotten in the countryside. Instead, it is right on the edge of Old Havana, looming over the city from a high cliff at the mouth of the bay.

Are there still prisoners there?

No, José says. It's a monument now, restored to recall its original purpose as a colonial fortress built by the Spanish to deter invaders. Cubans can visit for a peso. He's never been there, though.

To visit? You mean . . .

It takes a second for it to settle in.

I can go there?

I can go there. I almost tell José right then to turn the car in the direction of La Cabaña. I want to stand there. I want to see the cells. I want to know the place where they caged my father. But I think of Rosita and Alina, who have been so eagerly awaiting me. I still feel the excitement in their voices. Yet there is something between curiosity and a raw rage gurgling in the pit of my stomach as I think of the men who imprisoned my father so unjustly. And the place that represents all that repression stands on the edge of town, glaring down. I'm here for several days, I tell myself, and I feel the heat dissipating. But I know now that a confrontation awaits.

We drive through the heart of Havana, west toward Marianao, through a host of neighborhoods that make up the city. The high-rises become two-story duplexes and individual homes, low, squat houses with paint flaking, the sidewalks cracked and dirty, the streets riddled with potholes. The road curves through one section where majestic homes face the street. They are mansions, two and three stories tall, but in the same decrepit state as the rest of the homes, with lawns overgrown, layers of paint peeling to show previous layers, and windows cracked or missing altogether. José says these homes of El Vedado were for the wealthy years ago, before Castro. When the rich went into exile, the servants in these homes became the new inhabitants, and generations of those families have grown up in them. Families have restored some of the homes little by little, bartering in the gray market for paint and concrete mix and fabric to reupholster period furniture. These families rent out their homes as reception halls for married couples or as the backdrops for fifteen-year-old girls to take their *Quinceañera* pictures.

Farther down, where a neighborhood nears the sea, those majestic homes reach their full splendor: Crisp white columns and fanciful moldings. Intricate archways of sculpted stone. Perfect, green lawns behind wrought-iron fences.

Wow, these families have invested big bucks.

José laughs and shakes his head.

"No, *chico*, this is Miramar. This is where all government people live. Politicians. Military men. Heads of the *ministerios*. People like that."

At one intersection, red-and-white gates and armed guards limit access.

"We're getting close now," José says, rousing me as I wordlessly watch the scenery fly by.

He makes a turn, and we are on a wide road divided by a median of parked cars.

"That's it," he says, pointing just to the right, where I can see the very edge of a blue-and-white building. "That's La Plaza de Marianao."

I clench my jaw to stop the shaking that makes my teeth chatter. We park in the median and cross the street where La Plaza comes into full sight. Filling the corner where three streets intersect is this two-story building with simple concrete columns that make it look as if it is held up by stilts. Wide steps that span most of the front of the building lead to a covered area, where dozens of people from Marianao, *marianeses*, pass through a set of glass doors to the inside.

"I do a lot of my grocery shopping here," José says as we step through the glass doors and into an expanse with no walls and tables set up in long rows.

I am nearly stopped at the door by the din of a hundred conversations and an overpowering odor, as if the smell of fermented fruit and vegetables has been simmered down and concentrated into a noxious gas. It is an open-air *bodega*, and at the tables, local merchants display all kinds of perishable goods with handwritten price tags. There are heads of garlic and bulbs of onions. Stations with baskets of dried beans. Tables with fruits, green-and-orange speckled papayas, spotted yellow bananas. *Marianeses* shuffle between the tables, squeezing and considering the fruits, haggling over prices. They are yelling and laughing, and I cannot concentrate on what they are saying for the sight of meat being butchered, men with cleavers brutally chopping, chopping, chopping on craggy granite counters. Swarms of flies land hungrily on the pieces of meat, from oozing chicken thighs to bleeding pork shanks, and the butchers do not bother to shoo them away.

Closer to the back, I am stopped by the distinct stench of pig feces, and it is as if a landfill is on the other side of the wall. I step back, try to steady myself, and nearly trip over a lonely dog, striped with filth against his yellowing fur. He is licking at a pool of blood on the floor and begging for larger scraps. The chopping and haggling and licking and laughing all swirl together into a blinding white noise, and I do not remember how I find my way out.

I breathe in the simmering summer and scan the building for any sign of the quaint cafés and the restaurant that my father's stories have described for me over the years. I pull the scraps of paper out of my bag and look for the names of their three businesses here: Mi Buchito Oriental (My Little Sip of the East), El Tropicream, and El Restaurante Oriental (the Restaurant of the East). A hand-painted sign above a set of stairs says "Restaurant Bar," and I am hopeful.

José and I walk up the stairs into a large open area set up with tables and chairs and a small bar at one end. I wonder if this was the restaurant my father and uncles owned. I walk up to the bar, which is covered in cracked turquoise tiles. But the two women working the counter are young. The Frías Brothers of Marianao? Sounds familiar, they say, but no, they're not sure. They do know the upstairs has not always been a restaurant. Only recently did they start to use it to serve lunch to locals and to rent out on the weekends for receptions and *Quinceañera* parties.

José and I buy a couple of beers poured out of a tap into two small plastic cups and sit down at one of the tables. On his own, José goes from table to table asking whether anybody has heard of the Frías Brothers. Music plays out of a pair of speakers in the ceiling, behind rusted metal grates. A woman is singing a soft, sad song in Italian. I sit quietly staring into my cup, lost and filled with melancholy. I came here expecting an instant connection, to stand at the places my father knew so well and feel a bond of some kind. If anything, I had hoped to recognize façades, at least, where a business might have stood. I feel as if I have cracked a safe only to find it empty. And I feel just as empty inside.

José and I are soon alone with our empty cups. And I decide to call Alina.

"*Niño*, where are you?" she asks. "I was starting to worry about you."

Her voice, like a favorite aunt speaking to her favorite nephew, breathes life back into me, and although my emotions are frozen, she warms me at my center. I tell her I'm at La Plaza. I'm waiting for her.

"What are you wearing?" she asks.

I laugh a little. I am wearing a red-striped polo and khaki pants. Knowing I would be seeing her and Rosita today, I wore the best clothes I brought to Cuba. And so, I stand out.

You'll be able to pick me out. I look like a gringo.

I stand in the shade by a bakery on the first floor of La Plaza as people file past me purposefully. Coming up the steps, one small, thin woman is walking delicately. She glances at me and alternately looks down to climb the steps. When she looks up again, she is smiling. Alina. She hugs me even before we exchange a word and does not let go. I allow myself to be hugged as if I am loved for the first time in days. She adjusts her gold wire-rimmed glasses, grabs my hands, and cranes her neck. "Let me get a good look at you," she says.

People say that I look like my mother.

"That might be true, but I can see your father in you," she says. She studies my eyes, my mouth. "*Claro, claro,* you can see you are a Frías."

I introduce Alina to José and ask her to show me around, to tell me about this plaza and, more important, about La Plaza my father knew. She curves her arm around mine, and we walk back through to the *bodega*, as José follows behind. I am thankful to have her at my side and feel sturdier for it.

This building had been closed for more than fifteen years, she says, after the government took over all the businesses and closed them in 1965. When Cuba aligned itself with the Soviet Union, the Russians came in and gutted it. They tore down walls, reworked the layout, and turned La Plaza into a shell so it could be used as a covered open-air market. We come to a butcher and ask whether he knew the Fríases. He stops chopping and says his father had mentioned them, but he was too young to remember. He points to an older vendor on the other side of the aisle who is selling red and black beans and split peas, *chícharos,* out of great, tattered woven baskets. The man, also named José, remembers my family, but they would not remember him, he says. He was only seventeen and sold cutlery to the businesses of La Plaza to make a little money. Just enough to take a girl to the Gran Teatro de Marianao, the lavish movie theater up the street and, after, to buy himself and his date a cool *guarapo,* crushed sugarcane juice over ice, at the busy little café on the corner, Mi Buchito Oriental.

"La Plaza is what sustained Marianao," he says. "This never closed, night or day."

I ask Alina to show me exactly where the businesses were, the restaurant, El Tropicream, Mi Buchito. I want to stand there. I want to imagine them. She looks up at me and presses her lips together. I can see from her face that I have just asked to see the body.

We walk beyond the butchers, and the smell returns, the sweet and pungent odor of rotting meat, the acrid stench of pig feces. We come around a half wall, and the floor changes from a stained concrete to a cracked earth, caked with orange clay. We are standing in the trash room of the *bodega*.

"This," she says, waving her hand halfheartedly, "was the restaurant."

There was a long, chrome-edged counter over there, with spinning leather stools every few feet, she says, pointing to the back wall, where three large garbage bins overflow with remnants of produce. Husks of corn and boxes soggy with rotten tomatoes are pushed into one corner. There, she says, where workers are sweeping rotting fruits and vegetables into a pile, was a long, wooden bar and several small tables with white linen tablecloths. And here, she motions to our feet, was a beautiful granite floor of black-and-yellow squares where people used to dance.

What is that smell? I ask a young butcher who walks by.

The slaughtered pig carcasses are hosed off in this back room, he says. They don't always come in clean. Alina points to two small holes in the ceiling where she says a sign once hung that read simply "El Restaurante Oriental."

Back outside by the glass doors, she points to a large piece of machinery like a generator to our right, closed off behind a chain-link fence. There, she says, was El Tropicream, a little juicing stand where my Tío Felipe made the most delicious fresh fruit drinks. The line used to stretch down the steps, she tells me as she stands where the counter once was. She would lean on the edge of the counter and chat with him, laugh with him, and he would compliment her shimmering black hair that stretched nearly to her waist. She picks up there, as if in mid-conversation with the man who was her boyfriend forty years ago, and she is alone with him in another time, transported.

"Those were some times," she says, staring at me, her eyes busy as if she were watching an old movie.

We walk back toward the right side of La Plaza, and Alina points across the street to a great, towering building, the Gran Teatro. The roof is mostly missing, aside from a few metal tiles and beams. There is a great pit in the front wall, as if a wrecking ball has punched a hole. But that would be more attention than this building has received in the past fifty years. The theater is now great only in name and standing like the corpse of a once-great prizefighter.

"It's condemned now," she says. "But people still stand in the foyer and sell flowers."

Roaring diesel buses and whining motorcycles streak down the road in front of La Plaza, what was once called the Royal Causeway, La Calzada Real. Today, it is just called Fifty-first Street, its regal lineage only a story old people tell. When we reach the corner of La Plaza, Alina finds a column and marks the paces off with her foot. Stretching her arms out in front of her as if she is finding the right spot to hang a painting, she marks out the edges of Mi Buchito Oriental. There are only windows punched into the wall now, but there was once a long, open counter that several employees attended, she says. A man in one window, selling eggs in what used to be Mi Buchito, does not want me to take his picture.

"This little store was *un fenómeno*—a phenomenal little money-maker," she says.

At all times of day, people stood outside, buying cigars from the glass case, lining up for cups of espresso, drinking fresh-squeezed *guarapo*. But it was at night that Mi Buchito Oriental and the rest of La Plaza came to life.

Alina leans against the counter, and I picture her standing just so fifty years ago. Her descriptions and the stories of my father become watercolors; my mind is a willing canvas. And I begin to paint. I don't even need to close my eyes. The anecdotes and old black-and-white pictures I've seen weave into a detailed quilt, and my vision of La Plaza de Marianao that my father knew grows clearer and richer. I can see it. Actually see it, La Plaza as it was in 1955 . . .

The sun is just setting, and the lights of the Royal Causeway begin to illuminate the *marianeses* walking along the sidewalk in front of

La Plaza. People from all over the western part of the province are making their way here, to the largest municipality outside Havana proper, in shiny new cars of the fifties, Buicks and Pontiacs and Fords, zooming in front of La Plaza.

La Plaza, too, is shifting gears. The produce stands have closed down, and the morning masses are being replaced by a well-dressed evening crowd, men in guayabera shirts and slacks, and women in pressed skirts and blouses. And La Plaza is getting ready for their business. My father walks up the hall from El Restaurante Oriental to Mi Buchito to be certain the little café, first in the line of fire, is ready for the initial wave of moviegoers.

"Make sure we have enough coffee ready to brew," he tells them while he looks over the glass case facing the street, taking a visual inventory of the variety of cigars displayed: H. Upmanns, check. Cohibas, check. Behind him, rows of premeasured coffee grounds are laid out in front of the espresso machine. The *guarapo* crusher is pressing away at stalks of sugarcane with the sound of crackling fire, filling pitcher after pitcher to ensure the staff need only to pour the sweet yellow-green nectar over ice. The glow of red neon from their sign overhead—Mi Buchito Oriental No. 1 Hermanos FRIAS—reflects off the case and illuminates the sidewalk out front, where Rosita, the most trusted of my father's employees, is polishing yellow and black tiles to ensure a pristine look. Mi Buchito is ready for business. My father asks one of the waitresses to brew a fresh *colada*, and he samples it. A friend of Rosita's who has a new camera asks them to hold their poses. My father raises the cup to his lips. A flash. He is in the center of the photo under the sign.

He wants to make sure the little café is a gem. After all, it's the one that started everything. He joined my Tío Ciro, who was the first to leave the farm for the big city. Ciro had a business mind and always felt the family's best chance of making it was in Havana. Ciro had been selling food out of a lunch truck in Marianao when he called for my father to join him, to come help him make their fortune. My father was always up for something new. He joined his brother in 1952, working at a café in La Plaza. But the job was tedious and unrewarding for a man in his mid-twenties. He worked the late shift for six months before a fight with the owner—and a physical fight with an employee who refused to alternate shifts, as they had originally planned—left him looking for a new job.

The owner of a *bodega* at La Plaza, who had some space to rent and heard what had happened to my father, came to him one day and asked, "How would you like to open your own café, right across from that *cabrón*, and start working for yourself?" How would he like it? The brothers opened Mi Buchito Oriental that same year. They bought coffee and sugar on credit and started giving away the coffee for free, just to get people to the counter. Before they knew it, Mi Buchito was the last one standing.

The sound of laughter from across the street and the click-clicking of dress shoes against the sidewalk signal that the first movie has ended. Here they come. They swarm like ants to sugar, and Mi Buchito is ready. Pesos and coffee, at three cents a cup, exchange hands faster than the two waitresses and my father can handle. Cigars fly out of the case. The rows of cigarettes along the back wall get lower and lower. Business as usual.

My father wants to check on the other stores. The sound of the whirring juicer at El Tropicream is drowned out only by the many conversations of the dozens waiting in line. Felipe is pureeing mangoes and mameys as fast as he can while another employee lines up cup after cup with ice in an assembly line. The brothers nod at each other as my father moves to the restaurant to see how his other brothers, Ciro, Ramón, and Rafael, are doing. An old Cuban tune is pouring out of the Victrola in the corner as the smells of sizzling thin Cuban steaks and fried green plantains, *tostones*, fill the air.

My father yells to their best cook, a Chinese Cuban, who is preparing fried rice with fresh beef, pork, and chicken in the back. "How are you, my friend?" he tries to say in the only broken Chinese his cook has taught him.

Men and their dates are already sitting at the white-linen-covered tables, their feet tapping to the music, others taking to the speckled granite dance floor. My father puts his arm around his father, my Abuelo Pancho, who is ringing up checks at the cash register. From there, Pancho can look out to the side street, where

Alina is standing on her porch. She stretches and waves to him. He tips up his signature fedora, sees her by the glow of her porch light, and waves back.

"I would always see him walking up the street from their house. He had this elegant little saunter and always tipped his hat to women when he passed," Alina says as we are back sitting on her porch, staring at La Plaza of today.

The movie playing in my head has ended, and the houselights are up. Men in stained jeans are throwing garbage into a trash bin that sits beyond what used to be the entrance to El Restaurante Oriental.

That used to be the jewel of La Plaza. Look at it now, I say to José.

"From king to king's fool," he answers.

After fifty-three years, Alina still lives in the same house, on the same street, and in her eyes, you can see she is still living the same dream, watching the same black-and-white movie play in her mind. Between her little two-bedroom apartment and La Plaza of her memory is an expanse of time she navigates often and with ease. The aroma of fresh-brewed coffee floats in from her galley kitchen, where she cannot open the oven door all the way because it bumps into the refrigerator. We sit facing each other at her dining table, big enough for only two people, sipping from our cups. She lives here with a niece she has raised, who is away at work today, and makes me promise I will be back to meet her.

Of course, 'claro,' I'll be back. There is so much to know, still.

She rests her hand gently on mine.

"I still can't believe you're here," she says.

She asks me about my family, and I show her pictures of my wife and daughters. I have brought several prints of a recent picture we all took together to give to my family here, and I give her one. She asks me about all my aunts and uncles. And finally, she asks me about my Tío Felipe. Her old boyfriend.

I am surprised to learn she had kept in touch with him, sparingly, over the years, exchanging letters that took months to traverse a distance a plane can cross in forty-five minutes. She knows he is married. She knows about his two children, my cousins Felipe and Lily. She knows, too, that he has vitiligo, a condition that leaves his skin mottled between albino-white spots and patches of caramel. She figures that's why in all of the pictures he has sent, he is always standing far away from the camera. When she asks me about his health, I try to keep my expression from betraying the truth: My Tío Felipe had a grapefruit-size malignancy removed from his abdomen less than three years ago. Since, he has been cancer-free, but I have seen him somehow more delicate than I remember him from my youth. The illness aged him years in a matter of months. But he still spends afternoons working in his yard, trimming the mango and mamey trees, dutifully cutting away banana leaves with a machete. This is the image I give her, where he is strong and healthy, and she does not have to worry. I tell her Felipe's son and I grew up together and that, of all the cousins, I am closest to him. It makes her smile. She shows me the flower-shaped gold studs in her ears and tells me that, about fifteen years ago, Felipe sent those to her. She wears them every day.

Tell me about my 'los Frías,' Alina.

She raises her hands as if grabbing the memories out of the air, and she smoothes her hair, now bobbed and golden brown, carefully ordering the thoughts.

"Everyone knew the Frías Brothers," she says. "How could you not? Five brothers. They were all tall, handsome. To me, the best-looking ones were Felipe and Rafael. But Rafael was always so stern-looking, and he was always wearing this silly hat, *un sombrerón*."

She laughs when I tell her he still wears those hats, my *padrino*, my godfather. And I think he's the last person in Miami who can still pull off a fedora.

"Now Ciro," she continues, "he had the best business mind. But all he ever thought about was business. Business and playing dominoes."

I laugh again, because so few things change. The *Viejos*, the five old men, still get together at least twice a week to play dominoes. Most of the time it's Ciro who rounds up the troops, calling his brothers to "remind them" of the game that has been their routine for the past fifty, sixty years. In Miami, they all had owned jewelry stores, but Ciro is the only one of the brothers who still works. I joke with Alina that if you tried to take away either the store or the dominoes, you would surely kill him.

"Now the ones with the best personalities," Alina says, "were Fernando," my father, "and Felipe."

Of course. Felipe was the best-looking *and* had the best personality.

"*Ese* Fernando, he always had a joke, *un chiste,* to tell or a kind word to say. I remember if an employee needed an advance on her salary, she would go to Fernando. Ciro would get upset and make a fuss—*formaba un escándalo.* But Fernando would take the money out of his pocket and say, 'Don't worry, pay me back when you have it.' Ramón, he was the quiet one, the shy one," she says.

But the one thing she can say for sure about all of them is they were *tremendos mujeriegos*—unbelievable womanizers. "Women would throw themselves at them," she says. "Imagine." They were in their twenties and thirties, they owned their own businesses, and they always drove around in new cars, trading them in every two or three years. She remembers the time my father went to Miami to buy a new 1958 dark blue Pontiac. He had it shipped over on a barge, and the uncles went around town with different girls every week in that car.

"Did you know," she says, coming out of her trance, "that Ramón has a son here?"

No, I did not know.

A son?

Ramón's son lives in Marianao, she says. Alina sees him all the time at La Plaza, and she visits with him every so often. She says that at about the time my uncle got engaged to his wife of forty-plus years, a woman he had dated off and on showed up at his fiancée's house looking for him, insisting that he recognize the boy as his own. He had no proof that this was his son, and he was set to marry in a matter of weeks. Alina says she heard the woman threatened to burst in during the wedding, and groomsmen had to be posted at the door. My uncle left for the United States before claiming the boy as his.

"And he looks just like Ramón," Alina says. "They say that the son of an affair, *el hijo de un tarro*, always looks the most like his father. And this man," she says, leaning in to stress the point, "looks like Ramón gave birth to him himself. You know, he would love to meet you."

Ay, Alina, I . . . I don't know about that.

How must this child—no, this *man* who would be in his forties—feel after all these years, never knowing his father? Rejected, abandoned? How would he receive me? Would he take out the anger, the frustration of having been left behind on me?

"*Ay, chico,* it would mean so much to him," she says in my silence.

I have to think about it. This is . . . I sigh. I never imagined I'd be taking on this role of emissary. *This is big. I have to think about it.*

It makes me think about a lot of things. As I sip my coffee wordlessly, Alina is cleaning up in the kitchen, boiling beans for her dinner on a single electric burner, which is the standard-issue cooking device for Cubans. I am thinking about this lost cousin. I am thinking about my birthday parties at T.Y. Park, about family photos around the roasted pig in the backyard, about squeezing together at my Abuela Teresa's for Thanksgiving and Christmas dinners. And I am trying to imagine where he would be in the photo.

But mostly, I am thinking about that fight with my mother.

About ten years ago, I don't remember why, I was arguing with her outside her garage in Pembroke Pines, the home I grew up in. She had always been the one who protected me from my father's wrath, his style of country punishment that consisted of belts to the rump, the way his father disciplined him. Today I often wonder who this little old man is who walks around the floor on all fours like a horse with my daughters riding on his back and where this gentle soul was when I was kid. I struggled to please him, to be strong, gregarious, and outgoing, like he was. Try as I might, I was

Mami's boy, who went to the car dealers at night and looked at the new Fords with her. I was her partner at church; my father rarely went. I was her confidant, her sidekick. But in the years since I left home, after I became an adult, after I got married and had children of my own, I had grown to be less her little boy and more my father's companion. I began to understand him better, to see him more as a man and a father, as an equal.

Then, in an argument about him, my mother blurted out, "You think your father doesn't have his faults? All those Frías men were *mujeriegos*. Do you know he has an illegitimate daughter in Cuba?"

Her outburst had the desired effect.

No. I did not know.

It ended the argument with stunned silence. I could see from the look on her face that she had gone too far, said too much. And the mystery that was the life of my father before he came to the United States as a grown man took a new twist. There are holes in my knowledge of him that this place can fill. If I have the nerve to ask. I have never spoken with my father about that fight. He does not know that I know. And even now, as I sit on a lumpy orange couch in Cuba, owned by the woman who was the girlfriend of one of my uncles a half century ago, I am not sure that I dare myself to ask.

Alina comes back into the room.

I sit silently for another minute.

If you talk to him, I say finally, *to Ramón's son, tell him I'd like to meet him.*

I will face things one at a time.

Alina was more than just an uncle's girlfriend; this is becoming evident. She is the secret keeper of my family, the historian who seems to know where all the bodies are buried. Probably of all the people remaining in Marianao, she spent the most time in the family's old home here.

I have heard about this house, and I ask Alina if we can go see it. Of course, she says, it's only just up the street.

As we are heading out, my phone rings, and I see from the caller ID it is a Cuba number.

Rosita!

I have totally forgotten about her. I have spent most of the afternoon with Alina, at La Plaza, and I realize she is still waiting for me.

"*Niño,* what's happened to you? I've been worried sick waiting for you!"

I'm sorry, 'perdóname,' Rosita, I lost track of time. There's just so much to learn.

She laughs and says not to worry. She tells me she had called my dad's friend, the butcher Miguel, and he had been waiting for a while before going home. Don't worry, she says, she'll call him back over when I arrive. I have been lost on this journey, and I promise that I will come soon. But I have to see the house, even if just for a moment. Because I know something about it that even Alina does not. That there is a body buried there, too, so to speak. Buried treasure. And only my father and I know where to look.

José motors delicately over the cracked asphalt, navigating past ditches that are like canyons, with weeds growing inside. Alina says that first we have to swing by Mario's house. Mario is my father's cousin, who still lives here in Marianao. I have heard my father speak of him often.

We drive two blocks, and she gets out of the car and disappears between houses. She returns several minutes later, saying there was no answer, and we are back on our way. After one turn, Alina tells José to stop. That house, she says, is where my Tío Rafael used to live. It is a sort of triplex apartment building, each story painted in the remnant of a different color. It makes the house look like it has been put together from scraps of different homes: one, a fresh-painted salmon; another, a mottled cobalt blue; and a third section, a faint, peeling aqua.

One block farther, we reach a house next to a vacant corner lot. This is it, Alina says, and José parks along the street. I dig the scraps of paper out of my bag and find the address of the home my father lived in as a young man in Marianao. The number on the paper is the same as the one in black numbers by the glassed-in porch. This is it: my father's home.

From the street, I take it in: A narrow set of cracked terra-cotta steps that lead up to the two-story house divides a pair of concrete planters that are flaking to reveal bricks beneath. Lush green plants with blood-red hibiscus blooms—my mother's favorite flower— are on either side, the bushes growing wildly in every direction. Yellow paint is flaking off the walls, making it look as if the house has been painted with a camouflage stencil. To the right of the house is an empty corner lot, enclosed in a rusting chain-link fence twelve feet high, another flowering hibiscus climbing it like a vine, concealing what is inside. It is the empty lot my father and I have spoken of so many times. It is where the treasure is buried.

I climb the steps and knock gingerly on an iron door with glass panes that closes off the front patio. Some of the glass is missing or broken, and the whole glassed-in porch seems to rattle when I knock. No one answers. I knock again, call inside.

'¿Hola? Buenos días,' is someone home?

No answer still.

"We almost never see him," Alina says.

The old man who lives here alone is either locked inside drinking or out buying more liquor. Sometimes, he's gone for days, she says. I knock again.

'Señor,' I'm just visiting, and I'd like to talk with you. '¿Hola?'

"Let's go next door," Alina says, heading up the block with José. "There are some people that knew your family who would love to meet you."

But I do not want to leave. I stand in front of the door, trying to peer inside. I feel like I am being pulled by a force on the other side, and only the rule of law keeps me from pressing further. I do not want anything from this man, from this house, from all of Cuba at this moment. I just want to stand inside, close my eyes, and imagine the life that existed here. But no one comes to the door.

I walk back down the steps and to the side of the house, where a low concrete wall separates it from the vacant lot next door. My heart begins pumping wildly. Since learning I was coming to Cuba, I have thought only of this moment. My father and I have spoken about it, and it is as if I am seeing the memories before me. The day of his forty-second birthday—the day before he left for the United States—my father buried something in that yard. A metal urn. Inside of it, something more valuable than gold. Yes, he went on to become a jeweler in the United States, owning a little store, even taking a bullet once defending what was his. But, no, there is nothing you could call priceless by monetary standards in that urn: Some worthless pre-Castro Cuban pesos. A few silver American coins. Some old pictures and documents. It's nothing more than a time capsule. Finding it would be the real treasure. Knowing that one thing in thirty-seven years has not changed, the reward. I want to look at those trinkets to help me imagine a Cuba that exists now only in the memories of our fathers. And now the opportunity is here, right here in front of me, but it might as well still be ninety miles away. I put my hands on the fence, move aside the flowering vine, and look into the yard, where there are several trees planted in neat rows.

"Your grandfather planted that avocado tree from a sapling," Alina says, standing next to me.

The tree is now easily twenty-five feet tall. The branches are cut oddly, the tree misshapen, as if hurricanes and tropical storms have done the only pruning.

"He died before he could ever eat its fruit, though," Alina says. "We can come back another day."

She takes my left arm and pats it lightly. She must be able to see the frustration on my face. I take a deep breath. Of course, she's right. I snap a few pictures and walk with Alina, arm in arm, down the sidewalk my father walked as a young man.

Three doors down, Alina yells from the sidewalk into a house, which is separated from the street by a chain-link fence, like all the other homes. Its owner, a slender woman with dark hair, comes out and is happy to see Alina.

"You've been lost from around these parts—*Estás perdida*," she tells Alina.

"I'm going to make it up to you," Alina says, "because I've brought someone that you're going to want to meet."

We walk past a weather-beaten wooden door into the house. I sit on a velvety couch with a pattern no one in the United States has seen in decades and can feel the springs pushing up against my legs. Alina sits next to me, her hand resting gently on my knee. The woman inside tells her daughter to brew some coffee, and soon the air is awash in the sweet, mocha aroma. I still have not said a word.

"Take a good look at him. Doesn't he look like someone?" Alina says.

I try not to smile as I am being examined.

"I know that face," the woman says, squinting at me. "Who are you?"

Alina answers for me. "This," she says, softly stroking my shoulder, "is the son of Fernando Frías."

The woman's eyes roll to the sky, accepting enlightenment from the Lord Almighty.

"*Ay, Dios santo! Claro, claro*, I can see it. He has that same air."

Her father was the town doctor, who, of course, knew everyone. Then, another woman who is visiting from across the street says, "Yes, I, too, can see the resemblance." She was a close friend of my Tía Dania's and attended her wedding. After all these years, they still live in the same houses. They ask me about my family, from whom they have heard only through Alina over the years. How they miss their presence here, they say, in that house, on this street, in Marianao. The old man who lives there now, "that hermit," one of them says, they see only when he leaves the pump to the cistern running and floods his and the neighbors' yards.

But, oh, how the block used to come to life when *los Frías* lived there, they tell me. The single brothers lived in the house—how women clung to them, *se le pegaban las mujeres*, one of them adds—with my grandparents. But every Sunday, the married brothers and sisters all came by for dinner. Their cars lined up around the block as music flowed from the open windows. While the men played dominoes on the back patio, a pig roasted in the open air on the lot next door, and children, my cousins Danita, Solange, and Amado, played in the grass. They all had their own lives but wanted to be close, needed to be close to their family.

When I walk past the house on the way to the car, I try to see it as it was. I stop in front and hold still. I can hear the life inside, Beny Moré spinning on the record player, *los hermanos* arguing over dominoes. I can smell the pig roasting, the garlic and sour orange in the *mojo* sizzling and filling the air with mouthwatering pungency, the aroma mixing with the sharp smell of charcoal burning to an ashen gray. And I see my cousins playing tag around the avocado tree my grandfather planted. But the picture is fleeting, and soon it dissolves into flaking yellow paint, broken windows, overgrown bushes, and a misshapen avocado tree. My mind does not recognize this house as the one it had illustrated with years of anecdotes. The one that older *marianeses* paint with wistful nostalgia. The one I know exists only in quilted memories.

We rumble over the potholed streets back to Alina's house and leave her at her door. She says she can't make it to Rosita's because she doesn't want to be gone when her niece gets home. But she will call Rosita to tell her we are on our way.

"*Ay*, Carlos, you've given me new life," she says.

She asks me, if I have time this week, to please visit her sister, who lives in El Vedado.

"Just for a few minutes. She loved *los Frías* so much, I know it would make her so happy to see you." She gives me her sister's telephone number, and I promise I will call.

"And come back tomorrow if you can. Or the next day. I'll make you lunch. You know this is your home. You can stay here if you like."

She offers to sleep with her niece so I can have the back room to myself. I tell her not to worry; she'll have enough trouble keeping me away while I'm in Havana. She hugs me, and I can feel her hands trembling. She releases me, looks me in the eye, and hugs me again.

We are so late as we head toward Rosita's house. I was originally supposed to be there at noon and have kept her waiting the entire day. I feel a rumble in my stomach, and it reminds me I have not eaten. And neither has José. I've been fueled by knowledge and nostalgia, and frankly I feel like I'll never have to eat again. I am full with newly minted memories. José has been by my side all day, even calling his wife from my cell phone to tell her he is going to be late tonight, but he never even mentioned food.

'Coño,' José, *you must be starving!* 'Mi hermano,' *I'm sorry.*

He smiles and admits that, yeah, he could eat *un caballo*. I tell him to find a restaurant and I'll buy dinner not just for us but for Rosita and whoever else might be at her house. It's the least I can do for him and for her. We stop at a little storefront between houses, a café that is nothing more than a counter with outside seating. I want to buy something opulent, something that Cubans might not ordinarily be able to buy for themselves. I want it to be a feast. But I am not in a touristy section, and this little restaurant is made for the people who live here. I buy six roasted chicken quarters and two liters of soda, one a tuKola, the other a lime-flavored one. I do not buy more food because there is nothing else for sale.

José stops in front of a freshly painted aqua house with bright yellow trim and parks across the street. The house is narrow, like an old Miami Beach duplex, and pressed between buildings.

I open a low iron gate and step onto a tiled foyer just outside the entrance. The entire front of the house is made up of French doors, and all of the glass panels are clean and intact. The inside is hidden from view by a curtain that runs the length of the door. I knock, and after a few seconds, the curtain pulls away. A thin-framed woman opens the door, her short blond hair neatly styled into a small beehive, and she is smiling behind her gold-framed glasses.

"*Ay, muchacho*, what a relief!" Rosita says, and we hug like friends who have not seen each other all summer. "You forgot all about me, and Alina has had you all to herself all day. Well, now it's my turn. Come in, come in!"

We walk inside, and the house invites us. The ceilings are at least twelve feet high. Although I can tell from the pattern of the fabric that the furniture is old, the chairs and sofa are well-kept and neatly placed. I tell her I've brought dinner for us, but she has already eaten, and her husband is still at work.

"But I want you to sit down here and enjoy," she says, leading us to a small round table next to her kitchen. In fact, she says, she will make *tostones*. I tell her not to go to all the trouble of deep-frying the plantains. I know even cooking oil is a commodity, but she insists she makes delicious *tostones*.

"*Ay, niño,* for me this is a treat," she says.

I relent because those crispy cakes are my weakness. Plus, she'll heat up some rice left over from her dinner. That way, we can have a proper meal, she says. She calls Miguel, my father's friend, and tells him to start heading over. While the oil warms, she brews fresh espresso, and I find myself looking forward to that sweet aroma.

Rosita disappears into the back and returns a few minutes later with a handful of photos. We walk back to the main room, she opens the front door, and we sit in opposite rocking chairs as a warm but welcome breeze blows in from the street while we drink our coffee.

"You have to see these photos," she says and begins handing me an array of memories. They are pictures of her as a girl, some stained at the edges, some fading into a reddish mirage. I pass them to José after I see them. One is the black-and-white her friend shot of my father holding the coffee cup to his lips. The girl standing next to him in a fifties blouse with a wide collar, dark buttons, and rolled-up sleeves is Rosita. She was the principal waitress at Mi Buchito.

"You wouldn't believe the business that little Buchito brought in. Every night, there were lines and lines that never ended," she says and recounts the story of how, when she was sixteen, the brothers helped her lie about her age so she could start working to support her family. "They were so good to me."

But they were tough bosses, she says. Shirts had to be crisp and tucked in. Skirts had to be pressed. And the girls always had to smile. They used to tell her that the waitresses, not the owners, were the ones who made the businesses successful. There are pictures of her children and one with her husband, a man she has been married to for more than thirty-five years. She tells me he works at a newsstand, selling books, magazines, and newspapers like *Granma* and *La Juventud Rebelde*, the Rebel Youth.

Will he be home in time for me to meet him?

"No, I don't think so," she says. "He's working late today."

She hands me another photo. This one is in color, and from all the gray hair, I know it is recent. It is a picture of all the uncles standing next to her during her last visit to the United States. She has a daughter who lives in Miami now, and Rosita visits her every few years. Every trip, *los Frías* give her jewelry from the stores and wads of cash. They each pitch in, and she returns home with several hundred dollars. She is wearing a pair of gold bangles on her right wrist, dangling earrings with blue stones, and a thin necklace adorned with small white pearls. I ask her how she is allowed to visit so often. Most people, I'm told, aren't granted visas because they are considered "potential emigrants" by the Cuban government.

"You know, every time I've put in a request, I've always gotten it," she says, not looking surprised.

"Well, tell me, what's brought you here? What made you want to take this trip?" she asks me.

I've been dying to tell you, but I didn't want to say it over the phone.

As we sit rocking, I lower my voice and begin to tell her my story. I've come on a personal journey to know the land of my parents, I tell her, and to write about the experience. To know all the places they knew, to meet the people they met, to find my history. But I have only been able to come in as a tourist through Mexico.

You see, I am a journalist for a newspaper, and Cuban Immigration is turning away reporters because of Castro's illness.

You should see all the stories being written in the United States right now, people wondering what will happen when 'El Hombre' dies.

I am looking down at the pictures and sipping coffee as I tell the story.

Reporters are being turned away en masse. It's on every talk show in South Florida. And if he dies while I'm here, I would actually get to see the transition up close. Who knows, maybe one day I'll even be able to write a book about it all.

As I have done all day, I pull the folded children's notebook I bought in the city—the one with a cartoon soccer player on the cover—out of my back pocket and start taking notes. When I look up, I realize Rosita has stopped rocking. She looks worried. Her words become curt and strained.

"I figured there was something like this going on," she says.

She wrings her wrinkled hands and bites her lip. She is silent for a moment before speaking again.

"Look, Carlos, let me be up front with you," she says, taking a deep breath. "This is the CDR. And I want you to know that my husband is the president."

The wind has stopped blowing. The room has gotten noticeably warm.

CDR stands for the Committee for the Defense of the Revolution. This neighborhood watchdog group calls on citizens by oath to their country, to spy on neighbors and turn in dissenters. Every neighborhood has a CDR. And on my third day in Cuba, I have just outed myself at the local headquarters. I look from my notebook to her and realize that my mouth is hanging open. I shut it.

"Carlos," she says, trying to reassure me. "I just wanted to tell you how things are. But my friendship with your family means more to me than any of that."

I try to believe her. But I picture the people I have spent the day with—*my God, Alina*—all being hauled in front of some tribunal to determine whether they should be charged with espionage or treason. Rosita sits back in her chair stiffly, looks forward, and continues rocking. "Go ahead and ask me your questions," she says.

She is not looking at me. I hold my pen over the paper and stare blankly at the page. I manage to scribble only "Committee Defense Revolution" and "husband the president."

Tell me more . . . about my uncles.

I slowly fold the notebook in my lap. She starts rocking faster and begins telling more stories. I smile as she tells them, and she begins to smile, too.

I do not hear a single word.

The pounding of my heart is in my stomach now, and all I can think about is getting out of this place. I look at my watch and pretend to reach around in my pocket for my cell phone.

Oh, Rosita, my cell. I'm supposed to be getting a call from my family in . . . well, just my family.

I don't want to give away any more.

Hold that thought. Let me go see if I can find it in the car. I really can't miss this call.

I ask José if he can come open the door for me and help me look. I have to get out of here.

"Carlos, don't get cold with me," Rosita says warmly as I reach the opening of her front door. It sends a chill down my back. She has sensed me recoiling. I turn around and give her that "C'mon, you kidding me?" look. I cross the street and pretend to rummage around the car, looking for a phone I know is in my backpack, trying to quiet my heart.

She's in el Comité! I say in a hushed rasp to José.

"I would have warned you, but I thought you knew," he says. "I noticed it on the door when we came in."

I wasn't looking for anything like that, couldn't have ever fathomed it. And the husband, José says, it's more than coincidence that he's not around. You have to be a communist to work at one of those newsstands, and by this time—it is almost 8:30 P.M.—he should be home. They close at 7:00. He knows, he says, because his mother used to work for one.

"Look, I wouldn't ask anything else if I were you. Just talk about family, keep things light. Let's eat our dinner and get out of here."

I stop pretending to rummage and stare at him.

Dinner.

I brought dinner. I cannot just run out on her. Rosita has spent the whole day waiting for me, is cooking *tostones* for me as we speak. I can feel my mouth becoming watery with saliva and a tightness in my throat.

I have to break bread here.

As we walk back into the house, Rosita is in the kitchen, and I can hear the sizzling of hot oil. I swallow hard to keep my stomach in check.

There is a knock at the door.

"*Hola,* Rosita!" It is a stout man with a barrel chest and thick glasses.

"*Ay,* Miguel, come in, come in," she says, hurrying from the kitchen to grab my arm and take me to him.

"What do you think, Fernando's son?"

His handshake is a vise, his hands callused and thick. Oh, yes, this man was a butcher. He asks me about my father, a man he exchanges letters with to this day. Miguel's brother lives in the United States and, until the newer travel restrictions, visited Cuba often, taking letters between my father and Miguel.

"Your father was like a brother to me," he says. "No, we were more than brothers."

As we sit in Rosita's living room, Miguel tells me stories about when he and my father would go out on the town. A girl my father liked agreed to go out with him only if my father had a friend for her sister. Miguel agreed to the blind date only to find the girl was, well . . . the kind of girl you have to throw into a package deal. Another time, they each told the other about a girl they had met over the weekend who was perfect. She had beautiful jet-black hair, my father said. So did my girl, Miguel said. She was a dancer. So was mine. She had light green eyes, so did mine. "Is her name so-and-so?" Miguel asked, and it was! The same girl. But my father owed him from the earlier debacle, so he yielded to Miguel. Stories like these went on and on.

"But it wasn't until your father was arrested that we got really close," Miguel said.

When my father and two uncles were in La Cabaña, Miguel took cuts of beef—already hard to come by in 1965—every week to my family's home in Marianao, for *el Viejo* and *la Vieja*, my grandparents. After my father's eighteen months in prison were over, he was shipped to a work camp for another two years. The camp was a two-hour bus ride from Marianao, and although only family was allowed to visit, Miguel showed up one day with a bag of cooked meat and pleaded with the guards. They tried to turn him away, but he started screaming that they had to let him see his brother. "And I yelled and yelled until they finally let me in," he told me. "Your *Papá* asked me, '*Muchacho*, what did you tell those men to let you through?' I said, 'I told them the truth. That we are more than brothers.'"

He speaks about how bad things got in the years following the revolution, how he barely had meat for himself, much less any customers. Even today, he says, it's up to luck whether there will be chicken at the rations store.

"No, no, that's not true," Rosita says from the kitchen, where she is serving our chicken and rice and crispy *tostones*, her voice coming as a surprise.

"There was chicken here last week. I've never seen this rations station run out of chicken. Maybe that happens in other places, but I don't know about that."

Miguel looks back at me.

"And what brought you here, *now?*" he says. I stutter and look at José, whose gaze is fixed.

It just seemed like as good a time as any to visit.

"You picked a strange time for us. People here are nervous about . . . everything that's going on," Miguel says, lowering his voice.

"The boys have to eat," Rosita yells from the kitchen, our conversation cut short. Miguel hugs me like a grizzly, and I can tell he is hugging my father.

"Tell Fernando that I think about him a lot. And even though he's over there and I'm over here, that I still remain his best friend," he says.

My father has never had what you would call a best friend, not outside of his brothers. And I think now I understand why. He left his friend behind all those years ago.

We sit at our plates, and José dives hungrily at his chicken. I approach it as a science project. I skirt around the meat and taste the *tostones*. They are hot and salty and the lightest, crispiest, and most delicious I have ever tasted. But I can feel my insides trembling. I begin to force down enough food, despite the knot in my stomach, to prove to Rosita that I am not rattled, that everything is right between us.

As I eat, I can think only of Alina. I rushed away from her house, leaving her to make dinner for herself, and instead I bought dinner for Rosita, who could probably afford or acquire whatever she needs. She has already told me she will just refrigerate the leftover chicken, and maybe her daughter will eat the rest tomorrow. It dawns on me that, in my entire afternoon with Alina, I never saw her eat. She just moved with me, from house to house, every now and again sneaking outside to smoke a cigarette. In my rush to meet Rosita, I failed to appreciate Alina.

I ask Rosita whether she would mind if I took some leftover chicken to Alina. Of course not, she says, and she wraps it up in a foam container. I look down at my plate. I am pleased enough with my work. The chicken is picked at sufficiently, and I have eaten three or four *tostones*. They settle in my stomach like stones.

It is getting late, and José has to get back home to his wife and family, I tell Rosita. Plus, I am exhausted from this day. She says she hopes this will not be the last she sees of me. She decides right then that she wants to host a dinner at her house in my honor. We can invite Alina, she says.

"Let's not invite Miguel, though. I like him, don't get me wrong," Rosita says suddenly. "But every time he comes over, he just talks about the same depressing things, over and over. It gets exhausting after a while."

She leads us to the door and hugs me gently. She holds my hands in hers and looks me in the eye. There is conflict there. She is scared for me, and she is torn.

"Be careful. Please be careful," she implores me as we stand in the doorway. "Do everything you can while you're here. And don't do anything you can't."

As the Ford rumbles away from the aqua house, Rosita stands at the door. We make a turn, heading toward Alina's, and I tell José to be ready to pull over. I think I might be sick.

We drop off the chicken at Alina's, and I resist telling her what happened with Rosita. I am too tired, too sick to go into it all over again. I just hug her, tell her everything went fine, and say that I will call her tomorrow. When I look at her now, it is as if I'm seeing her for the first time. Her eyes are smiling as widely as her grin. She is holding my hands, and I can tell she does not want to let go. Nor do I.

"*Buenas noches*. I hope you sleep well," she says. And I wonder if I will sleep at all.

Our car ride back into Havana is quiet. The roads are dark between the occasional streetlamps, and people still step out into the road trying to hail us. I write in my notebook by the light of passing lanterns.

"Anybody can be a communist that way," José says suddenly, his eyes fixed on the road. A family in the United States, sending money back. A house that José says he could remodel to fit at least two other families. A husband who is the president of an organization that informs on other Cubans and gets special benefits. And everyone else, walking around wondering when the other shoe will drop. I tell him I didn't know what to do with myself when Rosita dropped her bombshell. I didn't know what would happen next, if I was in trouble, if *he* was in trouble.

"That fear you felt, we feel every day of our lives," he says. "The fear that something bad, *something*, is going to happen."

We reach the hotel, and José parks on the same back street where we began our day. We sit in the quiet of the night for a moment, and I sigh heavily.

"You know, I've driven around a lot of people, even Cubans who left and came back, who just want to see the pretty parts, go to the clubs, meet some women. But this was different," José tells me. "I feel almost a little embarrassed because I heard some things that I know were pretty *fuerte*, pretty hard to hear. But I really feel like I lived what you lived. I learned something important about the way things were."

As I tuck my notebook into my backpack, he warns me to keep it with me at all times.

"What you're carrying in that little notebook is *dinamita*—dynamite. That little book stays with you, *mi hermano*." Not in my bedroom at the hotel, not even in the room safe, he says. I put it back in my pocket.

I take out one hundred Convertibles and give them to him. He holds them in his hands, his eyes darting from the five twenties to me. "This is too much. No. No, no, no . . . this is too much," he says and begins to return it to me as if I have handed him a live grenade. It is equivalent to about ten months' salary for an average Cuban, but about what a round-trip cab ride to the airport costs me back home. I tell him he's earned it, if only for going without food for most of the day.

I ask him what he's doing tomorrow, and, unfortunately, he's back at the hotel. But he has a friend who also has a car and could shuttle me around. He will call him tonight and slip me a note under my door in the morning about what time to meet.

"Where are you going tomorrow?" he asks.

I decided before we left for Marianao.

La Cabaña.

His eyes widen, and he puffs his cheeks as he lets out a long breath.

Yeah. I let out a deep sigh myself.

I know.

DAY FOUR

"Ramón has a son over there!" my wife says, our voices running into each other's because of the delay over the phone.

I know, can you believe that? Wait, how did you find out? Alina just told me about it.

I sit on a bench in El Parque Central under the shade of a large tree. The cell phone connection is clear, but the delay makes it like using a walkie-talkie. Christy and I speak hurriedly because the calls cost more than a dollar a minute, and they quickly devour my prepaid phone cards. I want to tell her everything, *everything*, all at once: Alina. La Plaza. The house. Rosita. And she, too, is bursting with information. We fight to not talk over each other.

She says she spent yesterday at the birthday party of one of my cousin's kids, where all the talk, not surprisingly, was about *el atrivido*, the presumptuous young man who dared to go to Cuba. All the uncles and aunts milled around her, she says, since she and I have been talking or exchanging e-mails at least once a day. In the middle of a conversation, my Tío Ramón came up to her and said, "They say I have a son over there."

" 'They say.' He said it like he doesn't know for sure. He's got to know, doesn't he?" she says.

I don't know that he does.

"Well, he just came right up to me and said it, like it didn't matter who heard it. Either way, he says you should try to see him."

75

Man, I don't know. I mean, shouldn't this be Frank's job? Or Jesus' or Ray's?
My cousins, his sons.

Why do I get stuck with this?

"You have to do what you feel comfortable with." She pauses. "Speaking of which, did you decide what you're going to do about . . . you know. Your sister."

Right. What about *her?* Since hearing about my long-lost cousin, all I can do is think about the argument with my mother. Why did she say that? I don't even know what the fight was about, or whether it was relevant. Maybe I said something to make her bite. Maybe she'd had a fight with my dad that day. Maybe it had been eating at her all those years. All I know is that, in that second, things got more complicated. I thought I had put my arms around my dad's past. After all, it was a life he lived before coming to the United States. Before meeting my mother. Before me.

I had been raised knowing I have a half brother, Rogerio Frías, who was born in Cuba. I grew up being told that my father and Roger's mother had been married and divorced before coming to the United States. She left shortly thereafter for Los Angeles, where my brother lived most of his life. Before my father proposed to my mother, he told her about Roger and said that, if they were going to be married, she had to accept that part of his history. She went further. Because my father never had more than a sixth-grade education in the country, she was the one who wrote the letters to Roger.

When my brother was seventeen, he visited us for the first time. I was two. Roger visited South Florida every summer thereafter, and I, the *only* only child in my family, idolized him. Even though he is fifteen years my senior, I loved having a brother-for-a-week. He played the part perfectly—because, in a sense, he was an only child, too. He knew how to make the best French toast for breakfast. He drove us to the beach, and we'd spend all day swimming and playing football on the sand. We went on vacation to Disney World, and he would photograph us with his camera. When he left, I would spray one side of my bed with his cologne, Ralph Lauren's Polo, and pretend he was still there. It was the week of the summer I looked forward to more than any other. When he came to visit, I saw no difference in the way my mother treated us. The family just grew by one. Today, we live less than ten miles apart and are godfathers to each other's children. My parents sometimes pick up his kids from school, and they spend the afternoon at Abu and Abuelita's house. This is what family should be, at the very least.

So why had they buried my sister?

I blew it. I should have asked about her before I left.

"Do you . . . want me to ask your dad for you?" Christy asks.

I am thankful for the delay, thankful for the moment of silence to think.

Christy is the only one I've told. She's the only one who understands. We've spent hours talking about how this girl might have come to be and why my father has never spoken of her. Plus, she is the only one with enough guts to ask.

"*Lind*, did you hear what I said?"

Sorry . . . I heard you.

This is the coward's way out, I know. I need to ask my father myself how he could leave his own flesh and blood, a girl, behind in this forgotten world. I thought about asking him before I left but never could. Now I'm here, and it's too late. And I may never be able to come here again. I glance around El Parque Central and look at the faces: She could be one of these women, wearing mismatched clothing and flip-flops. I have a *sister*. She has a brother. No matter the circumstances, we are family. And so, I take the coward's way out.

Yeah. Yeah, ask him. And ask him for any details that might help me find her.

"You're stirring up a lot of stuff over there," she says, and we both burst out laughing.

Yeah, and I'm bringing it back home with me.

José is waiting for me outside the hotel. He is working the door today and breaks away for a minute to take me to his friend.

"Martín is a good guy—*buena gente*, he says as we walk toward the back street where he and I met yesterday. "And you don't have to worry about him, if you know what I mean."

We hear a honk. A man in a baseball cap pulled low is waving from inside a primer gray American *cacharro*, a rust bucket with mismatched rims, and he opens the door to let me in.

Martín wrestles with the three-speed shifter on the steering column of his '53 Ford, and we bounce, bounce, bounce from gear to gear. The sixty-six-horsepower Hyundai engine purrs like a motorcycle's as we cruise along El Malecón. The air is warm and thick, but when I stretch my arm out the window, I can feel the cool of the sea spray. I surf my arm over the wind, like a little boy allowed to ride shotgun for the first time. As I look out the window, I catch sight of *it* out of the corner of my eye. La Cabaña.

The great stone walls, a grayish brown, rise up against a searing blue sky and calm turquoise sea. I turn away, not wanting to take it all in just yet. I have a promise to fulfill first. I need to see Manuela, Alina's sister. I called her first thing this morning and told her to expect me. She had spoken to Alina the night before and had not left the house, waiting for my call. We drive the same path as yesterday along the ocean wall, and I stare forward. But I can see from my peripheral vision when La Cabaña disappears.

The streets in El Vedado are narrow, and we slow to a crawl as we pass other cars. The road is covered in a canopy of green, the August sun filtering down and flashing through the trees like a movie projector. With the ocean nearby and the diffuse sun, you can feel a cool breeze swirling.

Houses are set back off the road, not as in the city. Some have small courtyards out front, knolls of grass that range from neatly manicured to savagely overgrown, where weeds stretch freely over dusty gray-brown pits. We make a turn and drive along a narrow street with a wide sidewalk. There are businesses on the bottom floors of two-story buildings and apartments above them. A massive flowering tree, with leaves the color of a gecko and blooms of iridescent orange, marks the corner to Manuela's house.

I call her from my cell as we wait on the sidewalk outside, an eight-foot chain-link fence separating us from the small courtyard. A woman who looks to be in her fifties opens the door beyond it. She wipes the wisps of bobbed brown hair from her face and scrunches her shoulders.

"Ave Maria, Alina was right! You can see right away that you are a Frías," Manuela says, unlocking the fence and letting Martín and me in. I have never been told so many times that I have the air of my father. We hug, and, in a move that is becoming customary, she steps back to examine my features for the faces she once knew.

She leads us up a narrow stairway, over cracked marble steps, to her second-story apartment. The living room is filled with knick-knacks and picture frames. There are pictures of her, of Alina, of a young man with floppy black hair at all ages: as a boy, as a teenager, as an adult.

"That's my baby, *mi niñito,"* she says, grabbing a photo of her son as a boy and holding it for me to see.

She ushers us out to the balcony—"Sit down, sit down. We have too much to talk about," she says, almost giggling—before rushing back to the kitchen to set coffee to brew. We all sit under the shade of the flowering tree and enjoy the breeze, sipping our coffee, Manuela rocking briskly in her chair.

"You have no idea what you have done for Alina. You have given her twenty years of new life," Manuela says.

They spent hours talking after I left Marianao last night, reliving the moments of my visit, reliving the moments of the past. Manuela needs very little prompting to return there, and soon she takes us back fifty years, to when she was a preteen, living in the very apartment where Alina still lives in Marianao. The stories of my father come quickly. She was just a girl when she met *los Frías,* she says. Alina, her older sister by four years, was a teenager when she saw La Plaza de Marianao become increasingly filled with businesses owned by the brothers. They had come to her town, to her very backyard, and she was smitten right away. She had eyes only for Felipe, the prankster and smooth talker of the bunch.

"But of the five brothers, your father was the most *alegre*, the most jovial. And in my opinion, the best-looking," Manuela says.

When she thinks of my father, she pictures him in that gray McGregor shirt and blue suit, smelling of Brut 33 cologne, moving between the businesses at La Plaza. He rarely kept his jacket on, though, and usually rolled up his sleeves to the elbows so he could wipe down tables and help in the kitchen. These are the things a young girl remembers.

"I can still see him standing there," she says.

Manuela was about eleven when he once walked past their little apartment with a new satin gray windbreaker. He stopped to say hello, and Manuela was hypnotized by a triangular medal that hung from the zipper.

"I don't know why, but I just fell in love with that little *cosita*, and I kept saying, 'Por favor, Fernando, can I have it?' Who knows why I wanted that. It's just something that a child falls in love with. He said, 'Niña, why do you want that? I just bought this jacket, I don't even know if it will work if I take this off.' But he broke it off and gave it to me anyway."

She still has it, she says, in a box in her attic. She has a lot of memories in that box, things she put away years ago but are only a happy thought away. She still has a doll that belonged to my cousin Solange, thirty-five years after Solange and her mother, my Tía Dania, were the last of the family to leave the house in Marianao.

"*Ay*, that house," Manuela tells me, running her hands through her hair. "You know, Alina lived in that house."

When only my aunt and her daughters remained in Cuba, caring for my grandmother—my father and his brothers had already left for the United States—Alina basically moved in to help, Manuela says. She was twenty-five then. While my aunt worked, Alina took care of the children. Manuela came over occasionally, and it was she who taught Danita her colors and letters.

Six months before the last of the brothers left, my grandfather

Francisco passed away. Manuela and Alina were at the family's side to mourn with them. Alina's love for my Tío Felipe served only to draw her closer to them, to that house. My family had become her family, and Alina clung to them.

"She has never gotten over Felipe," Manuela says, picking up our coffee cups and taking them to the kitchen. When she returns, she leans against the railing, and the breeze seems to carry the memories with it. Manuela remembers Felipe coming by at night in the brothers' new dark blue Pontiac and Alina rushing out to meet him. Her straight, jet-black hair flowed behind her like a mane, and it was all the more impressive because of her thin, spritelike body. They sped off, and the sound of music and laughter seemed to follow them like a comet's tail.

In the months after the last of *los Frías* left in 1971, they became like all other Cubans who fled the revolution. Phantoms. Letters seldom made it through, Manuela says. Phone calls were unheard of. When people "went to the outside," as the Cubans call the emigration, they vanished. They were like missing children, and the Cubans here like tortured parents, holding out hope of one day seeing their loved ones walk back through that door.

"It's something very difficult, *muy fuerte,* to deal with," Manuela says.

She copes with it in poetry. It is the therapy for her torment. She sits on this porch, with the wind in her face, to avoid the overwhelming moods of melancholy, writing sad, dark verses about "the eternal pain of our separation." She turns her face from the breeze.

"But that is my escape. Alina has never allowed herself to move on."

When my family left, the Cuban government gave Alina the right to their house. She had spent more time there than anyone else and, under the new laws, was the rightful resident—not owner, because there is no such thing as private ownership in Cuba. She could live there as long as she wanted. But Alina passed it up. She moved back into her little two-bedroom home with a view of La Plaza. The government changed the locks on the house and gave it to some other family. Which was just as well. That empty house was too crowded for Alina.

"She couldn't live in there with all those memories," Manuela says.

Why doesn't Alina move in with you? It seems like you two could really use each other's company.

"*Ay, niño,* you don't know how many times I've asked, pleaded with her, 'Alina, you're alone. There's nothing left for you there. . . .' "

She has never accepted. Alina tells Manuela she cannot move because she needs to be with their niece, Magda, the daughter of their late older sister, a girl Alina has raised as her daughter.

But Magda is a grown woman. The truth is Alina can't bear to leave La Plaza. Moving would mean accepting that life has moved on, that she is an old woman. And that the greatest years of her life—the girl with the flowing black hair chasing the prankster with the Cheshire grin—are only a memory. The sisters see each other once a week but talk almost daily.

"And you'd be surprised how often we talk about *los Frías,*" Manuela says.

She has been laughing and telling stories but begins to slip into one of her moods of melancholy; I can sense it brewing behind her eyes like an afternoon thunderhead.

"Thinking about all of that does her a lot of damage, *mucho daño,*" Manuela says. Then she turns to me, puts her hand on my arm, and smiles, her eyes still stormy. "But it does her a lot of good, too."

Twenty years of good. . . .

Tell me about your son, I say quickly, and the grayness in her eyes passes. She vaults out of her chair and leads me by the hand back to her pictures. She picks up a recent photo.

"He looks just like his father." His father who has passed away.

It was just Manuela and her son for years. He is working as a waiter at a café near the center of the city, where he can make tips in dollars and Convertibles.

"He wanted to be an engineer," she says, looking from the picture to me. "But I told him not to waste his life by studying."

Before the revolution, she was a newspaper editor, a University of Havana graduate, and a literature professor. "But when I saw what they started doing to the newspapers, I wanted no part of it," she says.

Once, when she took food and clean clothes to the daughter of a neighbor who was under house arrest, she was caught and convicted of being an "untrustworthy citizen." She lost her job at the university and was blacklisted. That was fine with her, she says, leading me back to the porch. She started cleaning houses, still does, and makes more money that way than she would in any university. She lowers her voice and says she was reprimanded once and had to pay a fine for cleaning house without a license.

"In Cuba, you have to have a license to wipe your bottom," she says.

She continues working illegally, at her peril. She cleans the house of a diplomat, who is in and out of the country, and gets paid in foreign currency. Even though it hurt her to say the words, that's why she told her son not to pursue an advanced education. "He can't make ends meet with what they will pay him," she says, "and he'll never have the chance to leave the country because he would be considered a professional. He'll be trapped here."

My father always wanted me to be a dentist (and after some days in journalism, I wonder whether it's too late to rethink my career choice). But he always told me, "I don't care what you study, as long as you get a degree in something." It was his one requirement. Manuela, a college-educated woman, has counseled her son to be a waiter so he won't struggle to make a living. Yet he still insists on returning to school, she says, shaking her head and flashing something between a smile and the start of a long, hard cry.

You mentioned my grandfather. What can you tell me about him?

Manuela breaks out in a cackle, "Ay, Don Pancho," she says, calling my grandfather Francisco by his nickname. "I'll never forget the way he walked down the street with that little walk, *ese caminito*, like he was never in a hurry. You would say to him, *'Buenos días, Don Pancho,'* and he would just smile a little bit and tip his cap."

My grandfather died without ever finding freedom. He was

buried here. And his grave has not been visited by family in nearly four decades.

Manuela, do you know where my grandfather is buried?

Of course, she says. He is buried at the Cementerio de Colón, the largest, best-known cemetery in Cuba. My family, she tells me, has a burial plot there. All I need to find him is his full name, which I know, and the date he passed, she says. This I do not know.

"Alina does," Manuela says. "I guarantee you if you ask her, she'll tell you right away. That mind of hers, for anything that has to do with *los Frías*, is a steel trap."

Manuela clutches a small medal around her neck and says softly to herself again, "*Ay, Don Pancho.* May God have him in His Glory."

It is then that Martín, who has been an invisible presence, finally speaks.

"You believe in God, eh?"

Manuela is not as surprised by his question as I am.

"That is the one thing they did not take away from me," she says. She is wearing a square, gold medallion of the Virgin of Charity, Cuba's patron saint. She wears it always, she says, and I can tell from her tone this is not the first time she has had this conversation.

"My grandfather believed in God," Martín says.

You don't believe in God?

Martín shrugs his shoulders.

"I never really paid much attention to that, but I know some people who do. What I believe in is our daily bread, *nuestro pan de cada día,*" he says with a smirk.

"Well, I don't care what anybody thinks," Manuela says. "I am a believer in *El Señor*—even though 'they' tried to make life impossible for anyone who believed in something other than what they were teaching."

Her faith is not like mine, which was nurtured in Catholic school. I have the luxury of being able to question my faith, second-guessing the rituals and teachings of the Church, picking and choosing from the priest's Sunday homily as it suits me. Her faith is tested in fire. At the beginning of the revolution, the local CDRs took note of those they saw going to churches and "reminded" them constantly that to believe in a supreme being was anathema to communist philosophy. And that such belief was counterrevolutionary activity. But Manuela could not afford to waver in her convictions.

"I told them I didn't care. I believe in *El Señor,* and if that meant I wasn't a good communist, to hell with them, *para el diablo con ellos,*" she says.

On Sundays, she would attend a small, local church in the mornings. But most Sundays, she says, the service was interrupted by loud singing, drums beating, and a *güira* scratching. The government would organize street parties every Sunday just outside the doors of churches. The preacher raised his voice, she says, and the congregation huddled around him to hear the Word. Her faith was another reason she was labeled an untrustworthy citizen. It wasn't until Pope John Paul II's visit in 1998 that Cuba allowed—tolerated—open worship. Until then, "you were at your own risk," Manuela says. "Just ask Alina what she went through. Let her tell you."

When she walks us to the door, she tells Martín to go downstairs and start the car, adding that there is a picture she wants to dig up for me. After he leaves, she grabs me by the shoulders and looks me in the eye.

"I don't get such a great feeling from this driver," she says. "Don't you marry yourself to one. Switch around every day. Don't let people know where you're headed or when you're coming back. Don't trust anyone."

I had spared telling her I'm a journalist. When I took notes, I told her I was writing down stories to tell my family back home.

I'll be careful.

She smiles and hugs me like the doll in her attic. She sees me down the steps, and I watch her wave good-bye as Martín's *cacharro* puffs gray smoke into the air.

I decide I won't do what I did to José yesterday.

'Oye,' Martín, you starting to get hungry?

I ask him if he knows where Cuba's Chinatown is and whether it is too out of the way to see before we head to La Cabaña. He's not such a big fan of Chinese food, he says, but if that's what I want to eat, then, yeah, it's on the way. I had noticed the neighborhood marked on my map this morning. My wife's grandfather was born in El Barrio Chino. He is a Chinese Cuban, and if you ever met him you'd swear you'd seen him in the background of a martial arts film. Actually, you probably did; he was in at least one film in the seventies, playing a Chinese gangster. My wife got her thick black hair and porcelain complexion from him—not to mention the knack for making the best combinations of Cuban and Chinese food. If she can't be here, I can at least give her this one gift, walking in her history by taking pictures of the neighborhood where her grandfather was raised.

Martín's route leads us back into the heart of Old Havana. The lushness of El Vedado is gone, and soon the buildings climb the sides of the streets again, and laundered clothing waves to us from rusted, rickety balconies. Block after block, the scenery remains the same: The grayness of weathered concrete. The peeling and fading paint. It is like a swinging pocket watch, hypnotizing me into a trance of depression. We turn off a main street, and it is as if every color that has been sapped from the city has been poured onto this one block. Three red Chinese characters on a yellow sign, hanging beneath a jade pagoda, signal the entrance to El Barrio Chino. Roofs are tiled in pastel yellow and terra-cotta over the many shops along this corridor. A police officer leans against a garbage bin at the entrance. We park along the street and walk into the alley, lined with trinket shops and restaurants.

Ducks hang in the window of a butcher shop. Festive red-and-gold paper lanterns guide our way. Wooden railings, carved into Chinese characters, denote the restaurant seating areas. Golds and greens and reds and blues highlight our path. I allow myself to close my eyes for a second. When I open them, it is like I am walking down a street in San Francisco's Chinatown. But it is a short corridor, and we make it to the other side in less than five minutes. And then, more of the same mind-numbing grayness that haunts Old Havana.

This is it? This is the whole Barrio Chino?

Martín says the neighborhood is actually several blocks wide, but this is the section that the Cuban and Chinese governments have agreed to restore as a sort of downtown Chinatown. The Cubans have a long-standing partnership with the largest remaining communist government in the world, even as Cuba has rejected taking on the "Chinese model" for a hybrid communist-capitalist economy.

We walk back toward the pagoda at the entrance and find El Restaurante Guang Zhou. A waiter leads us up a narrow stairs, and a server coming down has to retrace his steps to let us through. We reach a room decorated in bright red and gold. It is small, perhaps the size of a bedroom, and there are three tables for four set up inside, where cold air-conditioning is blasting. We sit along a back wall, and when I look across, I notice another room on the other side of the entrance. In it is a bed. This is someone's house during nonbusiness hours.

It's on me, so order whatever you like.

There are some traditional items on the menu, the kinds of things you would expect to see in Chinese takeout. Egg rolls. Fried rice. Noodles, or *fideos*, mixed with different meats. There are also *tostones* and fried sweet plantains. And, for the first time, I see steak. Beef.

"*Coño*, it's been a long time since I've tasted beef," Martín says while looking over the menu.

My cousin Jorge has told me about this. For years, beef has not been available to Cubans. It is sold only at restaurants for tourists, who will pay handsomely for the meat. Cubans do buy the meat on the gray market, often not knowing the source or the health of the animal it came from. It is a crime, punishable by jail time, to be caught with red meat, the reasoning being that a steak a Cuban eats could easily be sold to a tourist for twenty or thirty dollars, depending on the cut.

When the waiter arrives, I am not surprised to hear Martín order a *palomilla*, the thin, pan-fried Cuban steak that is the only cut of red meat on the menu, and sweet fried plantains. I have an egg roll and the chicken with stir-fried noodles. When the meals arrive, Martín dives in. He cuts the steak into the smallest of pieces, each the size of a postage stamp. He eats one at a time, placing it delicately into his mouth and biting down slowly, as if to taste the juices' full flavor. He leaves one piece, turning to the plantains and rice. Then he comes back to the last morsel. He places the final piece of red meat in his mouth and chews it slowly, swallows it, and sits staring at the glistening empty plate for several seconds.

"*Gracias,*" he says, still admiring the plate before finally looking up. "That was delicious."

For the man who sees God in his daily bread, it was truly a religious experience.

We walk several blocks through El Barrio Chino. The streets are filled with people despite the heat. I live in South Florida, and still I have never seen so many women wearing such tight clothes.

Martín points out one woman standing by the door of a building as we cut through a back alley. "*Jinetera,*" he says. A prostitute. "You don't usually see them that blatantly anymore," he says, since the government has started to crack down. "But tourists who come here looking for them can find whatever they want. I've driven them around. I know where to look."

We pass several young girls walking together. One of them, who appears to be about thirteen, is pushing a stroller. Already, I've seen dozens of girls who look barely pubescent pushing their babies around the streets of Havana. Her hair is in long, tight curls, her arms and legs slender, and I imagine that she could outrun all of the boys on the playground with graceful strides. As she and her friends get closer, the dark circles below her sea green eyes, eyes that pop against her caramel skin, seem more pronounced. She is telling a story, flailing her hands and joking with her friends as she passes. Her childlike laughter startles me, as if it is all that remains of someone's little girl.

Martín looks back as they pass, paying particular attention to one dark-skinned girl with black, curly hair and shorts that end just where her legs begin.

"I think God has to be *un negro,* black like me," he says. "How else do you explain why he made *las negras* look that way?"

I look back myself and then to him.

Those are little girls.

"Those girls already know more than they should," he says.

I think about saying something else but think better of it.

I catch a scent of salt water tinged with sulfur as we drive back toward the coast, Martín's Ford picking up speed along El Malecón.

It comes back into sight, and this time, I do not look away.

The midafternoon sun is baking the great stone fortress on the other side of the Bay of Havana. An ocean breeze whips the red, white, and blue flag, its great white star in the center of a red field appearing to flash like an all-seeing eye from atop El Morro castle. A line of cannons faces the bay from a separate gray stone monolith, built on a grassy hilltop, menacing the world below.

"That's La Cabaña," Martín says, pointing out his window. He makes a turn, and the prison disappears from sight as the car plunges into a tunnel that crosses under the bay. The rumble of the engine reverberates inside the tunnel. Motorcycles and other cars pass, honk, rev their engines, the sounds melding into a hollow growl as warm exhaust fumes fill my head. Soon enough, the aching blue sky is above us again, the cool ocean air fanning us. We pass a billboard to our right: *"Seguimos Bien,"* it reads, "We are on the right track." It looks freshly painted—maybe since Castro fell ill.

Martín takes a ramp to the right, and we pass rows of small, gray, peeling houses that look to be the size of one room. The road turns past them and climbs gradually, the slope increasing as we wind up a hill. A severe rise tests the Hyundai engine, and the car growls louder. The road curves back to the left, past a sweeping forest of oaks and palms and an overgrowth of brush that makes it feel as if we are heading to a far-off place. There are no longer any homes, just a road cutting through wild vegetation as we climb higher and higher. Then, to my right, the domed spire of El Morro rises into the sky, against the backdrop of the bay.

The road curves away, and I see we are coming to a vast open field, a campus of grass wider than a football field. Behind it, a gray fortress atop the hillside stands wide, engulfing the entire horizon. The Ford rumbles into a paved lot where a handful of other cars are parked. Martín shuts off the engine, and the car lies still. Waves crash on a far-off shore, and salty sea air blows stiffly through our open windows. The car seems to still be moving. But it is my insides that are shaking.

Shirtless boys, browned by the unrelenting sun, play baseball barefoot on the grounds of the fortress where my father was held prisoner.

Other than a homemade wooden bat, the batter is uniformed with nothing more than a pair of swim trunks. He lines a pitch over his friend's head as we walk past on a stone path that leads to a towering, moss-covered stone archway. My steps become heavier, I can feel a weakness in my arms, and I am not sure I can go any farther as we approach it. A lifetime of stories are swirling in my head, horrors my father endured in this place. I can feel them tumbling behind my temples, and my head begins to pound.

I stand at the threshold of La Cabaña, and I take it in.

Fernando Frías Verdecia never saw this side of it. He was brought here, probably right over this same rocky drive, in a covered military truck in the fading light of September 17, 1965, his wrists tied in front of him as soldiers with rifles sat at the back of the truck, waiting to shoot anyone who dared jump off. This was his punishment, I think, as I look through the arch to see a path leading to a large stone fortress behind it. This is what he deserved for the crime of "abandoning" the revolution?

I have heard the story many times, and as I walk beneath the arch, it begins to play in my head.

Five days before being hauled to La Cabaña, my father decided he had had enough. By that time, the government had already seized and closed La Copa, a café just a block from La Plaza. The brothers had owned it for less than a month in 1961 before four soldiers in olive posted themselves at the front and back doors and by the cash register. Owners and employees had to walk out single file and hand the keys to the soldiers, who locked the doors behind them. The brothers knew it was only a matter of time before the rest of their businesses ended up the same way.

So my Tío Felipe barely let off the gas as the elegant Pontiac bounced and skidded through orange mud, down country roads in the westernmost province of Pinar del Río in the dead of night. My father, Tío Rafael, and a friend held on for dear life. It was almost midnight when they reached a small canal near the coast of Punta de Cartas, a town on the southern end of the province.

Felipe and his friend were supposed to drive the car back, but he decided that very moment he would join his brothers in their attempt to flee. As the car made its way back down the road and the taillights disappeared into the darkness, the brothers walked for more than a mile in a moonless night until they came to a rowboat docked near a canal. Fourteen others were waiting for them silently in the dark. They hopped in and took turns rowing for two hours, no one daring to make a sound, until they reached the point where a speedboat was supposed to be waiting for them. A bright spotlight and the sound of loading machine guns welcomed them instead. It was a trap.

The boat overturned as soldiers ordered them out at gunpoint, sending them all, including three children under three, into the water. For the next five days, the brothers were moved from one detention camp to another. The routine at each was the same: Guards came in the middle of the night and tried to convince them, gently at first, that the revolution was benevolent; why would they want to leave? When he insisted on leaving, my father was tossed back into his cell, called *gusano*, worm, until the next visit, when the guards repeated their routine.

On the night of their last transfer, as a truck loaded with prisoners rumbled down the Royal Causeway on the way to La Cabaña, my father peeked out through slits in the canvas covering the truck and watched the city of Marianao fly by. The truck stopped at the light directly in front of La Plaza de Marianao. My father could see the counter at Mi Buchito Oriental bustling as usual, customers bathed in the red neon of their sign. The light turned green, the truck rushed away, and that was the last time my father would ever see Mi Buchito open.

I finally am able to walk under the archway as I imagine my father and the others marching through, guards in front and behind them. Martín walks ahead of me but stops me just outside a small office and tells me to let him buy the tickets; it costs Cubans only one national peso to enter La Cabaña. Foreigners are charged four Convertibles. We walk in together, and a woman in olive fatigues with her blond hair pulled up in a tight bun is waiting at the counter. There are pamphlets for purchase, referring to this place as *el monumento*, the monument. I flip through them as Martín approaches the woman. There is all manner of colonial history in these documents, stating that this grand fortress was for quartering Spanish soldiers. That today it is used for an annual book fair, where parents come to buy government-approved literature and read to their children in the open air. There is no mention of the gulf in between, of its most recent, infamous history. That Ernesto Che Guevara himself presided as warden during the revolution.

Martín, wearing a fading blue Nike baseball cap and a threadbare plaid button-down shirt, untucked over his gray pants, hands her one peso. She looks me up and down and turns to Martín.

"It's four Convertibles for him," she says.

I got it, I tell her in Spanish, and she cocks her head as I step forward to pay. I look her in her blue-green eyes as I hand her the government's take, and she tears me a small green receipt printed in broken English: "Your Visit Remember's [*sic*] Parque Morro-Cabaña. Thanks." I tuck the receipt in my wallet, and I know it will stay there forever. As I walk away, I wonder how my father would feel knowing that I just paid to enter the place he would have given any sum to escape.

The asphalt road becomes cobblestone, and I lose my footing several times as I come upon a bridge that leads to the actual fortress of La Cabaña. It spans about fifteen feet over a great moat, now dry and covered in wild grasses. Walls of moss-covered stone stretch in either direction, and the building instills the feeling that there is no escape from this place. On the other side of a long tunnel, the sky opens up and sun reflects off walls freshly painted the color of canaries. Wooden shutters, framed in newly stuccoed white, outline windows that stretch along a hallway that runs in either direction, repeating endlessly.

I walk up a gray cobblestone path, and a vendor wearing a white apron and a paper hat like a soda jerk from the 1950s is standing at a portable ice-cream cart, selling ice pops to tourists paying in Convertibles. I continue up the walkway, and it opens into a vast stone courtyard, lined with manicured sod and shade trees. A stone wall at the other end of the courtyard runs the length of the complex, enclosing us.

Soldiers dressed in olive lean against different walls. Two of them march side by side, back and forth along a hallway, their black combat boots clip-clopping along the stone floor as if in a show for the visitors. The grounds are silent, the few visitors wordless as they meander around the great "monument." I search for La Cabaña that my father painted in my mind, but I am lost everywhere I look. There are rows of arch-crowned rooms with cold stone floors. They stretch as far as the eye can see. Most of them are locked behind large wooden doors, which have been installed recently to replicate their colonial look. Above each door, a small barred window is the only source of light. Were these the cells where my father and uncles were held? I cannot tell, and no one here will tell me, either. This place is for visitors now, not prisoners. And if these were the cells, they reveal very little about their prior purpose.

I enter the first one. It is a small café, set up with several aluminum tables and chairs. A European couple and their two children sit and eat ice-cream sandwiches and drink cold tuKolas as a small air conditioner refreshes them from the heat. The boy is wearing a shirt with the image of Guevara and the girl an olive cap with a red star, the uniform of the revolutionary soldier. I watch them eat and laugh, and I can feel my lunch creeping up my throat.

I swallow hard.

In my mind, this could be his cell.

On the night my father was brought here, he followed the line of men to his cell. When the guards opened the door, at that time made of thick iron with just a small barred window up high, they came face-to-face with their life for the next year and a half. Guards crammed them in, shoving them from behind, to where more than five hundred men were held. One hundred rows of bunks, stacked four and five beds high, reached the ceiling. And even then, there were not enough. My father slept his first night in jail on the cold stone floor beneath one of the bunks. My Tío Felipe crouched in a corner and was awakened in the middle of the night when the toilet near him overflowed with the waste of some five hundred men. Not that they managed to sleep much. An explosion startled the men of La Cabaña that night, the sound of firing squad rifles cutting through the air.

"*Coño*, they killed them, they *killed them!*" one man yelled as my father's cell squirmed with fear.

And then they began, single gunshots piercing the night's silence, each several seconds after the last. The coup de grâce.

Bang!

"*Asesinos*, murderers!" one man yelled after the shot.

Bang!

"*¡Comunistas, hijos de putas!*"

Bang!

My father covered his ears as men screamed and wept like boys. For all I know, he was one of them.

Bang!

After the seventeenth shot, the silence returned, the night littered only with the muffled sobs of raving men in cages.

I struggle to relive that scene standing in front of what is now a souvenir shop, where a man resting his head in his hands at a glass counter is selling T-shirts, hats, pens, all manner of souvenirs with pictures of Guevara. A couple looks through T-shirts, trying to decide which image of Che they would like to display on their chests. I think about going up to them and asking them a single question: *Do you have any idea who that man was?* I think of my father, who might have sat in this very room learning to play chess—a game he would begin teaching me when I was six—from a young Chinese man who had been accused of planting a bomb against a government installation. In the middle of one of their games, the iron door clanked open, and a pair of guards yanked the young man from his seat by his arms.

"*Bueno*, I'll see you later," my father told him, leaving the board just so as the young man was led away. He stopped at the door, turned to my father, and said, "No. No, I don't think you will."

My father never saw his chess partner again.

I walk across a hall toward another cell. I am stopped at the door by the sight. Dark wood pews line both sides of an aisle leading up to an ornate altar with a carved stone backdrop. To its side, in a sealed Plexiglas container, a statue of the Virgin Mary with Child. This room, in this place of all places, has been converted into a quaint chapel. A woman with dark brown hair and an olive uniform sits in a folding beach chair in the corner. A tourist sits in one of the pews toward the front, appearing to pray. This, in a country where religion was not only forbidden but persecuted. I think of Manuela and the pounding drums outside the doors of her little church as she strains to listen to the priest. I step back out of the room, thinking that even standing here is too much of a sacrilege to bear.

I spin around and am back in the parklike courtyard. I walk out to its center, where I am alone and can feel the eyes of soldiers posted against a long stone wall, next to the rows of endless cells. From this spot, I can see the Christ of Havana, the great white stone statue perched high atop the bay, His left hand pointing at His sacred heart. And I wonder where God was for these men.

I climb up a long stone ramp and walk along the edge of the wall that separates the courtyard from the sight of freedom. All of Havana is before me as the sun begins to disappear beyond the horizon: A Spanish cruise ship docks in the harbor. A red-and-white smokestack pours a black cloud into the sky. El Malecón winds and stretches into the distance. And I can picture the soldiers who must have walked along this wall, standing guard with rifles. A blast of ocean air blows in from the bay, cool and sudden, and I bite down hard.

How different he must have been, my father, before coming to this place. Before he ever learned to play chess from a boy who would be executed. Before he learned that his beloved Buchito Oriental had been closed while he was jailed. Before he learned basic English—"Eet ees imposibul for mee to get in tuch wit you een sach a short taym," he would recite—from Larry *el americano*, who was serving a term of thirty years in the same cell as my father. Whatever happened here, it shaped my father in a way that these freshly painted walls cannot reveal, in a way I never want to fully understand.

No, I decide, this is not the place my father knew. The iron doors have been removed, the stone floors scrubbed clean of the blood spilled here.

I find my way down the wall, back to the courtyard, where a pair of soldiers are paying special attention to a large cannon pointed out to the bay. I ask Martín what it's all about.

"*El cañonazo*, the cannon blast of nine o'clock," he says.

The literature at La Cabaña's ticket office says it's a tradition that goes back to the colonial days, when the cannon would fire to signal that the city walls were closing to protect Havana from invaders. Soldiers, dressed in scarlet eighteenth-century uniforms, reenact the ceremony nightly for clapping tourists. For my father and his two brothers imprisoned here, it simply meant lights out.

I have seen everything I am allowed to see, yet I feel like I have seen nothing at all. I take one last look at the ocean as night threatens.

'*Vámonos, ya.' Let's get out of here, Martín. This place has already claimed too much of my family's life.*

I try to rest in my hotel from a day that will not end.

In a few hours, the Cuban government will begin the festivities it has planned, starting at 9:00 P.M., to usher in Fidel Castro's eightieth birthday. I'll have to put together some coherent thought about what happens and send some copy to the newspaper on deadline. But La Cabaña is swirling in my head. And all I want to do is lie in this bed.

My brain finally overcomes the pounding in my legs, and I will myself out of the room, past the doors of the Hotel Plaza and into the night. Music is coming from I don't know where. The streets are active, alive, and people pass me as I trudge along El Prado. Someone hands me a flyer about a party—dancing and drinking, all free—that will be held tonight at El Monumento Morro–La Cabaña. I drop the leaflet. The ground is already littered with them.

Blue-white lights along the wide boulevard barely illuminate the evening. I move between them, as something inside me is also only half-lit. I walk, walk, until I find myself at the end of the street, back at El Malecón. Couples stroll by, bathed in salty sea air, making their way up the boardwalk with hordes of others to a starburst of bright lights along the coast where the festivities are beginning.

I sit silently on the seawall, turning to stare out at the black ocean, at the menacing outline of La Cabaña in the distance. I close my eyes, let the breeze blow my hair, the ocean spray coating me in a cool mist as waves crash softly against the shore.

And when the cannon blasts suddenly at nine o'clock, reverberating throughout the city, the jolt dislodges me from a thoughtless trance and shakes my tears from their poorly guarded hiding place.

DAY FIVE

She is sitting on her patio in a black metal chair, nursing a cigarette, when my cab rounds the corner. Alina begins to wave
immediately, dropping the butt and coming to her feet in one motion, the car still at the other end of the block.

"Have you eaten yet?" she asks before the cab has even disappeared up the street.

I grabbed something at the hotel, Alina. I'm fine.

"*Ay, mi niño,* but why did you spend your money when you could
have come here, and I would have cooked for you?" she says, taking me by the hand.

That's exactly why I ate there, I do not say. I do not want to eat
her food, her rations that she pays for with a pittance of a government retirement.

"Well, tonight you're going to eat here. I'm going to make
you my hearty red bean stew, a *potaje de frijoles colorado,* because a
muchachón like you needs to keep up his strength."

I try to argue that we can go up the street and maybe find a restaurant, that she shouldn't go through all the trouble. Her shoulders drop a little, and she tilts her head. "Carlos, for me this is *un
placer,* a pleasure," she says, her brow furrowed.

I am getting pretty tired of that hotel food.

"This food is going to give you *vida nueva,* new life," she says,
perking back up. But first, she says, we have to buy a couple of
things.

She closes the front door and then the wrought-iron gate in front of it, squinting as though threading a needle as she fishes for the lock with the key hanging on a lanyard around her neck. She loops her arm around my elbow as we walk up the street toward La Plaza.

As we pass others, we nod to them, and they smile. I wonder if they think Alina is my grandmother, and I pat her hand gently, assuring her that I, too, am holding on to her. La Plaza is bustling as usual, the glass doors swinging restlessly as *marianeses* come and go from the *bodega*. As we approach, a warm, buttery aroma of fresh-baked bread wafts from the bakery on one corner of the building. I close my eyes and take a deep breath.

It smells fantastic.

"I wake up to that smell every day," she says. "If only the bread were as good as it smelled. As soon as it gets cold, it's as hard as a two-by-four, *duro como un palo.*"

Besides, all that's left by now is the aroma, she says. The bread, when they have all the ingredients to bake it, sells out just after sunrise.

I barely notice when we are back inside the *bodega* at La Plaza. The smells are a little softer, the sights a little less foreign, the loud scrambling of noise a little more manageable. Having Alina with me numbs my senses enough to see La Plaza for what it is today.

Alina jokes with an old man, his head covered in white-and-gray naps, who is selling her a half pound of red beans. Next to them, a young woman in a simple white sundress with a pattern of purple and green leaves flirts with a man who sports a neatly trimmed mustache and is selling papayas. She flips playfully at the tuft of straight black hair she has tied in a ponytail. In the corner, a butcher who is cleaving at a leg of pork is asking the man across the aisle about the domino game tonight. He pushes up his black baseball cap to make a point, and I notice the letters "USA" written across the front, against embroideries of the Statue of Liberty and a bald eagle.

Fifty years ago, La Plaza was very much the heart of Marianao, a city with its own baseball team and stadium. People came to La Plaza from miles away to shop, eat, relax with *un cafesito* and a guava *pastelito* as they caught up with one another's lives. It was their meeting place, and in many ways, it still is—even if the heart of Marianao now pulses with a different beat.

When we arrive home, Alina's front gate is unlocked and the back door open, so a soft draft blows through the house. A pretty young woman in a red tank top and denim shorts comes out from the bedroom when she hears the gate creak open.

"*Mima*, where did you go? I thought you were waiting for . . . Ahh!" she says, smiling with perfect white teeth, "for Carlitos."

Magda is a version of the image I have of a young Alina, but taller with shoulder-length dark brown hair tied in a ponytail.

"I didn't think she would just disappear if she knew you were coming," she says as we kiss hello.

Alina pats her niece softly on her back, and Magda takes the bags we are carrying into the kitchen. Something about Magda seems so familiar, but I can't place her. She returns to sit on the couch and I at the small table so I can look into the kitchen as Alina rinses freshly butchered pork cutlets.

"She's the one that keeps me young," Alina says, as she fills a pot with water, dumps in the beans, and sets it atop the small burner.

Magda shakes her head. "What would I do without my Tía?"

Alina sits across from me, wiping her hands on a towel. "We'll have to wait a few hours for the beans to soften," she says, "but that will just give us more time to talk."

Alina is glad to see I am alone today. She liked the driver I was with the first day, but when she and Manuela spoke on the phone last night, Manuela went on and on about the one I showed up with at her house.

"You have to be careful. You never know how some people think," Alina says and leaves it at that. It reminds me of Rosita, and finally I tell Alina about my visit, about the CDR and about Rosita's husband, the president. Just recounting it awakens the queasiness in my stomach.

"I didn't know they were mixed up with that," Alina says.

In truth, she hadn't been to Rosita's house in a long time and usually just bumped into her at La Plaza.

"But you know, the CDR isn't what it used to be. A lot of people don't even believe in that anymore, in turning people in, *chivatear*. Things are so bad. People don't believe any of those lies anymore."

That reminds her, she says. Rosita called earlier because she wanted to host a dinner for me at her house. But my father's cousin Mario also called and insisted he wanted to prepare a special lunch for all of us before I return home.

I think that would be best, Alina. There's no way I'm going back to Rosita's house.

"Ay, *muchacho*, what a fright, *qué susto*, that must have been for you," she says, patting my hand.

Alina, don't you think you would be better off living with Manuela?

"Ay, Manuela keeps harping on that. I've lived my whole life right here," Alina says. "I like living here. Do you know how many memories I have of this place? I look out my door and imagine it just as it was. It was such a wonderful time, *tan lindo*."

She is looking past me, past the wall that is mended with painted splotches of concrete, to something beautiful that is far, far away. Her mouth is still, her bottom lip a perfect half-moon, and she pouts like a china doll. Her eyebrows are trimmed and arched, her skin smooth, and the only creases of her face, laugh lines. Whatever damage living in the past has done her, returning there often seems to have kept her body and spirit young. Memories are Alina's fountain of youth.

"Maybe someday, when I'm too old to take care of myself, I'll move," she says finally. "Right now, I'm okay right here."

She has had several opportunities to *permutar*, that is, to trade her home for another. She lives in a desirable neighborhood, she says, because everyone from the country wants to move to Havana Province. Some have offered her good money—which is illegal but customary—to make the move. But what would she do with that money living in a place she doesn't know? Here, she has La Plaza for shopping, her friends for gossiping, her niece, whom she lives with. And she has her memories.

As Magda jokes with her aunt—"What would this block be like without you?"—she says she has to go up the street to check on one of their friends.

"Send someone to tell me if you're going to be late," Alina says as her niece walks out the door. After a few seconds, she turns to me and says, "That girl is like my own."

Alina's oldest sister was never supposed to have children. Doctors had told her she had a condition that could prove fatal in childbirth. Still, her husband had always wanted children, probably more than he ever wanted to be married, Alina says, and eventually, her sister became pregnant. But as she reached term, she could barely get around. Eventually, she was bedridden. And hours after Magda was born, the doctors' predictions came true. Her mother bled to death in her own home.

"He *knew* she wasn't supposed to have children, and he made her get pregnant anyway," Alina says, the memory still roiling in her voice.

But that's not the worst part, she says. After her sister died, her husband wasn't about to play a maternal role. It was Alina and Manuela who raised the girl. Her father brought a new woman home every night. When Magda, as a nine-year-old, asked him why she had no mother, he told her it was her fault that her mother died in labor.

"Can you imagine what kind of an *animal* says that to a little girl, his own daughter?" Alina says.

It's no wonder the courts granted Alina custody of the girl; her father barely fought it. Alina took Magda to several therapy sessions so she could realize she was not the reason her mother died. And when her father died a few years later, they all took it as a blessing. Alina raised Magda as her own.

Alina worked for herself over the years, selling baked goods, *pastelitos* and cakes, doing manicures out of her house, she says, and I notice her nails are in perfectly shaped peaks. She had several opportunities to advance in the government, six to be exact, but there was one stumbling block she happily flaunted: She strokes a small gold crucifix around her neck.

"Every time they would ask me, 'Why don't you let us get you this or that job with the government?' I would tell them that I believed in God. They would say, 'Oh, no, then you can't work for the state.' " Every job application asked, "Do you believe in God? Check Yes or No."

She preferred to work for herself, illegally if need be, rather than hide her faith. Over the years, she got small boosts from an unexpected source: My Tío Felipe and Tía Dania continued to send money regularly, knowing Alina was caring for more than herself here. When they knew someone going to Cuba, they would send along not just cash but clothes, even the jewelry Alina still wears.

"I think about them *mucho, mucho, mucho*, because I know they have never forgotten about me," Alina says.

"*Ese Felipe*, he would go off with different girls, and then he would try to come back to me," Alina says, first waving her hand dismissively, her brow scrunched in a scowl. Then she settles and smiles. "But then he would say, 'You know that I like you very much, *que te quiero*. Don't stay angry at me,' " and he would earn his way back into her heart.

Alina is far away again, lost in the dimension of time. As she rests her hands on her lap, I notice she wears a thin gold band on her left ring finger. I know that she never married. And I can only imagine that Alina is wed to a memory.

It's a crazy thought, what I'm thinking. But when I realize who Magda looks like, I can't help but think it is more than coincidence. All week I have been hearing about my father's and my uncles' romantic relationships, and maybe that has led to this suspicion. But every time I look at Magda in the framed portrait Alina keeps in her living room, I can think only of my cousin Lily—Felipe's daughter in the United States. My mind floods with possible scenarios in which this woman is his daughter. One stays with me like an unverifiable truth: What if he had a relationship with Alina's sister, and this child, this woman, is the result of that union? It would explain why they have kept in contact over the years, why he and Dania still send money.

When Magda comes through the iron gate a few minutes later, I pore over her every feature, comparing them with my cousin's. The roundness of her cheeks, a defined chin, the arch of her eyebrows, the shape of her eyes. The more I look, the more I convince myself. It is as if she is physically transforming with each passing glance.

Magda, you know I haven't taken a picture of you yet. Do you mind if I take one so my family back home can 'meet' you?

"Ay, Dios, a picture, with me looking like this? Look at this hair," she says, before agreeing to sit on a wooden chair and smiling a sideways grin.

I take several pictures, not satisfied that the camera captures her. She looks more like my cousin in person.

Magda, I don't mean to be indelicate, but you look so young. Do you mind if I ask how old you are?

"Forty," she says. I do the math quickly in my head. She would have to have been conceived in the summer of 1965—a few months before the brothers landed in jail. The numbers work. I snap one more photo.

A whining from a motorcycle grows into a growl as it stops outside Alina's front door.

"Ah, those are my friends, *mis amiguitos*," Alina says.

A tall, strong man wearing a white construction helmet and a lived-in white T-shirt helps a short, stout woman off the back of his motorcycle. Armando and his wife, Marina, stop in often to check on Alina, who often babysat Marina here in Marianao.

"So you are a Frías," Armando says, shaking my hand, his hard hat under his other arm.

Armando has only faint memories of running around La Plaza as a boy, but his father has told him all about my family, about La Plaza, about life as it was in the "old Cuba."

Alina suggests that Armando might be just the one to help me with another task. He could take me to my family's old house and help convince the owner to let me look around. Armando has a friendly way, calling me *Papo* or *Muchachón* and Alina *Mima*, and you can tell right away that his charm and quick wit get him a long way. I feel my heart jump at the prospect. Alina insists on making coffee before we go, and we all sit down in her living room as the roasted aroma fills the air.

Marina is complaining about all the work she has to do before school starts. She is a teacher at a local elementary school and still has to go shopping for supplies.

Doesn't the school give you what you need?

She bursts into a quick laugh. "It's *my* job to take care of *my* room," she says, and that means buying some basics, from chalk to grade books. "If I don't, my students suffer."

With minimal supplies, the government demands the highest performance. Plus, she has continuing education: She and other teachers are tested on Castro's hours-long televised speeches. They have to be ready to write essays on the points he makes. "What are the five main points of the speech he gave last week?" If she doesn't know, it can cost her cuts in pay. How can she teach the philosophies of the revolution if she doesn't know them herself? That the old man is sick gives her and other teachers a summer respite.

Armando hands me his construction helmet and helps me strap it tight. "Now you can tell your family back home that you've ridden on a Russian motorcycle," he says as he kick-starts the bike and it screams to life with a high-pitched whine.

We take off down the dusty roads, Armando driving just fast enough to evade the potholes. We ride down the same streets José and I drove a few days ago, passing Mario's home, my uncle's old apartment, until we come to the vacant lot on the corner. Armando's bike falls silent in front of the cracked terra-cotta steps that lead up to my family's old house. He and I stand side by side on the sidewalk, looking up at the two-story.

"This must have been some place in its day," he says, and I nod without looking away from the glassed-in porch. I climb the steps and knock, and the whole porch shakes.

'*¿Hola?*'

Silence.

Another knock. Another pause. More silence.

"*¡Hola, oiga, señor!*" Armando yells. Still no answer.

"You know, we can always come back with a bottle of rum," he says.

"I don't think he's home," comes a call from upstairs. Standing on the balcony is a large woman, her salt-and-pepper hair in curlers.

A staircase leads to the top floor, and I ask if I can come up. A bright white smile contrasts against her ebony skin, and she waves me up. The woman, who is wearing a Daisy Duck shirt with the sleeves cut off, invites me onto her porch. I tell her about my family, and she says her family has lived here for thirty years and must have moved into the home just after mine. I know from my father's stories that the top floor was actually a separate home, where an old couple lived. The woman invites me in and lets me look around. There are large white tiles with a brown design covering the entire floor. At the far end, a kitchen is separated by a low wall. The woman says she hears very little from the man downstairs, only complaining when he has flooded the bottom floor. Other than that, she says, yes, he is usually drinking or gone.

Do you know who keeps up the lot next door?

She says the old man does. As disgusting as the house is inside, the man pays particular attention to "his garden." She calls her daughter in a back bedroom and tells her to unlock the gate for me. "This way, if anyone asks, you tell them I let you in," she says with a smile.

I thank the woman and follow her daughter, a tall, slender girl with onyx skin and hair in a pair of thick braids. The iron gate between the house and the lot is not locked. A hand-painted sign on the front fence says the property is protected by the Committee for the Defense of the Revolution and local police. The girl lifts up a lever, and the gate creaks open. She smiles and heads back upstairs, leaving me to the moment I have dreamed of since I was a boy. I turn to Armando, who is waiting by the sidewalk, before taking a step. He nods at me. "Go on, *dale.*"

The hunt for buried treasure begins, and I can feel my heart take off.

For years, my father and I have talked about this exact moment. We have pantomimed the steps countless times. We even had a final walk-through in the minutes before I left for Cuba the first time.

"You aren't going to try to dig it up, are you? What if someone sees you?" he had cautioned. If it looks safe, I'd assured him, I'm going to try.

As I pass through the gate, instinct takes over. I am no longer in control of my actions. I am walking rehearsed steps, hearing my voice tracing over the instructions of my father.

To your right, next to the house, there will be a concrete wall about four feet high, I whisper, reciting the instructions to myself. As I pass through the gate, I see it as he has described. A concrete wall about four inches thick stretches the length of the house. I walk this tight alley, between the house and wall, all the way to the back. My footsteps create an echo down the path, and every step feels loud enough to wake the dead.

To the left is the back entrance of the house. There is a concrete sink and steps leading up to two doors. I see them, both reinforced with sheets of plywood. One of the doors leads to the back room, by the kitchen, where my father and his brothers played dominoes, leaving the door open to feel the cool of the evening.

Behind you, there will be a break in the wall wide enough for about one person to step through, and you can easily cross over into the yard. I spin around. The wall, cracked and showing exposed bricks, stops where he says it does. My father's instructions continue playing in my head, and the sound is joined by the harmony of my beating heart. I quickly find the spot, just as he has described it.

Every indicator is right where he said it would be. I won't say exactly where it is—after all, this is buried treasure we're talking about.

I stand on the proverbial X. Beneath my feet is the prize.

The only thing different from the story is that now the spot is covered in gray stone squares, laid out in a path that spans the empty lot. I look around for something to dig with, but I have nothing except rocks and my bare hands. I could always come back another day, with a shovel or spade to quicken the work. And then I remember the sign: This property is protected by the CDR. What would someone say if I am caught digging here, trespassing? It splashes on me like a bucket of cold water: *This is not mine.* This whole property, it belongs to my family's collective memory, but it is no longer ours. I look around and see papaya and banana trees planted in neat rows. The blooming hibiscus that climbs the twelve-foot fence and conceals the property from prying eyes has been carefully tended by someone. And it is not someone from my family.

I look at my feet. I squat down and run my hands over the stone. It is rough and hot from a beam of sunlight hitting this spot. *It's right here.* I can imagine that metal urn, rusted but still sealed after thirty-seven years, beating beneath the ground like a telltale heart, the layers of rock and dirt and sand and stone keeping it in its perfect hiding place.

Footsteps coming up the path make me leap to my feet. It is Armando. He jumps back, startled at my being startled.

"*Coño,* you scared me. Is everything okay?" Armando asks.

'*Sí,*' fine, fine.

I imagine being caught, just like this, with the rusted urn, still sealed, torn from my hands. I have no right to it, they would say, and in that moment of haste, I would have lost a piece of precious history, a priceless artifact hidden for nearly four decades and idolized for just as long. My father's goal was always to return here. To dig up this urn and recognize his past life through age-old trinkets.

And so I decide to leave it where it is.

Instead, I walk around the grounds. I stand in the cool shade of the avocado tree my grandfather planted and take its picture. I lean down to the base of the trunk and grab a handful of dirt, orange and dry like infield clay, and rub it between my hands, letting it stain me so that somehow I may take home part of this. I call Armando over and tell him about the tree, about the house, about the parties that my family used to have on this very spot. I do not tell him about our treasure. I walk back to the path and ask him to take a picture of me standing . . . just on this spot. I content myself with a photo of my feet inches from my father's treasure.

We'll be back for it together someday.

As we motor back down the Royal Causeway toward Alina's house, Armando stops off at La Plaza to buy himself a soda.

I'm fine, I tell him, and I sit on an empty bench outside. As I watch the cars and people pass in front of La Plaza, an old American Franken-car rumbles past. In many ways, it is still the fifties here, yet I wonder whether my father would even recognize this place if he were sitting next to me. I squint my eyes and look up the street, and I wonder, If he did the same, could he orient himself by looking at the outlines of the buildings?

It has been days since I have spoken with my parents. At home, we usually speak every day, see one another a couple of times a week. Armando is still inside. And I decide I need to make a call.

"*Hola-lá,*" my father says as he answers the phone, his usual greeting.

It's me. 'Soy yo, Viejo.'

"*¡Anjá!* And what's the good word from the *habanero?*"

What to say first? How do I pick through the images that are trying to force their way from my mind to my mouth, all at once, rushing, jostling to be the first through. Should I tell him about La Plaza, the trash room, the stink, Alina, the house, the treasure, the drunk, Rosita—what, what, *what* do I say? I breathe.

I'm here. In your old stomping grounds, 'en tu tierra.' I'm in Marianao.

"In Marianao! I don't believe you. *Coño, dime, dime,* tell me what you have seen."

I laugh. *I've seen it all.*

I just wanted you to know I'm safe, I tell him, that I found Alina. That she showed me La Plaza.

I saw the house. I visited Rosita. I hugged Miguel, and he sends his best. And La Cabaña, I was at La Cabaña, 'Papi', and you won't believe what it has become.

It is all beginning to rush out.

When I get home, I say, when I'm home I'll tell you all about it. I cannot give him the details now. There is too much for me to say, and too much for him to hear. No, not now. Not over the phone. A clunking and fumbling sound breaks our conversation. Someone else has picked up another phone.

"*Papo! Papoooo!* So how do you like my *Cubita?*" my mother says with the excited laugh of a little girl. Someone opens the door to La Plaza, and the smell of overripe fruit blows past me. Something inside me breaks, and I feel a rush of energy from my heart to my eyes, and they begin to sting and water.

Your 'Cubita' . . . is beautiful, I say, clearing my throat and swallowing hard. She, who my father says has been roaming the halls at night like a phantom, unable to sleep, listless during the day, staring off into the distance quietly and suddenly wiping her eyes, begins to talk and ramble and laugh. And I am thankful for it. Because if I speak, I know my voice will crack. She has spoken to my cousins in Cuba, Jorge in particular, and she is glad to know he is coming tomorrow to take me to Cárdenas.

"That one, he really knows his way around. He's going to take care of you," she says, pleased, her work done. "Tell him to show you everything . . ."

"Iris, he's making a long-distance call!" my father cuts in.

"*Ay, claro, claro,* of course. *Bueno,* you'll call us again when you get to Cárdenas. We love you *mucho, mucho, mucho . . .*" She trails off as she begins to sob.

"*Ya,* Iris, *ya,*" my father tells her, calming her. "Take care of yourself, *Papo.* And don't worry about Christy and the girls. We're taking care of them."

"Your father is going over there every day," my mother adds.

'Gracias, Viejo.' I love you both. Yes, Mother, I'll be careful. Yes . . . yes,

I know things are different here. Yes, I already told you I'll be careful . . . I know . . . I know . . . I KNOW!

The three of us laugh as we hang up. And I think I can go on for another day.

"I thought you had run away with him," Alina tells Armando as we come back through her door.

She sits next to me on her couch, her hand on my knee. "Tell me: Were you able to go inside the house?" she asks. No, I say. She shakes her head. "Ay, that house. Every time I walk by it, I feel this thing, *una cosa*, inside. You can't imagine how different it was years ago." I can. I am beginning to. This time, when she reaches into the past, I reach in with her.

Alina, do you remember the date my grandfather passed?

"How could I forget? May third, 1969," she says without taking a second to sort through her mind. "How we suffered," she says, sucking her teeth, shaking her head. "*Ay, Don Pancho*, it's as if I can see him standing in front of me."

I tell her I am thinking of visiting his grave tomorrow before my cousin comes to take me to Cárdenas. She says she has not been there since he was buried and doesn't know anyone who has. The thought of my grandfather's lonely grave leaves me empty. The dead cannot tell us that they miss us, that they wish we would visit. That he has been alone and longing for the past thirty-seven years for someone to come to him. The grandfather I never met, so far from family, so far from us. I will go to him, I decide.

I will visit you, 'Abuelo.'

Alina tells me in the last couple of days she has been trying to think of people I need to see while I am here, people who knew my family, and she has thought of one, Teresita. She says my family will definitely remember her because Teresita was the most beautiful of the waitresses the brothers ever hired to work at any of their restaurants. Pretty girls brought in the business, and Teresita, coquettish to further accentuate her looks, was an attraction unto herself.

"It's been a long time since I've seen her," she says, "and I hear she's been sick. Whatever she has, I think it would do her a lot of good to see you."

She doesn't live very far away, Alina says. We can walk there. Besides, the red beans aren't quite soft yet and could use a little more time in the pot. And on the way, she can show me a few more of the places that are important to her, that were important to my family. Armando and Marina say their good-byes as Alina locks the gate, and we start up the street, her hand holding on to my arm.

"Would you like to see where your brother grew up?" Alina asks. Absolutely, I say, as we cross the Royal Causeway. She remembers him, my brother, running around La Plaza and the streets of Marianao. When his mother, Elsa, had to work, Alina often babysat at their apartment or had him over at her house. Elsa and Alina became close over the years, if only because they were both in love with Frías men. It was she, Alina, who took my brother Roger to meet our grandmother for the first time.

"When I brought that boy through the door, your grandmother Teresa looked at him, then looked at me, and said, 'That is Fernando's son.' She guessed right away."

When my father and Tío Felipe were conscripted to work camps after serving their sentence in La Cabaña, Alina and Elsa made the two- to three-hour trek on hot, packed buses to visit them in the city of Nueva Paz, at the Havana-Matanzas province border. On the day the brothers ended their sentences in the camp, Alina and Elsa were there waiting for them.

What went wrong between my father and Elsa?

Alina seems suddenly reticent. We walk for a few moments in silence. She looks ahead and says finally, "I think there was a rift between the two families. Plus, I don't think *los Frías* wanted anything tying them down because they were all trying to leave."

She stops at a breezeway between two buildings and to get her bearings. It has been years since she has been here, she says. We walk between what was a bank and a fire station, up a dark corridor with towering buildings on either side. The iron gate of the last apartment on our right is slightly ajar, and I can hear a television. A woman with skin of toasted coffee and soft curls opens the door. When I tell her my brother grew up in this apartment, she smiles widely and invites me to look around. I poke my head in enough to see the apartment is a studio with a wall that does not reach the ceiling, dividing a sitting area from a bedroom in the back. We thank her, head back down the path, and continue on.

"People made a lot of sacrifices to leave," Alina says suddenly as we step off the Royal Causeway and down a side street. "I know Felipe loved me. He would tell me, and I could see it in his eyes. But some things just weren't meant to be."

We walk a very short distance, and then Alina points to a building with a continuous wall that stretches for half a block, doors and windows punched in the side, only a mishmash of paint colors denoting where one apartment ends and the next begins. A door right off the sidewalk, flanked by a pair of shuttered windows against a yellow wall—this was the first house *los Frías* lived in when they moved to Marianao, she says as we continue past. She is like a curator narrating an exhibition she knows all too well.

The streets are silent except for the shuffling of our feet. We walk several blocks, moving to the road when the sidewalks are impassable. I have never walked this consistently in my life, and my legs are already tired. But Alina keeps a quick pace, and I notice how young and shapely her calves still look. We walk past a house, and a pair of younger men, who look to be in their early twenties, sit outside, their feet dangling off a porch. They watch us go by in silence, and I hold Alina close.

Aren't you afraid of walking these streets alone?

"*Ay, muchacho,* I've learned to take care of myself over the years," she says.

One afternoon, on the way to Mario's house, a young man tried to rip the necklace and crucifix off her neck. He managed to break her necklace, but she screamed and yelled and gouged at his eyes, and he ran off without his prize. I look back, and see that the young men are still watching us as we walk up the block.

This is the street, she thinks. It has been a long time. We walk past row after row of chain-link fences and yard after overgrown yard till we come to a two-story house, once white but now gray with abandon and trimmed in flaking rust red. I start toward the door, but Alina takes me to the side of the house, where steep wrought-iron stairs lead to an entrance high above. They squeak and shake as we climb them, and I grab the handrail to steady myself. At the top, Alina reaches through the iron bars and knocks on a wooden door.

"Teresita, it's Alina!" she yells out.

There is a clunking and fumbling. A lock begins to tumble, and the door swings open slowly. An old woman in a wheelchair stares at us from the other side of the bars. Teresita unlocks the gate and lets us in.

She wheels herself from the entrance in the kitchen to the adjacent small dining room, where the walls, like the rest of the house, are unpainted concrete.

"Sit, sit, make yourselves comfortable," Teresita says as we pull up to a small, square wooden table, the surface worn through its dark wood stain. She turns back to the kitchen, locking the gate but leaving the door open for a breeze that barely moves the air. The wheels of her chair are slightly askew, the tires worn to the rims in places. She wobbles back to the table across an uneven concrete floor, the rusted chair squeaking like a hamster's wheel. A beam of sunlight shining between the splintered window shutters catches a piece of metal on her left leg. But I look down to find that Teresita has no leg. It has been amputated below the knee. The stump is wrapped in a beige bandage, held in place by glimmering silver fasteners. The dressing is new. I try not to stare.

"So, you are Fernando's son," she says, taking my hand in hers as we sit across from each other. I am thankful that it forces me to look her in the eyes. "Of all the Frías brothers, he was the sweetest."

She's not sure how their tradition started, but she tells me that she and my father would always trade gifts on birthdays and the days of their patron saints, St. Fernando and St. Teresita. It's a big custom for Cubans, and I always received a gift on the day of St. Carlos, which falls on my father's birthday.

"I have something that I'd like you to see," she says, and she pushes herself away from the table. She wheels down a long hallway, where lightbulbs in their sockets hang bare from the ceiling. I hear her fumbling in a back room. She returns a few minutes later with a manila envelope. She opens it and spreads across the table a thicket of black-and-white photos.

She hands me one of a young woman at a cash register, who has turned in time to stare into the camera. You can describe her look only as sultry. The young woman stares out from beneath her thick, manicured eyebrows, a storm of wavy black hair surrounding her face like an aura. Her arms are long and slender, and a black belt accentuates an hourglass waist. The image was captured nearly fifty years ago, but Teresita's confidence in her beauty exudes even across the vastness of time. This was an arresting woman.

"That was when I worked at the restaurant," she says.

She shows me other photos of herself at work, standing by an espresso machine, by a milk-shake mixer, always exuding the same allure. There is one of her with my father at Mi Buchito Oriental, her hair pulled up into a bun. She is standing elegantly in a crisp white blouse, the restaurant's name embroidered over her left breast, her black skirt impeccably ironed.

"You always had to look that way," she says, "without a hair out of place."

They were demanding bosses, she tells me, but they were also friends. She shows me a picture of her with her husband. After Mi Buchito closed at night, she says, a group of them, owners and workers, and Teresita with her fiancé, would go out to clubs and dance until morning. Dance, dance, until they could no longer stand.

But that was a long time ago. Her husband died young, and she has been alone for years. She has two daughters, but they have their own lives, she says. She lives here by herself on the second story of this house. I cannot bring myself to ask her how she lost her leg, but I ask how she manages to get around. The steps are no problem, she says. She straps on her prosthetic leg, sits on the top step, and bumps down one step at a time, dragging a walker behind her.

"Don't worry about me. I get around everywhere with that thing," she says with an honest smile.

"I think it's time for a little coffee," she says and wheels back toward her galley kitchen.

Alina and I look at each other and shake our heads. I continue to leaf through the photos, but I keep coming back to her standing at the cash register. My eyes dart back and forth, from the picture to her, from the old woman to the girl whom my uncles called the most beautiful. She brushes her flowing gray-and-white hair out of her face and reaches chest high to the counter, where she places the coffee. The heat in the room has caused perspiration to gather on the wisps of hair above her upper lip, and her house gown clings to her, pronouncing the droop of her breasts as she slumps in her wheelchair. She is probably the same age as my mother, and yet, when I place the pictures side by side in my mind, I cannot reconcile the damage time and life have wrought on Teresita.

As she waits for the coffee to brew, there is a knock at the door. A man in his late teens whispers for her attention. He reminds me of one of the young men on the porch, who stared us down the length of the street. With just a glance at him, she wheels to a corner of her kitchen, grabs a pack of cigarettes, and exchanges them for the money he hands her. He goes back down the steps without a word. She pours the coffee and begins to carry it to us on a tray on her lap. Alina stands to help her, but Teresita waves her off, quickly making her way to the table. We sit and drink the coffee, looking through more photos. I think about taking one of her now, but I cannot bring myself to snap a photo of the girl who was the fairest of them all. Some memories I have to protect.

She opens the manila envelope again and shakes out a photo that falls in her lap. It is a stamp-size picture of my father, a neat pencil-thin mustache matching his waves of black hair. The date on the back reads January 1955. He would have been twenty-seven.

Neighborhood boys play baseball on the grounds of La Cabaña, the fortress where my father and two of his brothers were imprisoned for nearly two years for the crime of attempting to "abandon" the revolution.

Children play soccer over the ruins of what was once one of the brothers' restaurants at the corner of San Ignacio and Lamparilla.

This is the house where my father and his single brothers, the Frías Brothers of Marianao, lived with their parents, even when they were successful businessmen. Now, the windows that are not missing are broken and paint peels from every wall.

Were these the cells where my father and uncles were jailed with nearly five hundred other men, where they were dragged out at 3:00 A.M. and hosed with cold water while female guards laughed at their shriveling bodies?

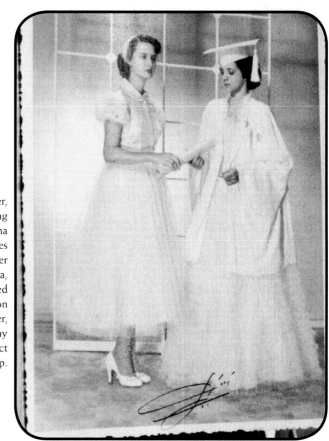

My mother, Iraida, receiving her diploma from Las Madres Escolapias. Her good friend Emma, who is pictured as her graduation godmother, remembers my mother's perfect penmanship.

The Frías brothers and sisters at the wedding of my Tía Dania in Havana. From left to right: Fernando Frías, Tío Ramón, Tío Rafael, Tío Ciro, Tío Felipe, Tío Mario, Tía Dania, Tía Aida, Tía Teresa, Tía Georgelina, and a family friend.

Mint, blue and yellow houses now stand in place of my mother's original home in Cárdenas. Her old wooden house, which stretched to the corner, was knocked down after falling into disrepair in the years after she left Cuba.

La Plaza de Marianao, which was closed by the government in 1965, reopened as an open-air *bodega* when the Russians partnered with Cuba. Here, I am standing in front of what was Mi Buchito Oriental.

My father opened Mi Buchito Oriental, the first of seven businesses he and his four brothers owned, in 1952. He is pictured in the center, frozen in time, about to sample the coffee from the little café. The restaurants were taken over and closed by the government in 1965.

In the 1950s, La Plaza de Marianao was the heart of the second-largest municipality in Havana Province, where my father and his four brothers owned three of their seven businesses. Today, it is an open-air *bodega*.

What was once the crown jewel of La Plaza de Marianao, El Restaurante Oriental, which belonged to my father and his brothers, is now the storage place for the plaza's trash.

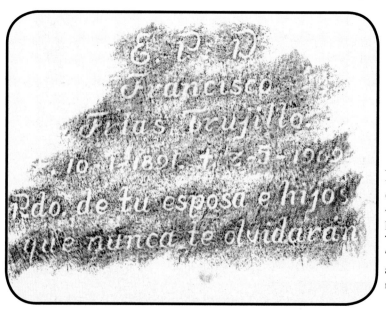

E. P. D
Francisco
Frías Trujillo
10-1-1891 † 2-5-1965
Rdo. de tu esposa e hijos
que nunca te olvidarán

A rubbing I made of the headstone in El Cementerio de Colón where my Abuelo Francisco "Pancho" Frías Trujillo is buried. It reads: "In memoriam: Your wife and children who will never forget you."

Old Havana has been beautified around the areas tourists visit. However, just one block away you can see the real lives of Cubans. Sewage backs up along the street and laundry hangs from the rusted wrought-iron balconies of the cracked concrete high-rises. Cubans here must take the stairs daily to fill their buckets at wells with water for bathing, cleaning, and cooking.

My uncles remember Teresita as the most beautiful of the waitresses they ever hired at any of their restaurants and cafés. Today, her left leg has been amputated and she gets around in a rusted, dilapidated wheelchair. She lives alone on the second floor of a house.

I am squatting near a spot where my father buried an urn filled with old Cuban money and pictures before he left for the United States. I didn't dig it up but hope one day to return to do so with my father in a free Cuba.

My mother's old school, Las Madres Escolapias, which she attended from the first through the twelfth grade. But it is no longer an all-girls Catholic school in a secular Cuba.

"Here," she says, handing me the photo. "Take this to your *Papá* so he can see that I haven't forgotten him after all these years." When we turn to leave, and she is not looking, I take a hundred dollars out of my pocket and put it on top of the pictures still on the table, where I know she will find it.

The hotel lobby is silent after midnight, and my pecking on the computer keyboard resonates through the empty marble corridors. Alina's dinner is still fueling me as I type an e-mail to my wife. The *potaje* of red beans and rice and the three pan-fried pork cutlets she bought at La Plaza did give me new life, just as she promised. And maybe heartburn. She spared no expense, slicing an entire avocado and even cracking open a beer, a real luxury since it costs about $1.50.

My eyes are heavy as I write to my wife about my travel to the countryside tomorrow. There are no Internet cafés where I'm headed, and it will probably be a while until I write again. Before I sign off, I send her a message to my father and my family.

"I know my dad remembers a woman named Teresita, who used to work at Mi Buchito," I write. "Tell him I took it upon myself to give her a donation from the family. I'll tell you later how much she needs it. No one in the world needs it more."

DAY SIX

I have passed these walls a dozen times this week without real-
izing what they enclose.

A walled city.

A city of the dead.

El Cementerio de Colón is a town unto itself. Regular streets
deviate when they reach Havana's largest and most historic cemetery, years of development not daring to trespass on sacred
ground. My cab follows streets along the twelve-foot wall, and we
pass miles with nothing but the enclosed cemetery to our left. Its
façade changes, the wall reflecting the neighborhoods it borders.
As we drive through one borough where low-slung houses are
particularly disheveled, the wall is flaking concrete, whitewashed
in uneven patches. Farther ahead, the cemetery borders a section
of El Vedado with stately, freshly painted two- and three-story
houses that my driver says are used by diplomats who make their
temporary homes here. The wall, dressed in salmon with coral
trim, bows to the neighborhood.

My grandfather is somewhere on the other side of that wall.

My knee is bouncing in the backseat of the cab, and I try to
steady it. I am going to meet Pancho Frías for the first time. I wonder what he will think of me. Will he recognize me as his own?

The wall begins to change again. Mustard sections with great
white crosses join with sections of wrought-iron bars, and for
the first time, the secretive wall divulges its secret. A white stone

cherub sitting on a grave marker. A marble Jesus crucified on a stone cross. A domed mausoleum with a terra-cotta roof. It is an endless garden of stone and marble amid towering sabal palms.

A great stone archway, a sculpture, really, sixty feet high, is the entrance to El Cementerio de Colón. It could stand confidently against the façade of any Gothic church in Europe. The cab pulls through the center arch, the main entrance, a pair of wrought-iron gates open to allow other cars to flow in and out.

I understand now why Manuela insisted I ask Alina for my grandfather's information. In every direction I look, marble and stone crypts, grave markers and towering family mausoleums disappear into the horizon. I am going to need help.

People are walking in and out of a building to my right, and I follow them to a small office. All of the doors to the office are open, but the air is still and hot. On a glass showcase, pamphlets and postcards and pictures of different views of the cemetery are for sale. There is a laminated map of the sprawling cemetery on one wall, covered in a film of humidity. It shows the grounds intersected by two main "roads," Avenida Cristóbal Colón and Avenida Obispo Fray Jacinto, which divide the cemetery into four quadrants. A series of smaller streets run north-south and east-west in a perfect grid. Laid against a map of the surrounding city of Havana, where the streets curve and twist and weave, El Cementerio de Colón is the model of order, its main avenue aligned with magnetic north.

A woman with red wavy, shoulder-length hair is sitting at a desk, fanning herself with a small stack of papers as she speaks to a man in a police uniform.

'Con permiso,' excuse me.

She turns slowly from her conversation, finishing before she looks at me completely.

I'm trying to find a grave. The place where my grandfather is buried.

I explain that I don't know where he is buried, that no one has visited the grave in years. Probably decades. She says there is an archival office on the other side of the entrance and that they should be able to help me find it. Then she notices my backpack.

"Do you plan to take pictures?" she asks.

Probably. Just a couple, to show my family back home. Is that a problem?

She grimaces, then raises her eyebrows to ask: "Do you think you'll take pictures of just the grave, or are you going to take pictures of the cemetery, 'tourist pictures'?"

I . . . hadn't really thought about it. I guess both.

Because I have family buried here, she won't charge me admission. But if I'm going to take "tourist pictures" of the cemetery, I'll have to pay one Convertible because I'm a foreigner.

I have to pay to see where my grandfather is buried.

She casts her eyes down as she says it and flashes her gaze up for a second to say softly, "I just don't want to get in trouble."

I understand. The government needs its cut.

I pay her the money and walk across the courtyard. A pair of workers pass me, riding on a gas-powered cart, shovels and small flowering plants in the back. Several trees are uprooted, and men are digging around them to plant more flowers. One of them is taking shade at the archival building, his blue short-sleeve shirt sweat-drenched and open to reveal gray and black naps of curls against his coffee-colored skin, a straw hat pushed back off his forehead.

There is a short line at a counter in the office. When it is my turn, I step up to the Plexiglas. A researcher, a man who looks to be in his mid-thirties, slender and with cheekbones well-defined, asks for the deceased's name and date of passing.

Francisco Frías, May third, 1969.

He turns to face a wall of maybe five hundred tomes, each about sixteen inches tall, about four inches thick, which contain the names of those buried here. He pulls one out of the wall and dusts it off, careful not to peel off more of the disintegrating light blue cover. The office is not air-conditioned, and I can feel a draft blow through the small opening in the window. This office, which keeps some of the most sensitive information about those buried here, is exposed to the heat and humidity of the outside air, and the priceless archives reflect that.

The young man examines one entry near the bottom of the

book before coming back to the window and asking, "Gonzalo Frías?" We stare at each other for a second. I know my father had an older brother named Gonzalo who died as a young man. He was the oldest of eleven. It makes sense that he would have been named after my grandfather. The researcher looks back at his book: "Gonzalo Francisco Frías Trujillo. A native of Manzanillo. Son of Rafael and Rosa?" In there, I find the name I recognize. Yes, I say, that must be the one. He goes back to the book to copy down the location of the grave.

What else is in there? I wonder. He mentioned Manzanillo, and from stories my father has told me, I recognize that as one of the towns in the farming province of Oriente where he grew up. And the book also lists the names of his parents? I need to see that book.

I ask the researcher if I can step inside and take a look at the book myself. He shakes his head at first, but I plead with him, *'Por favor,' I was born in the United States. I never knew my grandfather. I just want to see it.*

He speaks with a heavyset woman wearing a tight top, and I see her nod her head. He turns to the window and motions for me to come inside, where it is humid and warm and a fan in one corner of the room does little more than circulate the heat.

'Gracias.' I shake the young man's hand until the crack of a smile appears.

He turns the book around on a shaky wooden table whose surface is worn from years of use and points to an entry at the bottom of the page. The pages, translucently thin, have yellowed with age. Some are curled, brown at the edges, and the entire volume looks swollen from the humidity. I run my fingers over the entry. It is a standard form with blanks for new information. The words are written in neat cursive, fading black ink. I read it carefully, as if examining hieroglyphics.

It's all here.

Francisco Frías was buried on May 4, 1969, and it gives the location of the family vault. It lists his place of birth, his parents' names, even the funeral home in Marianao where he was viewed

and the name of the municipal judge who signed his death certificate. And there is one piece of information I am not expecting,
that no one in my family ever knew. Cause of death: ventricular
fibrillation. My grandfather died of a heart attack.

This was a great mystery for his children. A few years into
the revolution, my grandfather went to a local hospital with a
persistent cough. A chest X-ray showed a dark spot on his lung,
he was told. It could be anything. It could be nothing. Doctors
at the military hospital suggested surgery. A hardened man of
the country, Pancho Frías was not easily swayed by new thinking or new technology. He was as strong as an ox, peeled sugarcane with his bare teeth, my father remembered, and had the
rough, oversized hands of someone who has spent his life working the ground. But the doctors convinced him it was a necessary procedure. They opened him to find—nothing. His lungs
were healthy.

But the surgery left him weak. In the years after, the cough
persisted. He developed emphysema. He required oxygen and had
to go to a specific hospital, one for those who did not sympathize
with the revolution, for his treatments. One day, he checked in
and never left.

His sons would sneak in to spend time with him but, when
caught, were thrown out. Then one day they received a note at
their home in Marianao that my grandfather had passed away. No
further explanation. He died alone in the hospital. Not even his
wife was allowed to be with him. As I read the words on his burial
record, I now have an answer. I snap a photo of the entry.

The young researcher copies down the location of my family's
vault, and the directions are like a street address, indecipherable.
I ask him if he knows how to find it. He scratches his head as
he studies the directions. He peeks out the counter window and
points to the worker in the straw hat. He has worked here longer
than anyone else, the young man says, he should be able to help
me find it.

The man, who looks to be in his late fifties or early sixties,
pushes up his hat and glances at the directions for just a second.

"We have to walk *un poquito*, a little bit," he says, and I follow him.

He has worked here for more than two decades, he says. He's been part gravedigger, part groundskeeper, part tour guide, and he knows this place like his home. This cemetery covers about 56 hectares—almost 140 acres—and he says it is the third largest in the world. As we walk, he points out the graves of famous people I do not know, generals and soldiers and families of means. Most are family crypts, built aboveground in white marble or stone. Some are simple rectangular tombs. Others are adorned with angels and crosses and saints. Still others are entire buildings with family names sculpted into their façades. There is a small grotto to the Virgin Mary behind a low, iron fence in one. In another, a life-size angel, sitting and resting her head against the vault, whose stone cover has been sculpted to look like a fabric shroud. It is some of the most detailed stonework I have ever seen.

Sweat darkens our shirts as we walk easily a quarter mile, turning up cracked asphalt roads, past felled trees whose roots had been tearing up the roads and other crypts. The government is fixing up the cemetery, planting flowering and shade trees, my guide says, because it is a significant tourist attraction. Ficus trees are cut like topiaries, and the sod is green and manicured.

When we come to one main road, he stands in the dead center, where a white line had been painted years ago. He glances back at the directions, and then, taking giant steps, like a referee marking off penalty yards, he goes twenty-seven paces, mouthing the numbers to himself, and then takes a half step. He turns to face a corridor between two crypts. Then he takes another seven giant steps and finds himself directly in front of a simple rectangular aboveground vault. He crouches down at the foot of the grayish white crypt and makes out the engraving FAMILIA DÍAZ FRÍAS. 1959.

"Never fails," he says and resists when I offer him money for his help.

I rub my hands over the stone, tracing the name FRÍAS with my finger. It is hot to the touch from an August sun in a cloudless sky.

I pass my hands lightly over the top of the vault, feeling the fine grit of the stone.

I am here, Abuelo. 'Estoy aquí.'

I don't know who the Díaz refers to. I have never heard that surname attached to my family. I figure it must be a relative who either married in or the other way around. A large headstone bears a black-and-white picture on a porcelain disk, a bust shot of a man in a light suit and dark tie, with black hair, gaunt cheeks, and dark-framed glasses. My heart jumps for a second—*Abuelo?*—before I notice that carved above the picture is the name Serafín Diaz Alvarez, with the date January 8, 1958. There is no mention of my grandfather.

Then, I notice a loose, small marble headstone that has been placed on top of the vault. It is cracked from top to bottom but looks like it has been repaired to keep the two pieces together. The engraved words are impossible to make out, worn by the elements for the last four decades. I turn the headstone—it is heavy, weighing about twenty pounds—to face the sun and trace my finger over the glittery white rock. The noon sun burns against the stone, and I squint my eyes. When shadows fall just the right way, I can make out the first few letters: F. R. A. N. C. I. S. . . . It is my grandfather's name.

My hands instantly begin to sweat, and I feel a weakness in them. The headstone is so worn that I cannot make out the rest. Pictures fail to capture the image. If there were only a way to trace the words somehow . . . And then, in a flash of first-grade art class memory, I decide I can make a rubbing of the headstone. But I have only a pen and my little blue notebook, which is not wide enough to capture the entire inscription. I get my bearings and hustle back to the administrative office, and the same woman who charged me the dollar miraculously produces a plain sheet of yellow paper and a worn-down pencil. I jog back to my family's vault, my heart racing with anticipation. I wonder whether I am making a spectacle of myself. Do people run in cemeteries? I don't care. My legs can't get me back to my grandfather fast enough.

I gently lay the headstone flat, and as I begin rubbing the pencil on its side, the following dedication emerges in gray lead:

> E.P.D.
> Francisco Frías Trujillo
> 10–1–1891 + 3–5–1969
> Rdo. de tu esposa e hijos
> que nunca te olvidarán
>
> R.I.P.
> Francisco Frías Trujillo
> 1–10–1891 + 5–3–1969
> In memoriam: your wife and children
> who will never forget you

My sweat falls in heavy drops on the rubbing, and the pencil becomes little more than a mutilated nub. When I finish, I hold the rubbing, careful not to smudge the words, and read it aloud, over and over: *Your wife and children who will never forget you . . . who will never forget you.* No one has recited these words in thirty-seven years, and with each syllable, I feel I am summoning the spirit of Francisco Frías Trujillo.

I am here, Abuelo. We have not forgotten you. You are not forgotten.

I drop to my knees and begin praying. I pray an Our Father, a Glory Be, and a Hail Mary because it was what I was taught in a lifetime in Catholic school. I pray in Spanish, although I think I butcher the word for "trespasses," but, somehow, it seems more appropriate this way. As I kneel on the searing-hot, rustic granite squares at the base of the vault, I think of my father, who carries flowers to his mother's grave in Miami on her birthday, Mother's Day, and the anniversary of her passing. When she died, in Palm Springs Hospital at age eighty-six, we were all there, her sons and daughters, her countless grandchildren. It was the first time I ever remember seeing my father cry. He turned away from my grandmother's still body in the hospital bed and hugged me, held me tight, his eyes red and swollen with tears, repeating the words, over and over, "Our *viejita* has died, *Papo.* Our *viejita* has died." His father, his *viejito*, died alone. And my father had to leave him here all those years ago with no family member to tend his grave. He has been alone ever since. Until today. *I am here, Abuelo.*

I search for a place to buy flowers for my grandfather and find only a woman selling wilted sunflowers. Instead, I return to his grave. I pick leaves off the vault and sweep away several twigs and dust with my hand. I think of Abuelo Pancho and can imagine him walking the streets of Marianao in his fedora, sauntering slowly and tipping his hat to women as they pass. This time I stand and pray a personal prayer. One that will stay between a grandson and the grandfather he never met.

You are not forgotten, Abuelo. 'No te hemos olvidado.'

"Is your name Carlos Frías?"

I look up from my notebook to see the doorman at the Hotel Plaza as I sit in the lobby, waiting for Jorge.

"Your cousin was just here looking for you." I jump up from my seat, grab my bags, and hurry outside.

"Carlitos!"

I turn the corner to see Jorge stepping out of a bright baby blue van parked along the street, with the blinkers flashing.

"*Coño, primo!*" he says and wraps me in a bear hug. He looks me up and down. "You look good, you look good. But you're a little bit *flacón*, skinny," he says, patting my belly.

I've been doing a lot of walking.

I look him up and down. It's nice to see a familiar face. My cousin, the Cuban doctor. The only doctor in the family. Jorge has been here a week now with his mother, my Tía Sofía. I'm not used to seeing him this way, in shorts, a cut-off heather gray T-shirt, and sneakers. Even though he has been able to get only a radiology certificate in the States, he's usually in slacks and a collared shirt. His salt-and-pepper hair is a little messier than usual, his skin sunbaked by the Caribbean sun. He's always laid-back, a permanent smile and restful brown eyes. But today, right now, he looks at ease. He's home. A tightness that has gripped my stomach all week loosens with his hand on my shoulder.

Have you been waiting for me long?

About ten minutes, he says.

Why didn't you just come inside?

He grimaces and shakes his head.

When he went to the entrance, the doorman stopped him because he was wearing a tank top and shorts. The doorman mistook him for a Cuban citizen. They are not allowed inside hotels, much less dressed like commoners. Jorge, now in his late forties, was born here and, until eight years ago, had lived here his entire life. He now lives in Miami, but there is no hiding a native face. He didn't have his U.S. passport, and the doorman had only Jorge's word that he is a U.S. resident. If only he'd had a proper shirt, the doorman would have let him peek around for me.

"He did offer to lend me his," Jorge says. "I probably could have pushed it, told him, 'Look, I'm a *Yuma*,' but I didn't want to cause any problems for him. I knew I'd find you eventually," he says and shakes me by the shoulder.

Yuma? I've heard Cubans use that word to refer to me several times this week. I mean to ask Jorge about it when he says, "So are you ready to see where your mom lived in Havana?"

My whole life, I had heard my mother talk about growing up in Cárdenas, a large but slower-paced city to the east, along the coast and past the countryside. I never imagined my mother an *habanera*. The city seems so urban and fast-paced for her. And my mother, like Jorge, has a casual, laid-back demeanor, evocative of a childhood spent in a smaller town.

"During the summers, we would come and spend a couple of weeks with Tía," Jorge remembers. He and his two younger brothers made the annual trip. "For us, she was part of our vacation."

I wish I had known about it sooner. I could have gone there one afternoon. But I figure today I have the best tour guide.

'*Sí, vamos.*'

From the driver's side of the little blue van, a short, stocky man with thick arms and silver hair styled in a crew cut comes around to open the sliding door.

"This is Santiago," Jorge says, introducing me to a man he has known since he was in medical school. Santiago used to drive my cousin thirty or so miles home from school in Matanzas every weekend, he says, and they became fast friends. Over the years, they have kept in touch, and Santiago always picks Jorge up when he arrives in Cuba.

"And this," Jorge says, patting the side of the van, which looks to have been built in the late sixties, "is the Blue Bird." Santiago and the Blue Bird. It should be a band. "Don't worry, she runs better than she looks," Jorge says, waiting for a reaction from Santiago.

He perks right up.

"Don't you bad-mouth my little wagon. This is a rocket, *me oyes?* Do you hear me? A rocket!"

Jorge presses his lips together to hold back a smile. Santiago opens the sliding door, then props open small side windows with twigs he has whittled just for this purpose. "Don't lose those *palitos.* He almost killed me once when I threw one away," Jorge says, and Santiago shoots him a sideways look. The van kicks up with the sputter and *clack-clack-clack* of a Volkswagen engine, and we are off.

Jorge navigates from the passenger seat through central Havana and into a district of four- and five-story apartment homes built over businesses. A web of power lines crisscrosses overhead. The afternoon sun shines between the buildings, sunning trees planted along the road, their branches growing wild, unkempt. The breeze from the side windows blows into my face. The little twigs are doing their job.

"It's here, just past the bus station," Jorge says.

We turn up the street, and he tells Santiago to slow down in front of a four-story apartment that is painted in shades of blue. The bottom floor has been recently painted the color of sky, the second floor is shedding aqua, the third is flaking a splotchy mix of gray and blue, and the top floor seems to have just a blue wash. There, on the third floor, Jorge says, he used to spend his summers. Santiago perches the Blue Bird just up the street, and we walk to the apartment building. When I move toward the steps, Jorge grabs my shoulder.

"What are you doing?" he asks.

I'm going to see if there's anybody home and if they'll let me take a look around, take some pictures.

"Carlitos, you have to be really careful. People here are scared. The government is filling their heads with ideas that Cubans in the United States are coming to take their houses back," he says.

I look at him, ready to laugh. He is not laughing.

Are you serious? I look at the building. It is like a snake that is shedding its skin.

"Yeah, I'm serious."

A woman is sitting on her porch in the next building, and Jorge says that was a cafeteria when he was a kid. Once, he bought a chicken leg there, and as he walked down the street, a communist neighbor started accusing him of stealing it. He took off running and never looked back.

"*Señora*, do you know who lives in that apartment?" Jorge asks the woman whose porch was once outdoor seating. She says the woman who lives there is a sweet older person, but her husband is a bit of a recluse.

"And a little . . . unpredictable," she says. When I tell her about my mother's history there, she offers to guide me upstairs. Jorge and I follow her up a winding staircase, illuminated only by a pair of windows, until we reach the third floor. Flakes of black paint fall off a splintered wooden door when she knocks. An older woman creaks open the door. Our guide tells her that my family lived here many years ago and that I just want to take a look around. She smiles and lets us in.

"So you are from the United States?" the woman says, her voice hushed as she leads me inside. I tell her briefly about my mother growing up here, about my birth in the United States, and she pats her hands together, happy to be part of the story. She leads me past a galley kitchen, which is separated from the main room only by a low wall.

"Abuelo used to cook lunches out of his house right here," Jorge says. My maternal grandfather, Bartolomé, who lived to the ripe age of 107 in the United States, had all manner of jobs. I have heard my mother talk about him being a baker, a milkman, a *guajiro*, who worked the land with his hands. Now Jorge says he used to cook lunches out of his house, on the sly, for nearby workers. I remember him cooking for himself until he lost his sight at age 99. The man loved pork in every incarnation—bacon, fried ham steaks, roast pork—and ate it almost every day until the day he died. Take that, modern science.

The woman leads us into the living room, and there are two small bedrooms to our right. My grandparents slept in one, Jorge says, and my mother and Tía Hortencia shared the other. When he and his brothers came to visit, they slept on cots—*pim, pam, pooms!* as Cubans call them, for the noise they make when you open them. I nod at an old man sitting on a couch in the family room and offer, '*¿Hola, qué tal?*' He just stares at me until we reach the balcony.

I look out onto the street. Jorge grabs a large almond off a tree whose branches reach onto the porch. This tree was here when he was a boy, but it barely reached past the second floor, and they had to use an improvised hook to grab the nuts.

"Tata used to come out here to smoke," Jorge says.

The sound of her nickname, Tata, brings my Tía Hortencia back to me. It has been a long time since I've thought of her. And I, too, can picture her out here, her slender legs crossed, one long, thin arm moving to flick the ashes of her cigarette into that translucent pink ashtray she always used, her other hand casually fluffing her tight brown curls as she sits lost in thought. Jorge and I smile at each other, as if saying her name has flooded him with sweet memories, too.

My Tata was a kid in adult's clothing. When others were doing supposedly grown-up things, she was the one who would sit and patiently help me build plastic model cars, who taught me to play jacks and marbles on the cold tile floor of the home she shared with my grandfather, my Tío Julio, and my cousins Juli and Diani in Hialeah. She drove a racing green Camaro, and when she whipped around corners—before child-seat laws—my cousins and I would get scrunched to one side to our delight, and she would yell, "Hold on, *aguántate, tabaquito!*"

She was a seamstress by trade and never married. Her job, it seemed, was to keep that house, that family, all our family, together. She was there at my birth. And to us kids, she was the parent who was not a parent. She would never judge or scold us, and she listened to us as if our childish thoughts could change the world. She was the matriarch of a busy little family that could not keep its pace without her.

When I think of her, I still remember her with a cigarette in hand. In one of our famous family stories, Jorge's younger brother Ernesto, Tata's godson, defended her when someone waved away the smoke from her cigarette and said, "*Ay*, what a stink of cigarettes."

"It's not a stink!" Ernesto shot back, snuggling into a chair with her. "It's an *olorsito a cigarrito*, her sweet scent of cigarettes."

It was a rare, cool autumn afternoon as I sat with my Tata, my mother, and another couple of adults on a porch just like this one, I tell Jorge. I was seven. They were telling jokes, and Tata had just started laughing at one of her own when her laughter became a cough and we all watched her slide, slide down the frame of the door she was leaning against. She was still smiling when her eyes closed and she stopped coughing.

A doctor in a dimly lit hospital corridor looked ghostly green in a cold fluorescent light. There was nothing more they could do, he was saying, as I held my mother's hand. Juli, who had turned fifteen that month, startled me when he burst into tears and gripped my mom.

Nothing more? What does that mean? I didn't dare ask.

More than a week passed. The sun was setting, and I was in my Batman Halloween costume, perched on the couch, looking through the picture window at the impending twilight and the children with plastic pumpkin candy containers moving from house to house while my mother was on the phone. Our house was full of people I had never met. She sat next to me on the couch and stroked my hair.

"*Papo*, I don't think we can go out today," she said as she held my hand. "Tata . . . Your Tata . . . *falleció*, she passed away today."

No one in my family had ever *fallecido*. It was a new word for me. A new concept for a second grader. I didn't know what it meant, what it *really* meant, then. But I knew I didn't feel much like trick-or-treating anymore.

I'm never going to have a 'tía' like Tata again, my mother remembers me saying.

My Tía Hortencia died after an aneurysm in her brain ruptured while she laughed with her friends. Doctors guessed her years of smoking probably were to blame. A pang of loss chokes me when my daughters dress for Halloween, and I wonder how she would have loved to see her princesses dressed just so. But the pain is bittersweet. Because I know that my Tata, who so often tickled my cousins and me until we begged for mercy, died the way she insisted we live: laughing.

I wipe my eyes, and it is a few minutes before Jorge and I can speak again. He breaks the silence, clearing his throat, and points at the building across the street.

"I will always remember I was here on January first, 1959. The day Batista went into exile," he says.

Fidel Castro's revolution had triumphed, and news spread that the former president-turned-dictator Fulgencio Batista had fled the country. There was cheering in the streets, Jorge says, especially from the building across the street, another four-story like the one we are in.

"Your mother hadn't heard the news. She heard the cheering and said, 'I can't believe these people are happy about starting another year under *ese desgraciado*, Batista." Jorge shakes his head. "Everyone thought that something better was coming," he says, dropping his voice. "Anything seemed better. And what came to us, *lo que nos tocó*, was the devil himself."

I feel the stare of the old man on the couch and figure it is time to leave. I ask the older woman if I may snap a couple of pictures. She bites her lip and peeks inside to her husband.

"Out here is fine. But not in the house. *That one*," she says, nodding to her husband and speaking in a hushed tone, "is half crazy. He's gotten very suspicious in his old age." She drops her voice even lower. "He won't be here this weekend. If you want, come back then, and you can take all of the pictures you want."

That won't be necessary, I say. I grab her hand with both of mine, kiss her on the cheek, and thank her for letting me visit.

"See that park?" Jorge says, pointing out his window to a statue of a horse in a wedge-shaped park as we head back across town in the Blue Bird. "I used to climb up on that horse, and your mother would yell at me, '*Muchacho*, get down from there! What am I going to tell your mother if you fall and break your arm!' "

My cousins were my mother's little *compañeros*, they kept her company everywhere she went, Jorge says. They were an extension of her sister, my Tía Sofía, and even today, Jorge continues to visit my mother nearly every Saturday since he came from Cuba. He catches her up on his life, and together, they call Cuba to speak to my aunt, the only one who stayed behind.

The Blue Bird hums steadily past central and Old Havana, through the tunnel under the bay to the east, and emerges onto a four-lane road that hugs the northern coast of the island. A glimmering ocean greets us on our left. But just as we begin picking up speed, Santiago spots a car broken down by the side of the road.

"I know that guy," he says. "Let me see if I can help."

Santiago lands the Blue Bird just past the car, and Jorge and I wait inside for him to return. Jorge is staring through the driver's window at waves crashing against the shore, just on the other side of the road. He is lost, staring at the crests of waves turning foamy white as they reach the shore.

To think, it's just ninety miles away.

"It's a world away," he says, without turning to me.

Through the back window of the Blue Bird, I can see Santiago bent under the hood of the car behind us. Anyone who drives here has to be a mechanic. Jorge is still staring at the ocean. This drive home makes my cousin introspective.

We decide to cross the highway to the waterfront.

How do you see my Tía?

We stand in a stiff breeze from the sea. He scrunches his face, as if in pain at the question.

"She's not like you remember her. She's very fragile, very *lastimosa*, pitiable."

My aunt has visited the United States three times, the last time in 1994. Jorge shakes his head and turns from the sea to look me in the eye.

"I want you to be prepared for what you're going to see. For as much as I tell you, you can't imagine the conditions things are in at my mother's house."

He stops, and I know he means not just the things but his mother, too.

"It's so hard to come back here sometimes. You leave for years, and your life has changed so much. And then you come back and see that, for the people here, life hasn't changed at all." He thinks a moment as we walk along the coast. "And if it has changed, it's only gotten worse."

Santiago yells for us, and we dodge cars back across the roadway to the Blue Bird. With its rumbling song, we are off again.

The ocean stays to our left like a turquoise guide. So close to the sea, the temperature drops, and our hair is tossed by a cool breeze blowing into our little van. The city begins to fade away. There is only ocean and countryside, and rolling hills of green begin to dominate the landscape to our right.

"So what do you think of Cuba?" Jorge asks me. He looks at me like he has just asked a question to which he knows the answer. "*Choca*, reality crashes into you, doesn't it?"

He is the only person I've spoken with who can understand what I have seen, what I have learned. He is one of the few Cuban doctors to have been granted his unconditional release, so he is not considered a traitor to the revolution and can return to visit his family. He has seen both worlds, his Cuba and the United States, and can hold them side by side.

"Until you leave here, you can't begin to understand what the real world is like," he says.

I tell him everything I have seen. The inner streets of Old Havana, the buses called *camellos*—which he says are overrun with pickpockets nowadays; La Plaza; my run-in with Rosita and El Comité; the "dog pizza." What is it with pizza here, anyway? I ask him. Where are the *fondas*, the local Cuban food kitchens?

"Carlitos, you can't cook Cuban food when you can't buy the ingredients to make it," he says. He laughs and laughs when I joke that pizza and not the Cuban sandwich has become the national food, and then he just shakes his head.

"*Ay, Dios,*" he says. "There is no remedy for this place."

Jorge begins to point out the scenery. Those fields of lush green used to be hundreds and hundreds of acres of coffee and sugarcane. What I see now, he says, is nothing but *marabú*, a dense, fast-growing, thistly brush that, left unchecked, takes over the landscape, choking out whatever had been planted there. It stretches endlessly to the horizon. The sea begins to change color as we drive east, becoming more of a royal blue-green, a color of water that these eyes have never seen. And yet, it is hard to focus on the beauty between the oil wells dotting either side of the road, bobbing slowly, like giant metal birds poking their beaks into the ground. Jorge says the government has been drilling along the coast for years but has been able to extract only a poor-quality crude that can't be used for gasoline. That's why they rely so heavily on Venezuelan imports.

A few miles down the road, the sea disappears as the Blue Bird follows the curving road through *marabú*-covered hills. The air is cool, crisp, fresh mountain air, and it begs me to breathe deeply. But without warning, the air becomes venom. I can focus only on an overwhelming chemical smell that burns our throats and eyes. My lungs are on fire, and I wonder how long the burning will last.

"That," Jorge says, coughing, "is because of the refineries."

On the side of a hill, an ever-burning flame licks the top of a smokestack where natural gas is being siphoned from the earth. Cuban and Canadian flags fly side by side in front of the building, which was designed by the Canadians but approved by Cuba—only after the Canadians agreed to build bunkers beside the buildings. Why? For when the Americans attack, the Canadian engineers were told.

The sound of the wind buffeting the windows of the Blue Bird is broken when my cell phone begins to ring. It is a Cuba number, but not one I recognize.

Hello?

"Is this Carlos? Carlos *Frías*?"

The voice seems familiar, but I can't place it.

"This is your cousin Ricardo." There is a pause. "Ramón's son."

I sit up quickly as the wind from the open windows rattles into the phone.

Hello, 'primo!'

Alina called him this morning to tell him about me, my trip, and that I wanted to see him. He is speaking quickly: What brings me to Cuba? How long am I here? Will we have a chance to meet? When I tell him I'm here until Sunday, I hear him sigh.

"I'm actually not in Havana right now," he says, in a low voice. He won't be back until next week. "If only I had known. . . . Maybe I can come back into town early, catch a ride with someone. . . . *Ay*, I don't know if I can."

I am not sure if I feel loss or relief. And it is not until I tell him that I'm not actually in town, either, that I am on my way to Cárdenas, that I am forced to continue pondering it.

"I can't believe it! I can't believe it! I'm in Matanzas right now!" he says, his voice leaping. He is visiting his wife's family just thirty minutes or so from where my family lives. "This is destiny," he says. "It is our destiny to meet."

As I hand the phone to Jorge so they can figure out where and when to meet, I notice my hand shaking.

We agree to meet tomorrow at my aunt's house, and when I hang up, I can feel the smile across my face.

"*Coño*, how many questions he must have," Jorge says, as I tell him the story of this long-lost cousin.

My hands are shaking as I stuff the phone back into my bag, and I still can't tell whether I'm eager or anxious.

Occasional country shacks bordering the endless fields become slightly larger houses, little boxes that look like they could have been designed by children. There are more of them, closer and closer together, nearer to the street as the great highway becomes an urban road. We are approaching a city.

When we cross a bridge over a small bay, where boys jump from a pier into the ocean, Jorge says, "That's where we were supposed to leave from."

In 1965, a constant stream of boats headed in and out of the port of Camarioca, bound for the United States, until more than five thousand Cubans had emigrated in a mass flotilla. Jorge and his family—his parents and two brothers—were supposed to be among them, he says. It was his father's idea to take advantage of Castro's ploy to flood the United States with undocumented immigrants to get his family to freedom.

"My friends and I used to come here and watch the boats, *las lanchas*, speed in and out of the port all day, families sailing to freedom. But Fidel suspended the flotilla before we could get someone to pick us up at the port," he says, as more of civilization comes into view.

Santiago has to make one stop in the city of Matanzas to pick up a boy who is like family and drop him in the city of Varadero. This will delay our trip a bit, and the sun is already orange, casting long shadows, but I don't mind.

We cross over several metal bridges that are a hallmark of this waterfront city. We pass one billboard, freshly painted, that reads: "Don't leave for tomorrow the guard duty that belongs to you today."

"Since Fidel got sick things have been a little uneasy," Jorge says.

Who is supposed to do guard duty?

"Everybody."

To be a Cuban citizen is to be part of the military, and people have times and dates when they are supposed to "stand guard" at small outposts in every city and neighborhood. Beginning in the days after Castro's illness, men of military age, fifteen to twenty-seven, have been recalled to step up this guard duty and have been mobilized—sent away to train in different parts of the island.

We drive through one neighborhood, and Jorge and Santiago roll their windows up.

"Carlitos, if you ever want to get rid of somebody, you drop them off in this *barrio*," Jorge says.

"Here, they'll kill a man for ten pesos," Santiago adds, not taking his eyes off the pavement as the Blue Bird bounces over the potholed streets. Not even the police will respond to calls in parts of this neighborhood, Santiago says, as sometimes people in upper floors will dump pots of boiling water on them.

"But they've known me here for many years," Santiago adds, and those words are a sedative to Jorge, who trusts this man with his life.

There are few people on the streets, as if this is a bombed neighborhood that all the inhabitants have fled. A few blocks later, we reach the home of Santiago's friends and pick up the nine-year-old boy. "I can't wait," the boy says, "to jump into the beach at Varadero." He is quiet for most of the trip, clutching his backpack to his chest, staring out the window.

The main road wraps around the long, crescent-shaped bay of Matanzas. One-story houses and apartment buildings line the strip. If not for their decay, their lack of paint, the broken windows, the clothing hanging from their balconies, the scene could remind me of Miami Beach, before the glitz, when it was a sleepy little beach village. We drive past the homes and out of town, back to a wild country setting, where tall grasses and wide-open fields cover the landscape. Just a sliver of sun remains, and the world is cast in a warm glow, and Jorge is lost again, staring out the window.

The Blue Bird cruises down a two-lane highway and turns to cross a high-arching bridge, wheels humming on the steel beneath. From the apex of the bridge, I can see the dark blue ocean become a minty green as it washes over shallow white sand. The scene disappears behind rows of palm trees and homes, and if not for the boy in the backseat perking up and strapping on his backpack, I would not have known we just crossed into Varadero.

The beaches my mother has talked about since my youth are not visible from this road, and we turn down several streets, quickly, as if the Blue Bird is searching for a place to land after a long, hard trip. We park along the street, and the boy jumps out—"*¡ Hasta luego!*"—running for the house. Santiago follows him to the door while Jorge and I wait in the quiet van. A breeze cooling us through the windows carries the scent of the sea, salty and humid.

'Primo,' how's Barbara?

"You know, watching that little boy run out, I was just thinking about her," Jorge says, turning around in his seat. Jorge's youngest daughter left with him for the United States nearly eight years ago. She's doing fine, amazing, he says. She is twenty-three now, a college student. She just bought herself a brand-new Honda Civic with the earnings from her own part-time job and pays for the insurance and gas herself. She has even picked up a couple of traffic tickets, he says, and in that, she's like any American kid.

"I showed one of those Hondas to Santiago on the street, and he wouldn't believe that a kid could buy herself a car like that."

Jorge sighs and turns back around in his seat. After a minute, I hear him sniffle, and he rubs his eyes.

"You know when the breaking point was?" he says, suddenly turning back around. "We were here, at the beach in Varadero, and Barbara didn't want to sit on the hot sand." He bites his lip for a moment, swallows hard. "She went to grab a straw mat, and out comes this guy yelling and shaking his finger. 'Hey, who do you think you are? That's for the tourists! That's for the tourists!' This was just a little girl, a little girl! That night I went home and told my wife, 'That's it. I'm leaving. You can stay if you want, but I won't live another year in this hell, *este infierno.*'"

The next day, he started the process to find a way out of the country. He started by tapping into his war chest. His military dispatch to Angola had earned him the right to buy a car when he got home. And he had plenty of money saved, since his salary, paid in foreign currency, was put into an account for him. But he wasn't allowed to touch it until he returned to Cuba. They would release a little at a time to his family. "It's how they made sure you didn't desert." When he got home, he bought the car and used it to work illegally as a taxi driver, even after long shifts at the hospital. A year and a half after that day on the beach, he and his daughter were granted their unconditional release and accepted as immigrants into Venezuela. A month later, just before her fourteenth birthday, Jorge and Barbara arrived in Miami—where her mother was already waiting.

He begins to choke up as he speaks about his youngest daughter, and I cannot help but feel the emotion in my heart. My eyes fill as he speaks through it, determined to make his point. He thinks of Barbara now and compares her with the little girlfriends she left behind. One of her elementary school friends here nearly died in childbirth. Another already has a child and is unmarried. Still another is married, with a child, and has no prospects.

"What would have become of Barbara if she would have stayed here?" he says, wiping his eyes. "Carlitos, there is so much misery here—*tanta, tanta, tanta miseria.*" Barbara would cry in the days and weeks after reaching Miami, saying she wanted to go home, Jorge says, wanted to be back with her *Mima,* my Tía Sofía, who helped raise her, whose home she lived in for parts of her childhood. "Now, she's scared to visit. She misses her grandmother, but she remembers everything about this place. Everything. And I don't want to force her to come if she's not ready. But maybe someday."

When she returns, she will experience life here differently, just as Jorge has. As a resident of the United States, Jorge can come back with little fear of repercussions. He can stay in a hotel in Varadero if he likes, and, he says, "I can walk in there without a shirt on, if it suits me," but his mother, father, and brothers cannot enter, even if he pays the bill. He can visit the beaches meant for tourists, eat at tourist restaurants. But only because he first left.

"Now, they treat me differently," he says, "because I'm a *Yuma*."

Cubans call foreigners and emigrated Cubans "*Yumas*." *Yumas*, who send dollars to their family from afar. *Yumas*, who maintain girlfriends and mistresses on the island. *Yumas*, who emigrate and return like saints, their suitcases loaded with pants and shirts and toys and gifts for their families. *Yumas*, who return like devils, with rented gold chains, gold watches, and diamond earrings so they can show off to their countrymen. *Yumas*, who come into this country and are treated better than any Cuban citizen.

Jorge and I are *Yumas*.

"Humans."

Human beings.

"I had to leave Cuba," Jorge says, choking on his words, "to become a person."

Santiago returns, and Jorge turns around in his seat, looking out the window, looking away. Outside, the boy and his family are waving good-bye. He's barefoot, wearing nothing but shorts that are dripping wet. He has already been in the sea.

The last bits of light from a set sun bathe the horizon in soft orange as we drive west toward Cárdenas, back over the bridge and beyond a darkened ocean. Night brings with it an inky darkness and the three of us are silent as the Blue Bird brightens small patches of road with its pale yellow lights. There are no other cars on the road. Up ahead, the lights of the van catch a statue at the entrance to the city of Cárdenas. It is a white crab, about the size of a Volkswagen, its pincers in the air.

"They used to call this the city of the crab, because you could go off any shore and find crabs, to eat, to sell," Jorge says, shaking his head. "What the people here wouldn't do to get their hands on a crab today."

The statue is famous for another reason. In the early sixties, there was a shortage of food throughout the island but especially in these forgotten towns away from Havana, Jorge says. Someone spray-painted the crab with the words "*Tengo hambre, Fidel*. Fidel, I'm hungry." There was an insurrection; people came out of their homes clanking pots and pans, protesting in the streets, Jorge remembers. But the government dispatched tanks and soldiers to show that guns and metal can overcome a hungry belly.

Today, this is the city of workers, Jorge says. Cárdenas houses the workforce employed in Varadero's tourism industry, and buses take the masses back and forth throughout the day.

An occasional streetlamp casts an orange glow, revealing the city in bursts. A girl hitchhiking. A man stranded with a broken bicycle. A horse and buggy clip-clopping along. The Blue Bird splashes over sewage that has backed up and is stagnant on either side of these narrow streets. A pungent smell of decay blows in the windows. Buildings rise to either side of us, squat one- and two-story houses pressed against one another, grasping each other for support. Block after block, more of the same, flashing by in an unbelievable blur. It is as if all the blighted neighborhoods of the world have come together to mourn the loss of something beautiful. My eyes are heavy from the long drive, and the scenery makes me want to keep them shut. Fifty years later, this is the city where my mother grew up.

The Blue Bird lurches as Santiago wrestles with the steering wheel to make a turn. The scenery swirls as I lean my head against the window, disoriented, while row houses go by, one façade indistinguishable from the next. The Blue Bird is creeping now, creeping, finally stopping in front of a wooden door. It is rippled, dry-rotted, and damaged by termites, and you can see light shining through the cracks running vertically. Santiago and Jorge open their doors. Why have we stopped here? It's late. My Tía Sofía will be worried.

As I rest my head on the window, I see the front door creak open. And there in the doorway stands my Tía Sofía.

I step out of the van, and a dozen or so people are greeting me, shaking my hand, hugging me as I make my way toward the door. One of them takes my backpack. Another grabs my roll-aboard. They are all mere silhouettes. I can see only her.

My Tía Sofía is wearing a house gown, and her short silver-and-white hair is parted on the right, matted like a little boy's. She is smiling, and her lips are trembling. My heart begins pumping, and I am choking, choking on my emotion, as I hurry toward her and grab her with all my strength.

And still, I cannot shut out the sight of this slum: My Tía Sofía lives in this slum.

I know if I let go of this delicate little bird of a woman, this ninety-pound wonder standing with the aid of a walker, I'll collapse into a pile. I lean over the unsteady walker with the bent front wheel, and I hold her. Hold her. Bury my face into the crook of her neck and sob, uncontrollably. I tell myself not to squeeze too hard. I fear if I hug her with all of the pent-up emotions of my first six days in Cuba, I will crush her. But I cannot let go. Cannot stop shaking. Cannot contain the tears that have been waiting to flow. She is shaking, too. Sobbing. And I realize we are holding each other up.

The silhouettes become people, and soon I am surrounded by them. Jorge is with his brothers, my cousins Luis and Ernesto, and their wives and children. Jorge's two grown daughters are here with their husbands, and they are all smiling. The hugs and tears and kisses become one jumbled moment.

"Look at this, *primo*," my cousin Luis says, walking to a wall to show me a sign he has drawn on a square of torn cardboard in blue ink: WELL COME CARLITOS.

'Coño, primo,' you're a regular gringo.

He looks back at the sign through his round, wire-rimmed glasses and smiles proudly at his work. It instantly brings a smile to my face, despite tears that continue to flow.

So this is Luis. His face is round, his black hair speckled with gray, parted in the middle and feathered, and crow's-feet mark the corners of his eyes. I look around the room to Ernesto. His hair is a flowing nest of black with flecks of gray, his eyes large and round and kind. But it is his smile that reminds me of the boy I know from black-and-white pictures, the boy whose ears stuck out past his slicked black hair.

These are Jorge, Luis, and Ernesto; it finally sinks in. My mother's three nephews, her three *compañeritos*.

I know them as children in pictures. Boys are the characters in the stories my mother has told me. And here they are, men in their forties. With children. And grandchildren, *por Dios!* I know what I feel, and it is not loss. I feel cheated, cheated of the role they could have played in my life, cheated for my mother, who lost these nephews who were like her own children. Cheated for them and their summers in Havana that exist only in photographs. My tears continue to flow, and it is as if something inside of me has broken permanently, unexpectedly, and I am reminded of Jorge's words earlier today: "There is no remedy for this place."

We pull chairs from different parts of the house and sit in a circle in the family room under fluorescent lights. Some stand in this large, open room whose walls are painted in an uneven blue that reminds me of the washed "haint" blue the slaves of the South used in their homes to ward off evil. For furniture, there is only an oval dark wood dining room table and a curio cabinet, both looking of a style forty or fifty years old.

"Let's make *un cafesito*," says Jorge's oldest daughter, Elena, and she heads down a long hallway to the kitchen.

They insist I sit in one rocking chair, my Tía Sofía in the other. We sit close to each other, my left hand resting on hers as we rock. Her skin is soft, like silk paper. I bring her hand to my lips and kiss her delicate fingers. They smell of clean, like Ivory soap. Her husband, whom everyone calls Pipo, sits on the other side, smiling through thick glasses that give him an owlish quality.

"Carlitos, *caraj*, I can't believe you're here," he says.

"And what do you think of your Tía? Is she *muy fea?*" she adds in a squeaky little voice, squinting her eyes in a way that smacks of my deceased aunt, my dear Tata.

'Ay, Tía,' you look too good, *'de lo más bien.'*

"Good or good and screwed, *bien o bien jodida?*" she says, cracking up at her play on words and rocking herself in the chair.

I stroke her hand, partly to show her affection, partly to convince myself that I am really here. In Cuba. With my family. And even now, it is like *una mentira*, a great lie, a fantastic mirage that is no longer on the horizon. I have chased the wavy image in the desert and have caught it. And now, I don't know exactly what to do with it. This is my family, whom I know and don't know all at once. I stroke my Tía Sofía's delicate skin, at a loss for words.

"And what do you think of this hair? Isn't it true that I look like a little boy with this haircut?" she squeaks, patting down a cowlick.

"*Mima*, I think it looks great on you," Elena cuts in as she returns with an array of mismatched coffee cups on a tray.

The coffee is a salve. I hold the steaming espresso cup in my hands, let it heat my fingertips. The contents are hot and sweet but flavorless. And it is as if the farther we get from Havana, the more the world deteriorates. Even the coffee.

"Carlitos, you look just the same as you do in your wedding video," my cousin Ernesto says.

Come again, '¿cómo dices?'

My mother sent a copy of our wedding video seven years ago, he tells me. Apparently, Christy and I were introduced to them well before I made this trip.

"We know the whole thing by heart. That part where Christina and—Is that her mother? *Concho*, she looks young!—where they're dancing and dancing together, *ay, caramba*, that looks like it was so much fun. And that little boy that is shaking and shaking, dancing with that grown-up girl—oh, that's your nephew?—he was so funny, *qué risa*. What a great party!"

My wife and I think the same thing. We closed down our wedding reception, were the last ones to leave, and were sorry to see it end. How many times we wished we could live that day over and over again. My family in Cuba does, in their minds, what we only dream. They were at the party, too. They lived it with us. And they live the day over and over again.

How many times have you seen it?

Ernesto runs his fingers through his thick hair. "Too many to count. I put it on every time this *barbudo* comes on TV for one of his four-hour speeches."

That reminds me, I have something for you, Tía.

I reach into my bag to pull out a folder with a formal family picture of me with Christy and the girls, Elise and Amelia.

"What a beautiful family! Look at the blue eyes on that one! And look at the smile on that little one, *qué redondita,* how chubby and beautiful," she says.

Jorge's five-year-old granddaughter, Isabel, appears at my elbow to see the picture. She is inspecting my girls with her coffee-colored eyes when I say, *Do you know who they are?* She looks up at me, biting her lip, shifting her weight from one leg to the other, wordless.

Those are your cousins, your 'primitas.' Just like you're your 'Mami's' baby, those are my babies.

There are no little girls her age in my family here, and she traces the outlines of my daughters' faces with her fingers and pretends she's pinching the cheeks of my youngest.

"Why didn't my *primitas* come with you so I could play with them?" she says, finally.

They couldn't come this time, but they wanted you to see this picture so you would know them.

I reach into my folder and pull out a wallet-size copy of the same photo and give it to her. She giggles and holds the picture to her chest.

"Carlitos, can you put the picture over there for me?" my Tía Sofia asks, pointing into the other room. In the moment I get up from the chair, I feel a heaviness in my legs, as if a great weight, like the one pulling my eyelids shut, is testing my remaining strength. The room by the entrance is large enough for an entire living room set but is empty except for a glass coffee table and an old black trunk pushed against the wall. On the coffee table, there is a picture of Isabel and a framed picture of Christy, Elise, and me when Elise was only a few months old. My family in Cuba has followed our lives from the outside, assigning emotions and thoughts and dreams to the people they see in pictures over the years, pictures that capture how I've aged. They have watched me grow, like the biological parents of a child given up for adoption. I prop up the new photo next to the old one, a new still frame in time.

"*Oye*, I can't believe we don't have the game on," Luis's son, Luisito, says suddenly and heads for the television. A university championship is being played in Havana, and it is all the talk because the United States is playing in it.

"*Mima*, do you mind? Do you mind, Carlitos?"

Are you kidding? I've been dying to see Cuban baseball.

He turns on what looks like the first color television ever made, sporting rabbit ears and encased in a scratched wooden box. The sound comes on before the picture, which fades in from a greenish blue. The screen is barely bright enough to make out the game, and it buzzes with wavy lines, the picture bouncing and scrolling at times, the way televisions did in a bygone era. Cuba is playing Taipei. Luisito tells me the Americans have already won, and the winner of this game will meet them for the gold medal tomorrow.

"We're pulling for Cuba to make it to the finals," Luisito says with a smile. "But then, we'll cheer for *los Yanquis*."

When I tell Luisito that I am a sportswriter for a newspaper in the United States, he freezes in his tracks. "Do you know Derek Jeter?" he asks.

"That's his favorite player," Luis adds, even though his son is now playing first base. When I tell him that I covered baseball for three seasons, he barely pays any attention to the game. When I tell him that I spent a week at the Yankees' spring training earlier this year, interviewing Jeter, Alex Rodriguez, and Mariano Rivera for a story, his jaw drops open with each name. Luis says that, at his job, he has access to a limited Internet that includes a portal for MLB.com. Every day, he prints out stories in English so he can bring them home and decipher them with his son. A friend of a friend sent them videos of the 2005 World Series, and that tape has become part of the family library, Luisito says.

We'll have to have a catch while I'm here.

Isabel looks bored, running in front of the television and bouncing between her mother's arms, sometimes curling in her father's lap like a baby. I have extra notebooks in my bag that are meant for schoolchildren, and I remember the pens I bought in Cancún.

Do you like to draw? Will you draw me something pretty?

I let her pick between the motorcycle rider and the soccer player covers—she picks the motorcycle—and I give her a yellow pen with a clear plastic dolphin on the end that glows when you press the tip to paper.

"*Gracias,* Carlitos," she says. She sits at the old dining room table, fascinated, losing focus of her scribbles to watch the dolphin glow red. Every few minutes she walks over to show me a new scribble in fresh black ink.

The game between Cuba and Taipei goes into extra innings tied at 1, and yawns replace excitement. It is well past midnight. Everyone is still up, but Jorge must see the weariness on my face.

"*Bueno,* Carlitos, we should be getting you back to Varadero to get you a hotel," he says.

Varadero? No, Jorge, I'm not staying in a hotel.

"*Mira,* look, Carlitos," he says, "you'll be a lot more comfortable in Varadero."

I can have all the amenities that I'm used to, he says. There I can have running water, a soft bed, air-conditioning, a warm breakfast at the café downstairs. And then I can take a cab back here in the mornings.

No, Jorge. I want to stay here. I want to stay with Tía Sofía.

"You're not used to this, Carlitos," he persists. "There is no running water in this house. You'll have to take a bath scooping water out of a bucket. The mosquitoes will feast on you," he says, pointing out the square holes in the concrete walls that used to be wooden window frames. "Look at that roof," he says, pointing to the corroded steel bars exposed through the crumbling plaster ceiling of this seventy-nine-year-old house. "I'm afraid the house is going to fall in on *Mami's* head. The extra bed won't hold you; it is stuffed with newspapers to give it volume, and they are waiting to have the frame fixed, but until then, it would fall onto the floor if you lie on it," he says. "Isabel is the only one who can sleep safely on it."

I don't care about any of that. I am not going to Varadero, Jorge. I am staying with my family.

More than anything, I want to take shelter right here, with my Tía Sofía, who feels safe, like home. After a week of concealing who I really am, of searching for places that were important to my family only to find ruins, I just want to sit wordlessly in her arms and not have to feel anything anymore. We compromise. Elena offers to let me stay at her house, which is just around the corner.

"*Sí*, Carlitos, come stay at my house!" Isabel says, excited enough that she is fighting to keep her eyes open.

My Tía Sofía lifts herself from her rocking chair with her walker and hugs me with one arm, patting me rhythmically on the back.

"Sleep well, *mi niño*," she says. I swallow hard so I will not pick up where we left off just a few hours ago.

I follow Jorge just around the block in the moonless night to where his oldest daughter and her husband, Tomás, live.

Tomás carries Isabel in his arms, and she looks over his shoulder at me, smiling, her eyes closing as we walk. Elena says they have an extra room, but when I get there, I realize they do not. Beyond a front door reinforced by an iron gate, the house is split into two. Tomás, a stonemason, has built a wall between the living room and the room where his brother sleeps.

Tomás, my cousin Elena, and Isabel live in what amounts to a five-by-seven living room, and all sleep in the attached master bedroom on the other side. Sometimes, Isabel sleeps in the treacherous extra bed at my Tía Sofía's house. Tomás' brother is out of town for the week, so the three of them will sleep in his "house." I will sleep in their room. I start to protest, but they insist the other room is going to be empty all week anyway and so, I relent.

Their master bedroom is really only a shelter. It has three full walls, and the back wall is about four feet high with a walkway that leads to a small kitchen they built under an overhang. The room opens up into a courtyard and out into the warm, still August night. It is modesty that makes up the walls in this home. Elena makes the bed with fresh sheets, positions an oscillating fan over the bed, and hands me a towel so I can bathe.

The bathroom is tiled in white and clean. The water pressure is not strong enough in this part of town for the water to make it out of the showerhead. So I fill up a yellow plastic bucket with room-temperature water and scoop it over my head and down my goose-bumpy body with an aluminum cup. The bath cools me, but as soon as I step out of the tub, I am covered in a sprinkling of sweat as the constant heat permeates the breezeless night. I close the louvered wooden door that leads to the living room and lie on the bed, staring at the starry night where a wall should be.

I try to write in my notebook but lack the energy. My Tía in the walker, the crumbling roof, the bucket and cup, the sewage on the street, the missing wall, every sight and sound tramples over logic and words. My family must live this way. It is the best they can ever hope for. And all I can do is lie in this bed and sob and lament and know that in a couple of days I will go back and leave them like this, no better for my visit.

I turn off a lamp in the corner, and the mosquitoes come almost immediately. I cover myself with a sheet and give them my neck and face to feast on, the buzzing constant in my ears. They eventually find their way to my ankles, and I decide, instead of swatting them away, to give them their fill. They will eat and either burst or fly away.

I am not sure when or how, but I finally fall asleep.

The constant hum of the fan disappears, and I awake groggy to find that the power has gone out. There is an audible groan outside. Everywhere, people's fans have gone off. The night is still. I fumble for my watch and see that it is just after 3:00 A.M. Dogs bark. Voices murmur. Even at this time, you can hear the clip-clopping of a horse and buggy. A lone mosquito buzzes in my ear.

This is everyday life for Cubans. For my family.

There is a pop after about twenty minutes, and the power is back on. The whirring fan resumes its business, and my sleep returns with total emotional exhaustion.

DAY SEVEN

The sound of splashing water wakes me.

Sunlight fills Tomás and Elena's room, and I can see a band of blue sky beyond the wall that isn't there. The fan is still oscillating. The bed is warm and soft, and I'm not ready to keep my eyes open. I close them and listen to the splashing, like a hose that has been turned on full force, and the water is crashing against a cement floor. A few minutes pass before I roll to the far side of the bed, toward the doorless closet that spans the length of the room, the family's clothes hanging in plain view, open to the elements. Beyond the missing wall, I see Tomás in the open courtyard wearing nothing but a pair of shorts. As if standing under a rinse at the beach, he is taking his morning shower under the only showerhead with enough pressure to work properly.

I roll back onto my pillow and stare at the ceiling for I don't know how long. Outside, horses clip-clop and diesel engines clack by. The splashing water stops, and other rustling stirs inside the house. The rest of the world is alive, and I must be the only one still in bed. My arms, my legs, my eyes are still heavy. I know this room borders the kitchen and wonder if Elena and the others have hesitated using it because I am here. I sit myself up, open my luggage, and begin to dress. When I come to the money belt, my portable Fort Knox, I decide not to put it on for the first time since I came to Cuba. I grab a few Convertibles, stuff them in my pocket, and leave the belt in my bag. It has never been this safe. Nor have I.

When I come out of the bathroom from brushing my teeth, I see Elena in the kitchen filling the espresso maker and cutting a loaf of Cuban bread into slices as Tomás sits at a wrought-iron table.

"How did you sleep?" Elena asks, handing me my first cup of coffee.

Great, I lie. When they are not looking, I scratch at the welts under my ankle socks. The front door creaks open.

"*Oye,* is everybody up in here?" Jorge yells as Luis follows him into the house. Everyone wakes up with the sun except the *Yuma* who is used to a chirping wristwatch. For the first time in a week, I did not set the alarm. Jorge, Luis, and I hug, and Jorge kisses his daughter on the cheek as everyone sits down for coffee. I eat a couple of slices of crusty bread and wash it down with the bottled water I carry with me at all times. Jorge was up early getting his hands on a car. A friend works at a repair shop and sometimes has a car available to rent. For twenty Convertibles a day, we have a white Lada hatchback that is not much to look at, he says, but runs well enough to shuttle us around.

A ringing and buzzing interrupts us. My cell phone calls from the other room. I look at the number and recognize it from the day before. It is my cousin Ricardo. I take a deep breath before answering.

"*Buenos días, primo.* Are you in Cárdenas?" he asks.

'Sí,' I'm here with my cousins, my aunt, all my family. But when am I going to meet you?

He says he is in Cárdenas now, visiting one of his wife's family members, and could come over for a while. I hand the phone to Jorge and he quickly offers to save Ricardo the drive.

"You're sure?" I hear Jorge say. "Really, it's no trouble. We have a car, and we'll be driving Carlitos all over Cárdenas today. We can easily meet you at . . . Okay. *Bueno,* if you prefer that. Here's how you get here. . . ."

"It's strange," Jorge says after hanging up. "He insisted we not meet him at his family's house. 'No, no, we'll go to see you.'"

What could that mean?

Jorge shrugs his shoulders.

"Maybe the house is very humble," Jorge says, "and he's embarrassed for you to see it."

"Maybe it's opulent," Tomás says, "because his family are communists. Do you know anything about this cousin?"

I tell him all that I know, which is close to nothing. No one in my family has ever met this long-lost relative. Our eyes dart at one another's in silence. In Cuba, there is an institutional mentality of paranoia, and I find that I, too, am beginning to chase shadows. I feel guilty at suspecting such a thing of this cousin, this man who has already been made to feel so apart. But I have learned my lesson from Rosita's CDR headquarters in Marianao.

Tomás asks to see my cell phone. I hand him the old Nokia that I would have considered obsolete ten years ago. He has never used one but has seen others who have them. Not in Cárdenas, though.

"Here, someone talking on a cell phone is the same as a UFO landing in the middle of town," he says.

Pacing is the only thing that calms me.

I find myself unable to sit as the moment of meeting Ricardo nears. I pace to the bedroom, where I pack and repack and shuffle things around in my bag. I pace to the kitchen, where Elena pours me a second cup of coffee. I pace and pace, and Elena grabs my hand as I pass, pats it. I nod and breathe out long and slow as I sit down at the table. I am drinking Cuban espresso, ironically, to settle down. Although I barely have it at home, I drink it five and six times a day here. The coffee is a balm, calming the tremors at my core.

A knock at the door makes Elena and me stare at each other for a second.

Jorge goes to open it. Beyond my line of sight, I hear the voice on the telephone. In person, it rings truer. It is deeper, raspier, friendlier as I hear him greet Jorge, Luis, and Tomás. I stand up from my chair and wait to see him come through the bedroom door.

Framed in the rough concrete opening to the kitchen is a man almost six feet tall, who looks to be in his late forties. He wears his hair in a black crew cut, and his hairline is receding. But it is his face, *his face*, that seems to have reached across the proverbial ninety miles to bring me a piece of the Frías family that I know. There is no doubt, not for a second, that this man is my blood. Forget that he has never met his father; Ricardo's smile is undoubtedly my Tío Ramón's. His eyes tell the story.

There are no greetings, no words that need to be spoken. We embrace like we are holding something important in place. He hugs me the way my daughter Amelia hugs a stuffed toy. He is not letting go. We loosen our grip just enough to step back and look at each other. He searches my face for clues. I know I find answers in his. He has no idea how much he looks like his father—more so than any of my uncle's other three sons.

"Carlos, you can't imagine how long I've dreamed of this moment," he says, and his eyes, behind a pair of oval antique gold glasses, begin to redden and fill. "I thought I would live my entire life without . . ." His voice begins to crack. He hugs me again. His wife, Gisela, puts her hand gently on his shoulder. Her eyes, too, are instantly full, and her bottom lip quivers through a smile.

Elena rushes in to offer coffee and tells us to sit down. She brings in the fan from the bedroom and points it at the table. I look into the other room and can see my cousins peeking to see what is going on. They begin to talk among themselves as Elena busies herself with the coffee. We sit close, the three of us.

"Carlos, what made you want to find me?"

I tell him about my conversation with Alina. I even tell him about my apprehension.

I didn't know how you would receive me.

"Coño, *mi hermano*, my brother, how else could I possibly receive you? We are family."

As he speaks, I pick out features that I recognize. His eyes are my Tío Ramón's. His nose is my Abuela Teresa's; she is his grandmother, too. The hairline, well, it seems that now all four of Ramón's children share the unfortunate heredity. The more I look at him, the more he seems familiar. Meanwhile, Gisela records us with a handheld camcorder, saving this moment for her husband.

"As a kid growing up, I thought a lot about my father and my father's family. What they were like. What their lives were like," he tells me.

Tell me about your life, Ricardo.

He and his half sister were raised by his mother in Marianao. He grew up hearing about *los Frías,* who were so well-known in the city that he could not escape the name. It became a part of him, he says, *los Frías de Marianao.* He was one of them—and not one of them all the same.

"A long time ago, I put away thoughts about my father's family. You drive yourself crazy thinking about why things turned out the way they did," he says.

He studied dentistry in Matanzas, where he met his wife. They settled down there after school, before the promise of a better life called to them from the city. They both practice in Havana now but visit Matanzas several times a year, particularly because "the kids miss their *abuelos,*" he says. His mother gave him her last name. He does not say what she told him about my uncle or my father's family, and I do not press him for details. Whatever his truth is, it has not made him bitter. He smiles as he tells the stories of his youth, of his life, not like someone trying to show how well he turned out "despite," but like someone who turned out the way he has "because." It breaks down my guard, because I know we are talking to each other not as strangers but as long-separated family.

His own mother, he says, left for the United States about three years ago. Even so late in life, she applied for an exit visa and, when she got it, left with Ricardo's older sister. She has a lot of health problems, he says, is hypertensive, and they all felt she would receive better medical care and have an easier life in the United States than spending her twilight years bouncing between Cuban clinics without the necessary medicines. It left Ricardo truly alone, gripping tightly to his wife and his two children, Magaly and Julio.

"*Gracias a Dios,* I have an amazing wife and smart, wonderful children," he says, as he and Gisela hold hands. "Let's take a few pictures," he says, pulling out the video recorder that also takes photos. I wonder for a second how he can afford such a luxury as I sit in a kitchen that is a kitchen only because we say so. My mind goes there: Is he with "the party"? I silently curse Fidel Castro for intruding on our moment and stall before taking a picture so I can get the thought out of my mind.

Have you ever thought about trying to join her, your mother? Even just to visit?

I ask because I am curious. But also because I am testing him, I'm ashamed to admit. He grabs his wife's hand, and they give each other pitiable smiles. "That is the dream of every Cuban, to live in freedom," he says, turning back to me. "But I'm sure you know by now how deep a hole this place is to climb out of." They are both professionals. Ricardo and Gisela are "theirs" now. Cuba will never just let them go.

Gisela takes several shots with both our cameras as Ricardo and I hug and pose.

"And now one of you with Gisela," Ricardo says, grabbing my camera, "so they can see what a babe, *qué pollo,* I married."

Ricardo says he has people waiting for him back at his wife's family's house but asks what my plans are while I am here. I tell him that tomorrow my cousins and I are going to Varadero Beach. "Another coincidence?" Ricardo says. He will also be at Varadero. His son, Julio, will be there, too, and he wants us to meet. Another cousin. We trade cell phone numbers—again, I fight the urge to ask the question, "How can you afford a cell phone?"—and I promise to call when I reach Varadero. I walk him to the door, and he hugs me tight as we say our good-byes. When we let go, I see his eyes moist again. He puts his hand on my shoulder.

"I feel like this was meant to be," he says.

Destiny.

I am starting to believe.

"He doesn't know where she is," Christy tells me.

I know instantly what she means. My father. My sister. It is not going to happen. After our conversation last week, Christy had been trying to find the right time to talk to him. A time when my mother wasn't around, when he wouldn't feel pressured or embarrassed or uncomfortable. Yesterday, she says, he stopped by the house to visit and brought miniature *Manzano* bananas from his yard for the girls. While they played in Elise's room, he sat watching television in the office, drinking Cuban coffee my wife made for him. We stock decaffeinated Bustelo—something I once thought defeated the purpose of coffee—just for him. But now I understand. Cuban coffee is not a beverage, it's a ritual, like a Japanese tea ceremony.

She pretended to work at the computer as she got up the nerve to ask him. And then, she did what she always does: She popped the cork with confidence. She told him I left without having a chance to ask him an important question, and I had asked her to intercede. Carlos knows about his sister in Cuba, she told my father. Since this is a once-in-a-lifetime opportunity, he would like to try to find her.

"You could tell he was surprised for a second when I brought it up, but he didn't seem uncomfortable talking about it," she tells me.

He told Christy that he was young when my sister was born, probably eighteen or twenty. That would have made it the late 1940s, when my father's family was still in the country, in Oriente. They were just kids, both of them, he told her, neither in a position to be a parent. But the baby came. The child's mother never asked anything of him, and he didn't offer. "We just left things like that," he said.

When he left for Marianao, he lost track of the girl. The more Christy and my father spoke, the more the conversation became strained. She let it go, and they sat silently in the presence of the television.

"He thinks she's in Oriente, but he's not sure. I'm sorry, my Lind."

No, I'm sorry to have put you through that, my love.

"I didn't get the sense he was embarrassed to talk about it. You know how your dad is. He doesn't like to air dirty laundry, but once it's out there, he doesn't shy away from it. So maybe when you come back . . ."

I can do what I should have done before I left.

For right now, there is nothing more I can do. I don't even know her name.

Destiny.

Maybe it just wasn't meant to be.

The front door to my Tía Sofía's house is propped open. She is rocking slowly by a pair of open doors that lead to a courtyard out back, her walker propped up next to her. She is grinning, as she always seems to be, her eyes smiling as I enter the room.

"Did you sleep well, *mi niño?*" she asks as I kiss her forehead and feel the light sprinkling of perspiration on her brow. An oscillating fan feathers the hair that is now clipped back with a silver barette. She is wearing a thin pink house gown with a flowery pattern, one of the five or so that my mother sent her recently.

"Did you already eat breakfast? I can make a quick *café con leche,*" she says and starts to reach for her walker.

No, 'Tía,' I already ate at Elena's house. Some 'frijoles' they had left over from the other night, I lie.

She sits back in her chair, and I sit in one opposite her to rock and wait for Jorge, who has gone to fill the tank of the Lada so we can drive around Cárdenas.

"If your mother were here, she would recognize these chairs," she says. Like all the furniture in this house, these chairs with the wicker seats and backs have been around since the early 1960s. Every few minutes, while she rocks, she closes her eyes for just a second, and the smile on her lips dares to slip into an almost imperceptible grimace.

Does something hurt, 'Tía'?

"Ay, *niño,* even my soul hurts," she says, smiling again and resuming her rocking. "But, you learn to live with the pain."

A lot has happened to my aunt since 1994, the last of her three trips to the United States on a visitor's visa. In 2000, she had a stroke that paralyzed her left side, from a droopy left eye all the way down to a twisted left ankle. She fell and lay on the cold, green-and-white faux marble tiled floor until Jorge got to her house.

"Imagine me, sprawled out on the floor with my legs in the air like a cockroach," she says with a squeaky laugh.

Jorge drove her to the hospital in his car, because ambulances are scarce in Cuba, and sometimes it can be hours before they respond. It was better that he drove anyway. It gave him time to pack up towels, bed linens, sheets, a few gowns, a toothbrush, all of the things we take for granted at U.S. hospitals that Cubans must provide themselves. She needed physical therapy for thirteen months to regain use of her left arm. But her left foot still is at an angle. As she rocks in her chair, she pushes off with her good foot.

A year later, because her foot never regained its full range of motion, she tripped, fell, and broke her hip. A botched operation required another surgery with screws, and now the pain in her hip is constant, and so is the use of the walker.

"But what can you do? There's no choice but to keep on living," she says with a smile, her smile.

At least she has the walker to help. She is unstoppable around the house in that walker, she says, one that has become an awful, pathetic legacy in our family. My late grandfather broke his hip at age ninety-nine in the United States and learned to walk again with it. Later, it went to my mother, who broke her hip in her late sixties, but is now able to walk again without it. And finally, my mother sent it here to my aunt, who couldn't buy one even if she had the money.

As I watch this frame that is barely strong enough to shift her rocking chair, I know this is not the body of the aunt I remember. Not the one who is captured in my memory, in pictures at my mother's house. That aunt had her hair coiffed and styled and her nails done. She was plump after a monthlong visit and wore a new outfit for her trip home.

"When Jorge came to pick me up at the airport, he walked right by me. Now look at the little old lady, *la viejita*, that someone has left in her place," she says, showing the spirit that remains inside her.

"Carlitos, let me put that water in the refrigerator for you so it will be nice and cold when we leave," Luis says when he sees the half-empty water bottle in my backpack. I follow him back through the long, narrow house, through Sofía and Pipo's bedroom, through the room with the guest bed that cannot accommodate a guest, to a small kitchen.

"You did the right thing drinking bottled water if you're not from here. I work with guys who come here from other countries, and I've seen them get sick from *los parásitos*, the parasites, in the tap water," he says as he puts my bottle alongside others in my aunt's refrigerator. Luis is an engineer and works with foreign engineers at his job. "They tell us to boil our water, but we're already used to the parasites," he says. "We've become the best of friends."

He tugs at the door of a small but new refrigerator three times—"piece of trash," he mutters—before prying the seal open with his fingers. Until recently, they had a thirty-year-old General Electric that ran like a top. But the government recently began to stress energy efficiency and forced them to give up their old, working fridge for a Chinese model they must pay for in monthly installments. They did the same with their old rice cooker and the electric burner. The new rice cooker alone cost forty-three Convertibles, about four months' worth of Pipo's retirement income. They have a gas stove, but the government allows them to use it only "in times of emergency," Luis says. I look around the room. There is a hole in the wall where a window should be, and I wonder if they are not living this emergency.

I hear Jorge arrive at the same time as his two daughters, Elena and Andrea, who come by daily to help my Tía Sofía keep her house clean. Isabel, Elena's daughter, bounces through the door and rushes to the back of the kitchen, her mane of golden brown twisted into a thick braid. She clings to my arm and curls her little index finger, signaling me to "come here," and I bend down so she can wrap her arms around my neck. "Carlitos, I'm going to go with you today," she says.

She is ready for the trip. She wears a pink spandex tank top with a picture of Minnie Mouse saying *Aloha!*, baby blue athletic shorts that pinch her meaty midriff, and matching flip-flops.

Good, because I need you to keep me company.

Before we get going, I need to use the bathroom, and Luis asks me, "Do you know how to use the bucket?"

Behind the wall adjacent to the kitchen, I open the door to a rustic indoor lavatory, the color of unfinished cement. A salmon-colored toilet is separated from a shower only by a curtain that is pulled back. In the shower, there is a bucket of water, the bucket my Tía Sofía uses to bathe. I can't flush the toilet because there is no running water, Luis says, so when I'm finished, I have to chuck in the bucket to make the toilet drain. I've done this before at home, but only when the water isn't running. Here, the water never runs. A plastic bucket is the flush handle. And, there is no toilet seat. All over Cuba, outside the tourist areas, this is the norm. Back home, we take things like clean water and cable television for granted. Here, they covet a ring of plastic to keep their bottoms off a cold porcelain bowl.

"Where should we go first?" Jorge asks when we meet in Tía's living room.

I want to see everything. All the places that were important to my mother. The house where she grew up. The places she went as a girl.

"Her old school?" Luis interjects.

'Sí,' exactly.

Jorge and Luis talk over the friends of the family who are still around and the places we should visit, and they chart a course. The flood of possibility fuels me in a way that two slices of Cuban bread and a cup of coffee did not; I am going to piece together my mother's youth. As we head to the door, Luis snaps his fingers and rushes back to the refrigerator to grab my bottle of water.

"Carlitos," he yells from the other room, "is yours the water with *parásitos* or without?"

As we walk out the door, I see Elena mopping the tile floor

while her sister, Andrea, who bathes my Tía Sofía every morning, leads her toward the bathroom. My aunt walks ahead of her, moving the walker inches at a time, madly shuffling her feet for locomotion, and I'm reminded of that old Tim Conway character from *The Carol Burnett Show*. But this person, my Tía Sofía, is real. Sadly, painfully, beautifully real.

Jorge takes the wheel, and I sit next to him as Luis, Luisito, and Isabel pile into the backseat of the white Lada hatchback, which is about the size of a Ford Focus. Jorge wrestles the manual transmission until we ride at a pace just above a sprint. The roads are packed, but not with cars. Horse-drawn buggies clip-clop along, sharing the road with people who step off the sidewalks, which are cracked in places. Our movement sends a subtle cloud of dust into the air as we pass two-story buildings with businesses on the bottom floor. There is a fruit stand, a café, an anthill of movement as people cross the road, darting just seconds ahead of speeding cars. We zip past the horses, and I'm surprised they barely flinch. These Cuban horses are rarely spooked. One cart slows as its horse defecates, and the steaming balls of dung land on the street. When the horse finishes, the driver whales a switch tirelessly against the horse's rump to return him to speed.

A few other cars begin to emerge as we reach a main road called La Calle Real, the Royal Street. It is a wide main drag with expansive sidewalks encouraging foot traffic and buildings three, four, and five stories high on either side.

"Once upon a time," Luis says, and I can feel him going back into his memory, "this was one of the most beautiful avenues anywhere in Cuba. People strolled down the street, well-dressed, to eat, go to the movies . . ."

Meticulously kept horse-drawn carriages, with drivers in suits, shared the road with modern cars, a mix of the old and new worlds, he says. When I look down the road, I can see Jorge's memory bathed in an acid wash, the colors and the buildings faded and running. We turn down the road and head east toward the sea. We leave behind the urban buildings of Real and come to a park at the edge of town, where a monument, a great spire that reaches into the sky, was erected to commemorate the first time the Cuban flag was raised during the war of independence. Just beyond the park is the minty green sea. Lovers used to stroll at night here for the cool ocean breeze, and children played on the grass during the day, Jorge says. But like the rusting factory next to it, this park is abandoned but for us. Even the view of the ocean has changed. Piled high, concealing part of the horizon, is a veritable Mount Trashmore next to an industrial building. I look closer and can see the mountain is made up of old refrigerators, white, pastel blues and yellows, avocado greens, and browns.

"I'll bet you our old refrigerator is in there," Luis says, with a hint of nostalgia for their reliable relic.

We drive along the coast, a road just at the edge of the water, and the brothers, Luis and Jorge, point out the house of an uncle they used to visit in the summers. They would run less than fifty feet from the glistening ocean back to the old wooden house, which has now mostly fallen in on itself, the wood siding stripped of all but a few flakes of white paint.

On the way back into town, I feel a rumble in my stomach and know that my cousins also must be hungry. We come across a small café just off La Calle Real, and Jorge parks the Lada out front. The restaurant is situated beyond a small courtyard with red plastic benches and tables and matching umbrellas overhead, where a handful of people sit for shelter from the midafternoon sun. The menu is familiar at this point: more pizza. I order personal-size doughy pies for each of us, and we sit under the shade eating our fill. Isabel's fingers are mottled with tomato sauce, and she sucks them for every scrap.

"Niña, eat like a person," Jorge tells his granddaughter and wipes her fingers with a napkin as she wags her tongue at him.

"Did you stay up for the game last night?" Luisito asks me.

I couldn't keep my eyes open. Who won?

He and Luis look at each other.

"Taipei," Luisito says. Cuba lost. They can do no better than third place, in the capital city of their own country.

"Heads are going to roll," Luisito says. "If the *barbudo* wasn't dead yet, that probably did the job."

While we eat, a man at another table talks loudly. He is wearing a royal blue T-shirt with the sleeves cut off to accentuate the pair of gold bracelets on one arm and the gold watch on the other. He has a thick gold chain and medallion around his neck, and the diamond studs in his earrings twinkle against his caramel skin as he speaks and shoves slices of pizza into his mouth.

"Ridiculous, right?" Jorge says when he sees me eyeing the man. That, he says, is a Cuban who left the country legally and now can return as a *Yuma*, with his U.S. citizenship as a prize, to show off his wealth to his former friends and family.

Jorge stands up from the table, unable to watch any longer. As he does, a stray dog wanders over. The many missing tufts of its matted, filthy gray fur reveal fleshy rib bones beneath. Still, it wags its tail as it looks ahead with cloudy gray-blue eyes. Luis begins to shoo it away before Jorge, the oldest brother, says, "*Déjalo, chico.* Leave him alone." Jorge picks up the scraps of food from our foam plates, piles them onto one, and places it on the floor. The pooch eats the pizza scraps slowly, like either it is savoring the meal or even the soft bread is too painful to devour quickly. It wags its tail languidly as Jorge rips a paper cup in half and pours water from his bottle into it.

"He's gotten very sentimental about animals since he left," Luis whispers.

Before continuing on, we walk to a church across the street, La Parroquia, where my Tía Sofía was married more than fifty years ago and where my mother attended Mass on Sundays. It is a stately building, with twin-tiered towers on either side and a long aisle leading to a perfect dome over the altar. Stained-glass windows are cracked or missing, and the building is condemned these days because chunks of plaster fall periodically from the roof onto the marble floors, says a priest who knows my pastor at St. Bartholomew's back in South Florida. He says the Church is renovating it but lets us peek at the interior through a rear door, and the 150-year-old church smells as you would expect, of ancient wood and a lifetime of incense. An altar of reddish wood is shrouded in a white cloth just in front of a sculpture of a crucified Jesus. Light from the cracked windows catches on a haze of dust, as if a centuries-old tomb has been opened. Stenciled above the entrance are the words "Thy Kingdom Come."

We pile back into the Lada and head across town on the main road toward my mother's old school. As we drive west, more buildings appear to be recently painted. Turquoises and minty greens, salmons and Tuscan yellows adorn the roadway. Several colonial-style buildings seem as if they have put their makeup on for the day. When I ask what is with this infusion of life, my cousins simply say, "Elián." The boy at the center of the international custody battle lives right down the street, and many of the buildings along the main road were repainted in 2000, when media from all over the world came here to film his house and cover the story. The government moved his father from a tenement in La Marina, broken-down apartments near the coast, to a new house along this main drag. It was better for the cameras, my cousins say, and better for the boy, who became "Castro's patron saint," Luis says.

Jorge points to a two-story building that makes up one entire corner as we pass. It is covered in scaffolding, and there are workers moving in and out. That, Jorge says, is where my Tío Julio, my mother's late older brother, studied. It was an all-boys Catholic school run by a brotherhood of Trinitarian priests. Jorge, too, studied there, until the government took it over and closed it down as part of the state's atheistic vision.

Now, it is being transformed into a sort of college prep school, making up the tenth through twelfth grades, that will focus on computer sciences, Luisito explains over the loud hum of the Lada. Not surprisingly, Elián has said that's the field he wants to study. The closest of these pre-universities is in the city of Matanzas, and Luisito's grades earned him a scholarship there. These are all boarding schools, and he does not see his parents for a week or two at a time if they can't afford to send for him. But this "pre" under construction means Elián will not have to leave his parents. Right now, just as he prepares to enter the equivalent of junior high, the government is fixing up that school, too.

"If Elián wanted to study to be an astronaut, they'd build him a rocket," Luisito says.

Jorge pulls the hatchback off the road and parks across from a wide, one-story building that looks like it was painted during the Elián saga, an off-white with peach and salmon trim. This is it, my mother's school, Las Madres Escolapias, the all-girls Catholic school she attended from the first through the twelfth grade.

Isabel grabs my hand as we cross the street and walk through an open iron gate and up the stone stairs to a veranda highlighted by fluted columns. On the façade is a plaster crest with the date 1918, presumably the year this building was built. The wooden front door is open, and a breeze blows into the hallway, past a foyer with high ceilings and through a doorway to the courtyard. Finger paintings and handwriting assignments are posted just outside the doors, and I can almost hear the rush of children running from room to room. A woman in a tank top, shorts, and flip-flops sits on a wooden chair, papers piled high on a scratched and distressed pupil's desk in front of her. She looks up with a smile and blows a wisp of hair out of her face. *"Buenas tardes,* can I help you with something?" she asks.

My mother was a student here in—I do the math quickly—*I guess, the late forties, early fifties. I was just hoping we could take a look around and take some pictures.*

"An alum? What was her name?"

Iraida, I say, and give her my mother's maiden name.

"That name sounds so familiar. Did she have sisters?"

Yes! Two of them. But they didn't come here.

"*Ay, mi madre,* I think my mother might have gone to school with your mother," she says, her face lighting up. She is an administrator here and grew up in Cárdenas. "I'm very much interested in the history of the school. We have old photos in our archives and are trying to identify a lot of the old students."

She writes down my mother's information and the year of her commencement, which I remember from the side of the graduation ring she always wore, before it broke.

"I'm not supposed to let anyone in when the school's not open," she says, but she puts a rock atop the papers to keep them from blowing away and begins to show us around. Besides, she can get back to that work later. School starts in a couple of weeks, and she's just trying to get a head start.

She leads us out into a courtyard whose walls are flaking pink paint and down a set of steps. "This was the center of activity," she says, as girls moved from class to class and, for the girls who boarded here, to their dorms in the other building.

"Right here," she says, motioning to the courtyard, "is where they had all their graduations."

I imagine my mother taking these steps, now cracked and missing tiles, two at a time as a girl and climbing them ceremoniously as a graduate to pick up her sheepskin fifty-three years ago. I sit on the steps to take a picture, and Isabel sits next to me, props her elbow on my knee, and rests her head in her hands.

There, beyond those iron gates, where a rusted swing set now stands, was the play yard, the woman says. That must be where my mother has told me she learned to play baseball from one of the nuns who taught here, running to imaginary bags at the crack of the bat.

"Your *Mami* used to play baseball?" asks Isabel, who has not let go of my hand.

'Sí,' and she used to take me to all of my T-ball games and cheer like a crazy lady—'Run! Run!'—from the bleachers when I ran the bases.

I grab a handful of the sandy earth and watch it fall from my hand, this earth, my mother's earth.

"When your mother was here, that used to be the chapel," the woman says, pointing at a building that in a secular Cuba has been converted into a day care.

"A lot of things have changed since your mother was here," the woman says. She says the government has designated the school a historic building, and that means they have to stick to strict standards when they restore it. They keep telling her the restoration will start soon, but she has been hearing that for years now. There are other places my cousins want to take me, and I thank the woman for her time.

"Tell your mom her *escuelita* may be very different, but it is still here," she says.

We are close to where a friend of Jorge lives, and he suggests we stop by for a few minutes, "so you can see how Cubans *resuelven,* how they make do."

We continue west on the main road, and the houses remain a pastel treat. I look down side streets as we pass, and the world beyond fades into a grayish beige. This makeup is only skin deep. Jorge pulls the Lada into the drive of a mint house with white trim around the windows. It has its own little yard out front that leads to a porch with terra-cotta tiles, and I wish my Tía Sofía had been lucky enough to live on the same block as the boy who floated across the Florida Straits.

Jorge knocks on the varnished wood door, and after a few minutes, a stocky man with thick, curly hair and his shirt open to reveal, well, more thick, curly hair, wraps my cousin like a bear.

"*Coño,* Jorge, I was wondering when you were going to come see me," he says. Jorge introduces me to Silvio, whose hands are like paws, thick and rough. Jorge hugs Silvio's wife, who has her hair in curlers and is wearing a white house gown with a flowery motif. We sit on a couch and a pair of rocking chairs in his living room, while two fans circulate the warm air. After a few minutes, Silvio says, "Jorge, I have to show you the upgrade I've made," and Jorge winks at me.

Silvio leads us to a porch in the backyard, where finches in a cage chirp and bounce from twig to twig. In another cage, a canary sits songless, watching the strangers go by. They distract my attention for only a second before a growl and a bark make me snap to attention. Beyond a fence, where there is a small green space, a growling mongrel, which looks to be mixed with pit bull, is pressing its face up against the chain-link fence, growling, drooling.

"Down, Diablo," Silvio tells him, and the dog's tail begins to wag.

He leads it to a cage in the corner of the yard and locks it in. From the other side of this makeshift crate, it growls low and steadily.

"*Ay*, I can't tell you how afraid I am of that dog," Silvio's wife tells us.

"But he's a great watchdog," Silvio adds.

On the other side of the yard is what the mongrel guards. Silvio has cut a steel drum lengthwise and turned it into an oven. It has a temperature gauge built into the side so he can keep the heat constant. Silvio works where he has access to baking supplies—flour, yeast, lard—and brings home leftover ingredients so he can bake and sell bread on the side. He has to bribe local authorities, who could crack down on him at any time, Jorge says, and Silvio tries to keep good relations with his neighbors, offering them bread for free. But this is the way of life in Cuba, where stealing is built into a system that cannot provide the bare necessities for its people.

"Didn't I tell you that Cubans *resuelven?*" Jorge says.

The extra money clearly helps. The house appears well-kept, and when I ask to use the bathroom, not only does the water run but they also have a toilet seat.

"One day they'll decide he's gone too far, and they'll break him, *lo parten*, or some neighbor will get upset for whatever reason and turn him in, *lo chivatéa*," Jorge says as we drive back down the main road. "But he'll make do as long as he can."

At the edge of town, we loop around a quaint plaza with a monument of a carriage—this is, after all, the city of the horse and buggy—and Jorge says the road keeps going into the deep country, where his mother was a teacher years ago. He loops around slowly and nods his head to a freshly painted white-and-blue house bordering the picturesque little park with the manicured lawn.

A car with a blue government plate is parked out front, and under the shade of a porch, Elián González's father, famous for his televised pleas for his son's return, sits drinking a beer next to his personal driver. I reach for my camera, and Luis shushes me from the backseat, quickly shaking his head. They watch us go by, and we are a block up the street before anyone speaks.

"They watch that house carefully. You can't just take pictures," Luis tells me.

Jorge turns down a street, and we leave the painted road behind us. He slows the Lada enough to evade the large potholes and absorb the smaller ones with only mild teeth rattling. We are on the way to see an old friend, he says, a woman whose family grew up with my mother's, and the two families still keep in touch. He points out a spot between a row of houses where my grandfather once owned a *bodega*, which is now a private home.

We make several more turns until we come to a wide boulevard. A median down the center is lined with decades-old ficus trees that cast welcome shadows on the road and the one-story row houses that line it. Their façades are flat, as if walls have been erected on either side of the street. Barred windows. Barred doors. The pattern repeating.

We park the car and walk a short distance up the block. Isabel runs ahead and stops at a double door, one side of which is open. She pokes her head in and out and waits for us just outside. Jorge knocks on the open door—"*Hola*, Maribel, it's Jorge, Sofía's son"—and a boy, about four, who is watching a black-and-white television at the back of the room, turns and smiles. Isabel squeezes past a couch and runs through the narrow hall to sit and watch with him.

"Jorge, what are you doing around here?" comes a voice from another room, a squawk like that of an old hen that has learned to speak. In comes a tall older woman, about five foot ten, reedy, with a long face, a hook nose, and thick glasses, her hair a shoulder-length nest of gray and white. She has several moles on her face, including one bulging by her eyebrow, with several sprouts of gray hair. Maribel and my mother were just a year apart in school.

Maribel asks her daughter to make coffee while we sit on the couch in her living room and chat. She studies me through her glasses, which make her look as if she is staring through a fishbowl, and says, "*Dios mío*, I can't believe how much you look like Iraidita." This is the reaction I have gotten from people who see my mother and me side by side. "It's like looking at a picture of her."

She and my mother were part of a small group of girls who always stuck together. Maribel wasn't a student at Las Madres Escolapias, but their little group was united by church socials and the neighborhood.

Maribel walks to her front door and points to several houses across the street, painted yellow, blue, and mint green. There, where those three row houses now stand, she says, used to be my mother's house. It was a wooden house on a corner lot with a huge backyard, and all the kids would get together to play baseball there. My mother was the youngest of the bunch, but they all played together. And though she was a girl, she was just as adept with a bat as the boys, Maribel says.

"You may not know this, but your mother and I used to skip rope together. Area jump rope champions, your mother and I."

The kids lived between these houses, Maribel says, my uncle coming over in the early morning and whispering for Maribel's brother at the window so they could go fishing while everyone else slept. When the adults caught on, her brother tied a string to his big toe and let the slack out of the window, so my uncle just had to tug on the string to wake him.

After my mother's family left for Havana, the old wooden house rotted and crumbled to the ground. These new houses have been here for several years now. I can picture my mom's little gang of neighborhood kids. But as I look out on the street, where ficus trees have been damaged and misshapen by decades of storms and her house exists only in Maribel's stories, I wonder how much of this place she would recognize.

Maribel tells me I can't leave Cárdenas without visiting with one of my mother's best friends growing up, Emma. She went to school with my mother and lives just a couple of miles away. After pulling Isabel away from the television, we kiss Maribel good-bye, pile back into the Lada, and head for Emma's.

"Maribel we see every now and then, but it's been a long time since we've seen Emma," Luis says.

We pass a school along a back street, and Jorge says my Tía Sofía used to teach there, back when she was allowed to teach. A chain-link fence and overgrown weeds keep the abandoned school at a distance. It's a long story, he says, but tells me to ask my aunt all about it before I leave Cárdenas. "It explains a lot of things," he says.

Just beyond the school, we turn up a street where the houses are no longer pressed against one another but stand apart with their own small yards. We stop in front of one with a cement-and-iron fence and a wrought-iron gate. The house appears freshly painted, white with a salmon trim, and a cement walkway leads to the front door. Four of us wait at the car while Jorge walks up the path and knocks. I hear him talking through the window to someone. He steps back from the door to let it open, and an older woman, dressed neatly in a white blouse and dark pants, waves to us as we make our way up the path. She lifts a pair of glasses that hang from her neck on a tether and puts them on. As I get closer, her smile beams with white teeth.

"*Dios mío*, who would have guessed that Iraidita's son would one day be coming to visit me," she says and hugs me. "Come in, come in!" she says, hurrying us into her living room.

The tiled floors are bright and clean, and the white kitchen just on the other side of a high counter makes the room feel airy. As we sit in her comfortable living room, a fluffy white-and-golden dog, some sort of Pomeranian mix, comes in wagging its tail, and Isabel squeals with joy, jumping off the couch and crouching, blowing kisses to call the dog over.

"That's my best company, *mi compañerito*," Emma tells us as the dog licks Isabel's fingers. He has helped keep her sane since her mother fell ill, Emma says. Her husband, "May God have him in His Glory," passed away seven years ago, and it has been just she and her mother living here. Her mother is in the other room sleeping, so we keep our voices low. Emma asks me about my mother's life, and I fill her in, telling her everything from her late-in-life marriage to my father to the passing of her father and two of her siblings, my Tío Julio to cancer and my Tía Tata to a sudden stroke.

"I have always wondered what became of her life," she said. "I had heard about your aunt and uncle. I know how hard that was on your Tía Sofía."

When she heard the news, my Tía Sofía wailed and wailed for days, "Ay, Dios, my little brother. My little brother is gone," Jorge says, and we are silent for a few moments as Isabel giggles and pets the dog.

Emma, how do you manage here alone?

She shows me a picture of her two sons, who emigrated to Canada in 1980 and 1990 and are living and working there now. They send her money monthly, and that helps with the bills. Cubans like to say that, to survive in Cuba, you have to have *fe*, faith. Except that *FE* stands for *familia en el extranjero*, family overseas, one of those plays on words that Cubans love so much. Her third child, a daughter, still lives in Cuba. She has other pictures, she says, and retrieves them from another room. There are pictures of her sons, both married to Canadian women and surrounded by all the grandchildren she has never met in person. They speak to her over the phone with their accented Spanish.

So it's just the two of you? Do you ever think about joining your sons?

She has thought about it, but she is scared of that world. She and her young husband moved to South Florida in 1956, before the revolution, disenchanted with Batista's dictatorship. But there, they encountered harsh racism, postings on restaurant doors that read, "No tank tops. No sandals. No Negroes. No Cubans." And although she easily could have been confused with a white American—her skin is fair, her features fine, her black hair coiffed in a fifties hairdo—her accented English gave her away.

"I missed my family too much," she says. "I spent my life crying, crying, crying."

They moved back in 1961, two years after Castro's revolution took hold, and never left.

As I look at her well-kept house, where all the walls are painted a fresh white and the stainless steel appliances of a sixties kitchen are clean and functioning, I wonder whether her family bought into the revolution, as so many others did, and whether her husband made a name for himself within the party. And the fact that

her son is in Canada, not the United States, makes me more suspicious. But I ignore the subject of politics and ask her to tell me
about my mother as a girl.

"Wait till you see this," she says and hurries back into the other
room.

Emma returns with an envelope of old photos. She hands me
one close-up of several girls in Sunday dresses, buttoned up to the
collar, with black shawls over their heads, all standing around a
young priest who is reading from a booklet.

"See if you recognize anyone in that picture," she says.

My eyes quickly come to the second person from the left,
a waifish young woman. I recognize that chin, that nose, those
cheekbones on my own face, and I feel a smile coming on.

"She must have been fifteen or sixteen at the time," Emma says
of my mother. Her lips are thin and painted, her wavy hair parted
under the lacy black shawl as she looks at the priest in a moment
captured nearly sixty years ago. My cousins gather around the picture.

"Your *Mamá* was *linda, linda, linda,*" Luis says.

"That's just how I remember her," Jorge adds.

There are other faces I recognize here, and Emma and my cousins and I quickly pick them out. There, with those sculpted cheekbones and piercing black eyes, looking over at my mother from
the other end of the row, is my Tía Tata. Next to her is Lolita, a
woman who was like another aunt to me when I was a boy. Her
family and mine apparently go back to the time when they were
teenagers attending the same church. Her family were *los panaderos,*
the local bakers, Jorge says, and my grandfather was the milkman,
and that connection goes back just as long. At the other end of
the line in the photo is Maribel, the jump rope co-champion of
Cárdenas.

So many pieces of my family puzzle are fitting together to form
a richer portrait. For Cuban-Americans of my generation, these
pictures, this knowledge, fills a void I feel few others can understand. There are no such things as family heirlooms for us. We are
children of a lost generation, for whom memories are priceless

artifacts. I trace the outlines of my mother's face with my finger, holding proof of a life that existed.

Emma looks through her envelope and produces another photo. This one is of six youngsters, huddled around one another, the neighborhood clan. One of the four boys who look to be in their mid to late teens is my Tío Julio, his arm resting casually over his knee, his thick, black, wavy hair parted on the left. Behind him stands Emma's future husband, also wearing a long-sleeve shirt and a gold watch.

"And this boy," she says, pointing to a young man leaning back against a wooden fence, "was Carlín, Carlos, a boy your mother had a crush on."

They all knew one another. I watch her eyes studying the picture, and I know that she, too, is part of my unwritten history. Emma, Maribel, and my mother, the three of them, would fix up their hair, don pretty summer dresses, and go to the fair at the parish, she says, at La Parroquia, where all the local girls were married. They'd stay up as late as 9:30, gabbing as girls do, about fashion, hairstyles, about that boy my mother was so fond of. Emma keeps digging through the envelope, looking for another picture of her with my mother. Emma was my mother's graduation godmother, a tradition at their Catholic school in which an older alum sponsored a graduate. A few years back, the church sponsored a reunion of the girls who were still around, and more than fifty attended.

"Wait until I get to tell everyone at the next reunion that I met Iraidita's son," she says, patting my hands as we sit next to each other on her couch. She has that picture here somewhere, she says, and asks how long I'll be in town so that she can bring it over if she finds it. Plus, a visit will give her a chance to catch up with my Tía Sofía, whom she hasn't seen in a long time.

At her door, she hugs me tight and long. Isabel is patting the Pomeranian good-bye.

"Tell Iraidita that I think about her, about those days, a lot, *mucho, mucho, mucho*," Emma says, "and that it has given me great joy to meet her son."

A red-orange sun hangs low on the way back to my Tía Sofía's house, and Cárdenas is a silhouette. The blur of dark shapes that were foreign to me a day ago becomes familiar in the fading sun and the emerging sodium light. We pass my aunt's old school. We cross the tree-lined street my mother grew up on. That road, I know, leads to Las Madres Escolapias. This one, up to the old church. I guess the street to my Tía Sofía's house well before we turn, and when we park out front, it feels good to be home after a long day.

Home.

I push open the front door and find my Tía Sofía just as I found her this morning, rocking and smiling, wearing a fresh house gown. I feel the cool perspiration on my lips when I kiss her forehead, and she pats my face lightly.

I am home.

DAY EIGHT

"When Isabel comes in, make sure you tell her how pretty she looks," Elena says, joining Tomás and me at the table in their outside kitchen.

She has spent the morning in front of the mirror with her five-year-old, trying to stave off a tantrum. Isabel wanted to wear baby blue today, and there was no dissuading her. The white T-shirt with baby-blue lettering would not do. No, she wanted to wear the matching baby blue sweatpants, although it is already close to eighty-five degrees this morning, with baby blue sneakers and a baby blue headband. Elena yielded to her daughter's wishes because it's easy to do. Isabel greets everyone each morning with a hug and kiss. She disarms you by speaking like an adult, and usually when her parents have to tell her no, she goes down without a fight. But not this morning. Her mother had to braid her hair and adjust her headband just so, before she posed in the mirror and asked, "*Mami*, do you think Carlitos will fall in love with me?"

Elena covers her mouth and chuckles into her hand at the memory.

"It's easy to want to spoil her, to *malcriarla*," Tomás says.

At least once a week, he likes to go out with her, just the two of them, and they bond over an ice-cream cone as she rides the mechanical horse outside a nearby café. "Life is going to get harder for her, as it does for the rest of us," Tomás said. And so, a kid should be allowed to be a kid and eat ice cream every once in a while. "If I can give her that one joy . . ." he says, trailing off.

One week, he scrounged enough money to take her to the café to buy her a cone but not one for himself. When she asked to ride the mechanical horse, he had to lie and tell her it was broken. "Do you know how it feels when your child asks you for something so simple, and you know you can't give it to her?" he says. I don't. My wife and I worry about scraping enough together to send ours to private Catholic school. Ice-cream cones are luxuries we take for granted.

"You know what she told me? 'That's okay, *Papi*, I'll just sit on it and pretend.'" And that's what she did. The five-year-old girl, who sleeps with her parents in a room with only three walls, sat atop a motionless horse, licking the ice cream dripping down her hand.

"I don't care that I'm poor," Tomás says. "I know that, because of my poverty, I'm more in touch with my humanity. I know what's important in life. And that's what I try to teach her."

During the war in Angola, Tomás stood up to the government and said he was not going to fight in a war that had nothing to do with Cuba when there was so much need in his own country, in his own home. For that, he served time in jail and several years working in an agricultural camp. And, he is forbidden to work at the higher-paying government jobs because he will not list himself as a party member. His position never softened. "The president of the *Comité* comes to my house, says, 'Hey, why aren't you doing guard duty?' and I tell him, 'Because that is no concern of mine. I'm not a communist, I never have been, and I never will be.' And if he wants to report me, he can do that, too. But I don't believe in any of their lies. And I'm not going to play their game." He clenches his jaw and drinks the last shot of his coffee as Elena strokes his hand.

This is a critical time for them with Isabel. She is just beginning to learn about the world she is living in. At school, Isabel and her classmates begin the day with a poem to Che Guevara that concludes, "We are pioneers for the revolution, like Che!" When Isabel repeats it at home, her mother rolls her eyes and very gently tells her, "*Mamita*, you say that at school, but not at home, okay? That's for school."

Isabel is learning about the double life many Cubans must live. I worry for them all. I remember sitting in my car, showing my daughter Elise the emerald ring we had bought *Mami* for Mother's Day, but warning that she couldn't tell her anything or it would ruin the surprise. When my wife got back in the car, Elise blurted out, "*Mami*, we have a surprise for you!" before I could shush her. I imagine Isabel divulging a conversation between her parents during phonics or social studies, something like "My *Papi* says all communists are liars." I start to ask how they will deal with that day just as Isabel walks into the room, her hands behind her back, resplendent in baby blue.

She looks like a fashion doll, like any American kid, juxtaposed against the backdrop of the room with three walls and the cracking cement above the doorway. I can smell the clean Russian Violets baby perfume her mother has sprayed into Isabel's hair, the same kind my wife uses on our daughters back home. It has been more than a week since I have held my own babies, and I miss their smell. Isabel's ploy works. I am in love with this little girl.

Wow, 'Mamita,' you look so, so 'linda' in that outfit! Are you a princess? Because you look like a princess.

She bites her lip and twists her toe into the ground, then covers her face and hides behind her father's chair. I reach in and pinch the baby fat around her love handles, and she chirps with laughter.

Are you coming to Varadero with us today?

"*Sí*, Carlitos," she says, stepping out from behind Tomás. "And I have a bathing suit that my *Mami* and *Papi* bought for me and I'm going to wear it today, but I don't know how to swim so my *Papi* is going to carry me, but my *Papi* is teaching me and I'm not scared . . ." I can't help but smile as I listen to her monologue and watch her little hands gesture as she rolls her eyes to the sky, searching for new points to expound on. She asks me to carry her as we walk around the corner on a warming late morning to my Tía Sofía's house, where Jorge is supposed to meet us with the car.

Tía Sofía is in her usual spot, rocking in the path of a draft, when I bend down to kiss her forehead. *'Buenos días, mi Tía.'*

Andrea has already given my aunt her morning bath, and she is here with her husband, Joaquín. When I said we were going to Varadero Beach today, it meant everybody.

"So you're going to swim at Varadero, eh? *Ay*, how your *Mamá* loved Varadero," my Tía Sofía says, rocking, closing her eyes to envision the memory. "When she came to visit from Havana, she would spend almost every morning there. She would go with *los muchachos*, my kids, and they would all come back *tostaditos*, bronzed from the sun."

When I spoke to my mother back home last night, she asked specifically to speak with Jorge and told him she would never forgive him if he didn't take me to Varadero. So, the trip was set. Not that anyone needs much encouragement to bathe in the always-warm waters of the best-known beach in all of Cuba. I didn't bring swim trunks but figure I can buy some at a shop near the beach.

Elena quickly grabs a mop—a rag draped over the end of a wooden T-shaped pole—and begins giving the floor a quick once-over while we wait for Jorge, Luis, and Luisito to arrive with the car.

A ringing from the corner of the room startles me, a classic bell-and-hammer sound that we hear only simulated on cell phones anymore. Telephones in Cuba, especially in an out-of-the-way city like Cárdenas, are few. The sole reason my aunt has one is that Jorge, who was given the right to buy a phone line when he was a doctor here, transferred it into her name before he left. It is one of the only phones on the block, and often friends and family of neighbors will leave messages here.

Elena picks it up. It is Jorge. He is still finishing up in Matanzas and later will stop by to pick up Luis and his son. He suggests we pick a place to meet at Varadero, and he will join us there.

Jorge's call reminds me I have one to make myself, a visit to co-ordinate. Ricardo is supposed to be at Varadero today visiting his wife's family, and his son is with him. As I look up his number, I can feel my heart quicken. It is like the first time we spoke; I am eager and anxious all at once. And when I think of his son, I wonder how this boy will receive me.

'¡Hola,' Ricardo!

"*¡Mi primo!* I brought you with my thoughts. Your ears must have been ringing since yesterday, because I have been talking about you all day. And you should hear my son, Julio. He keeps talking about *los Frías*, and he's dying to meet you."

I doubt Ricardo notices when I breathe a sigh of relief. We agree to meet on the beach at Twelfth Street, which is near the entrance to Varadero.

"All of this, *mi primo*, feels like a dream to me," he says, and we hang up.

"*Bueno*, what are you all waiting for?" my Tía Sofía says. "Get him to Varadero early so you can enjoy the day."

I worry about leaving Tía Sofía and Pipo alone. Her support system is going off to the beach. What if she has an emergency? I ask her. What if she has another fall? She tells me her youngest son, Ernesto, is supposed to come by in the early afternoon. He does nearly every day, and she shoos us out the door.

Dig out that old bikini and join us, 'vamos, Tía.'

"*Mira*, what a *descarado!*" she says with her high-pitched laugh. "*Muchacho*, people will go running in the other direction if I show up there in a bikini."

There are six of us and no car, but Elena says the best way to get to Varadero is on the bus. Since most of the workers in Varadero's tourism industry live in Cárdenas, buses run back and forth during the day. Going to Varadero Beach is an escape for *cardeneses*.

We walk along the cracked, stained sidewalks, kicking up dust as we pass. It has not rained since I've been in Cuba, and the streets are dry, the air thick with late summer heat. We walk in a group down several blocks, trying to stay in the shadow of the one- and two-story row houses right up against the road. We cross the street at a corner where garbage is piled up: a plastic bag that held a baby's milk, pieces of a broken chair, greens that look like they came from shucked corn, concrete rubble from some sort of construction. Or destruction. The smell of spoiled milk and rotting vegetables wanders farther than the buzzing flies.

We follow Elena across the street to a two-story house where several families, including her mother, live. We have to make a quick stop here, Elena says, to pick up her *other* daughter, Luisa. Isabel bolts to her older sister the second she sees her waiting in the living room downstairs.

"Come here, my little termite!" Luisa says as she grabs Isabel, puts her on her hip, and swings her around and around in one motion, Isabel cackling uncontrollably.

Luisa is a pretty girl of about seventeen with a round face, smiling eyes, and a bright, white smile, Elena's daughter from a previous relationship. Elena kisses her older daughter, who is almost her height, on the forehead and strokes her hair. I cannot imagine that Tomás and Elena would not want their daughter to grow up with this half sister, who is now blowing raspberries into Isabel's belly. But I know their living situation, that even at times, when parents need their intimacy, Isabel must sleep at my Tía Sofía's house. And however good a father Tomás may be, he is still not Luisa's father and would have to live in close quarters with a girl who is becoming a young woman.

No, there is room for only one daughter in that house right now. Elena has been forced to choose between her children and has decided that, right now, Isabel needs all of her attention. I wonder where I, staring between the blue ocean in my daughter Elise's eyes and the hazel woodlands of my baby Amelia's, would find the strength to do the same.

Luisa is waiting with her boyfriend, a boy of about seventeen, handsome with flowing, wavy, black hair, chiseled cheekbones, and a striking smile. He is wearing flip-flops and a black tank top that shows off his athletic arms. He puts one around Luisa, and they join our group for the walk to the bus stop.

When I see them together, boy and girl, walking like man and wife, I wonder if this is the new Cuba. I think of those girls pushing baby strollers through the streets of Havana, girls who have no hopes of careers, who see no future in the "education for all" that Castro extols. I understand now why it was so important for Jorge to leave and take his youngest daughter with him. Jorge married his first wife and had Elena in his teens, Elena had Luisa in her teens, and now, Luisa threatens to continue this legacy. Jorge needed to break the cycle.

Several others are waiting at the bus stop when the eight of us finally reach it after walking about half a mile. My light blue polo is dark in spots with sweat. I squint in the glare of the late morning sun. We wait for about fifteen minutes, until the roar of a diesel engine comes up the street. What looks like a twenty-year-old city bus approaches, the sun glistening at odd angles from the dented chrome panels along its side. The bus stops with a hiss and a moan.

Elena pays my fare in national pesos, and we take open seats in the back as the bus lurches forward. Isabel scampers from her seat next to her parents and sits beside me. The sun is beaming through my window, and the torn vinyl seats and chrome tubular metal are hot to the touch. Isabel sits in my lap to avoid the hot, sticky seat.

The bus moves unhindered, passing buggies on either side. We cross over the street my mother grew up on, and I watch the pale blue, yellow, and lime green houses that replaced her childhood home fly by. The road curves, and Tomás points out the cemetery and the monument to the Cuban soldiers from Cárdenas who have been killed in foreign wars. I wonder how he feels every time he passes it, knowing he could have been just another casualty.

As we head out of town, we pass the concrete crab, which is still hungry, I know, even if its open pincers no longer carry the town's spray-painted sentiments. The bus picks up speed and hums down a road with tall, wispy grasses growing on either side, the scenery unchanging for about thirty minutes until, amid all the dry earth, a sliver of shimmering turquoise emerges. The breeze brings with it the salty scent of the sea, and soon the bus is swimming with the smell of the ocean.

Elena begins searching her large canvas bag for money. Unless we tip the driver, she says, he will take us all the way to the main bus stop, farther into the island city of Varadero. And then, things can get a little dicey, she says.

For many years, since Cuba started to revitalize hotels for tourists in the late 1990s, Varadero was strictly closed to any Cuban national who does not live or work there. Police wait in a guardhouse at the mouth of the bridge that crosses into Varadero, the only way on and off the island, stopping cars periodically. The enforcement, if not the rules, has been more lax in the last few years, Tomás whispers from the backseat, but there are still officers who wait at the bus stop inside Varadero, occasionally asking to see the government-issued IDs that Cubans must carry at all times. We have to tip the driver with enough money to make it worth the risk of letting us off before the regular stop.

I grab money out of my wallet and give Elena five Convertibles, about 120 pesos. She makes her way up to the front, holding on to the rails and the backs of seats as the bus shifts. I watch her lean over, talking to the driver as the bus approaches the high-arching metal bridge.

Officers stand in the guardhouse, and I immediately get the urge to turn my face and slump in my seat. When I look up at Elena, she is beckoning us to the front of the bus. Tomás carries Isabel, and I follow him up, behind Andrea and her husband and Luisa and her boyfriend, as the bus shimmies over the bridge. We are all standing at the front when the doors open, the bus still moving and the road flying by.

"*¡Rápido, rápido!*" the driver says as the bus slows to a crawl and we step off onto the street, several other passengers following us out, momentum carrying us for several steps. We look around to make sure we have all made it off, and the bus is already gone, plowing along with a puff of black smoke. We cross the street quickly to avoid any prying eye.

Palm fronds rustle in a slow-moving breeze that carries the bouquet of the beach as we all walk down the sidewalk, which is covered in a verdant canopy. Sunlight filters through the trees, and seagulls screech overhead. A flock of red-bellied, green parrots, heavily into a squawking symphony, sails overhead, silhouetted against an impossibly blue sky. The streets have the feel of old Key West, from the shaded roads to the cottage-style houses set off from the road by small yards and fences. But their condition changes from house to house. This one has been freshly painted the color of limes, trimmed in sparkling white. Right next door, a chain-link fence restrains an overgrowth of weeds surrounding a dilapidated wooden cottage that stands only by the grace of God. Paint hangs from the siding like scales. There is no glass in the windows, and a bare wooden door muffles voices coming from inside. Some of the trees in the yard appear as if they have had limbs torn off carelessly, and I can only imagine what the next hurricane would do to this house.

Some houses have been repaired, Tomás says, because the owners have been given a government license to rent them out to foreigners. These *casas particulares* are quaint alternatives to the larger hotels on the island and can mean good money for the owners, even though the government takes a heavy licensing fee. That's why some will fix up their houses in secret to rent illegally to tourists—which is why modifying a house is against the law in Varadero, he says, even to make it more livable.

The hotels are farther down, at the other end of the island, where only tourists can use the facilities, Tomás says. We're headed where all the locals can go.

I remind Elena that I still would like to buy a pair of swim trunks, and we find a store that sells some of the bare essentials. While the others wait, Elena and I join a line outside one store for about ten minutes as a guard lets in one person for each one that leaves. When we finally get inside, the store is hot from the sun pounding through a pair of fixed floor-to-ceiling windows, and the fifteen or so people there slip by one another to different glass showcases. Behind the counters is the merchandise, from sunblock to T-shirts and hanging women's bathing suits. In the glass cases are disposable cameras and snorkeling masks that look to have been sitting there waiting to be purchased for years. Most people circle around the flip-flops and Lycra tube tops, the more disposable and inexpensive items that make up the attire of locals.

I ask the woman behind the counter if she has any *trusas,* men's bathing suits. She walks over to another section and returns with several pair of Speedo-style trunks. They are black with varying colored stripes. And very, *very* small. I stare at them for a second, then at Elena, then at the woman, as if someone should recognize this faux pas, offer an apology, and bring me the longer Bermuda-style shorts I'm used to before we all have to blush. Instead, they are both looking at me, Elena nodding and grinning as if to say, "Do you like them?" It's as if red wine has spilled onto a white carpet, and no one is rushing to get a towel. Has my face not done a sufficient job of betraying my horror? Maybe they would understand if they knew I used to go the whole day sweaty and sticky rather than share the showers after first-period gym class in high school.

Uh . . . no, I don't think so, I say and push them back across the counter. Modesty forbids that I do as the Romans. No way, brother, am I squeezing into a banana hammock.

This is not exactly what I'm looking for. Don't you have any 'trusas' that are a bit . . . longer? You know, 'trusas,' shorts!

Elena and the clerk look at each other, and the woman shrugs. She leaves and brings back a pair of khaki shorts. I point to my own gray Dockers shorts to show that they would not be much of an improvement. We turn up the block to another store and repeat the humbling process, which seems embarrassing only to me.

Never mind. I'll just go in the water with my shorts, I say as we meet back up with our group.

"But I don't understand. What was the matter with those *trusas?*" Elena asks as we walk down the street. I try to explain American sensibilities (read "prudishness") to my cousins, that while those little *trusitas* are fine for the Europeans on South Beach, they are not our regular swim attire back in the States.

"But why?" insists Andrea, and they are all looking at me for a logical answer that I can't give them. How do you explain that

Americans as a whole aren't comfortable enough with our bodies to . . . put ourselves out there, so to speak. Just then, we come to an intersection and find Jorge, Luis, and Luisito parking the Lada along the road. Jorge will help me explain.

Jorge—'¡Gracias a Dios!'—can you explain to these people why we don't wear those 'trusitas' in the United States?

He and I stare at each other for a second and immediately start to cackle. He himself is wearing Bermuda-style trunks. The rest of them are looking at us as if waiting for the joke and the punch line. But it's our own inside joke, one he might never have gotten had he not left for the United States and become a prude himself.

"We just don't wear those over there," he tells them. "We," he says. We Americans. They stare blankly, and he tries again. On his first trip to Miami Beach with friends, Jorge tells us, he pulled off his pants to reveal the Speedo he was used to, ready to try out the water. His friends, immigrated Cubans who had been living in the United States for several years, were mortified and shamed him into putting his pants back on. "They told me, 'Muchacho, are you crazy? You can't wear those! No, no, no.' "

My cousins still look confused. We lack the tools to explain mores and cultural norms, especially when there is no word for "prude" in Spanish that I can think of. I'm sure they still don't get it, but at least I'm off the hook as we turn up the street and, finally, head for the water.

We walk up a small ridge at the end of the street, and as we reach the top, a cloudless sky meets a color of ocean I have never seen before, blue like the feathers of a macaw, like an oil painting still wet to the touch. The Caribbean sun reflects off alabaster sand, blinding, warming.

Varadero.

When Cubans speak of this place, it is like a soft bed after a long journey. Like a lover's expecting embrace. It is a feeling more than a place, a memory that warms the heart. As I take off my sneakers and let my toes sink into the powder, the heat rises into me, up my legs, raising goose bumps as it travels, warming my heart and clearing my mind. And I can only conclude that whatever energy lives in this place has discovered where I keep my soul.

"How your mother loved this beach," Luis says, appearing next to me and waking me from the trance. When she visited from Havana, he says, she would grab one of her nephews, her *compañeritos*, and walk barefoot along the sand here, her sundress rustling around her ankles, pretending to ignore the men whistling and staring at her as she passed. When the five-year-old would go at the men to defend her honor, she would shake him by the wrist and shush him under her breath. "*Muchacho, cállate*, quiet, boy!"

Now I know why my mother so desperately wanted me to come here. So I could feel what she felt. This is where she hid a piece of her heart when she left Cuba forty years ago.

Sand like confectioners' sugar slips through my toes as we walk toward the water, looking for an empty spot on the beach. School is out, and it seems like every six feet or so, a group of teens or a family has staked their claim. Looking in either direction, as far as the eye can see on a curving, crescent shore, people dot the perfect white sand like the pips of a domino. I want to stay near Twelfth Street so Ricardo and I can find each other, and eventually, a family of five packs up their things and leaves us a clearing. Elena and Andrea lay out a pair of towels, and everyone strips down to their bathing suits. I take off my shirt and let a breeze flow over me like a current. The wind cools the perspiration on my skin, ruffles the curls on my chest, but a perfect sun in a cloudless sky bathes me in warmth. I am standing on the edge of the world, the world that I know.

As the others make their way to the water, I feel a little hand slide between the fingers of my right hand. Isabel, wearing a pink one-piece with ruffles along the straps, looks up at me, shielding her eyes from the sun with her other hand. "Take me in, Carlitos. Take me into the water!"

She leads me toward the water's edge, and I hold her back for just a second, aware that an ebbing and flowing ocean the color of reflected sky is just inches from my toes. For me, this is a moment of baptism, and Isabel is tugging at my hand lightly, pulling me forward, eager to be my unknowing sponsor.

I step in slowly, and the water feels like it has been drawn for a baby's bath, warming me as I advance up to my waist. Isabel reaches up for me—"Carry me, Carlitos!"—and I put her on my hip as we move forward through water that is so still waves barely break on the shore.

Ready to wet your hair?

Isabel nods and pinches her nose closed. I am ready, too.

'Uno, dos, tres . . .'

We plunge underneath long enough for me to feel the entire warmth wash over me, then break back through the surface of the water, wiping our eyes, Isabel giggling the way she does. And I am reborn Cuban.

My cousins and I wade together in water that is chest-deep, even though we are a good hundred feet from shore. Tomás holds his hands under Isabel's belly as she kicks and splashes, holding her breath like a puffer fish. Jorge, Luis, and I take turns dunking our heads and swimming short distances underwater. I keep my eyes open when I swim, and the mild stinging only reminds me this is not all just a dream. The salty seawater leaves the skin on my face smooth, Varadero tenderly caring for me.

Luisito carries Isabel back to shore, where the women have lain out on the towels, tanning in the afternoon sun, leaving us, the four men, still wading and diving and swimming in the clear blue. Off from the rest of us, Luisa and her boyfriend are by themselves, wading in the water so only their shoulders are above the surface. She is sitting across his lap, and his arms encircle her. Their faces are close. And they are lost in each other's eyes, smiling. Jorge sighs. "God forbid they make me a great-grandfather so young," he says.

Tomás has waded farther from us and is standing alone, waist-deep, staring not at the shore but off into deep water. I wade over to him, and he barely moves, as if he's far off somewhere over that horizon. A small fishing boat runs parallel to the shore, motoring steadily across the water.

It's a long swim to Miami.

He looks at me with a serious face, his brow furrowed, and then softens into a smile. "I was almost there."

Several years ago, he says, before he married Elena, he tried to reach the United States by sea. Everything was set. He had a deal with a boat captain who was ready to leave the island himself with his teenage daughter. The captain knew these waters well. He knew they had to leave before dawn, timing their departure between patrols by the Cuban navy. The day before they were set to leave, a neighbor learned about the trip and asked the captain to take him and his son along.

"He said no at first, but people were at the point where they were *chivateando*, reporting to authorities just out of sheer jealousy. We couldn't take the chance; we had to bring them with us," Tomás says.

He is silent for a moment as he moves his hands through the crystal water, seeming to steel himself to finish the story. "We should have known right then that there would be trouble."

Everyone showed up on time the morning they were to leave. But the son of the latecomer seemed agitated. He was sweating, even in the cool of twilight, and pacing as they got onboard.

"I don't know about this," he kept telling his father, Tomás remembers, as the little fishing boat pulled away from port and into the dark, shifting sea. The captain had planned well. They had not come across any Cuban vessels as the sun rose out of the ocean and climbed higher into the sky. The day was clear, Tomás remembers, and they could see all the way to the horizon. But this man, this young man with the sweating and the pacing, grew more and more unsteady.

"No, no, this isn't a good idea," he would say. He stared out at infinite ocean in all directions. "We . . . we can't do this. We have to go back. We have to go back!" Tomás says, his eyes becoming turbulent as he plays the part of the young man. He rubs his hands through his hair, tries to pace in the waist-deep water as he relives the moment. "He started to lose his mind. He wouldn't be quiet. All he kept saying and screaming was that we had to turn back."

Tomás eventually had to restrain him, and the man started screaming that Tomás was trying to kill him, writhing in his arms. The captain went faster. The young man slipped free and, in a second, got hold of a knife the captain kept onboard to gut fish, grabbed the captain's daughter around the waist, and held the sharpened blade up to the girl's tender throat. "Turn this boat around! Turn it around right now!" he screamed.

Despite the chaos, Tomás could see something on the horizon that clear morning. Land. American soil. No U.S. Coast Guard skiffs in sight. Nothing to stop them from reaching freedom but a raving young man holding a knife to a terrified and bawling Cuban girl.

Tomás turns to me, looks me in the eye. "What was I supposed to do?" he says softly.

Tomás is strong and stocky, with tight biceps and a barrel chest, what a pit bull might look like as a person. Should he try to strip the knife from the man? What if the girl was hurt, or worse? And if he overtook the man, would he have to throw him overboard to die? "I couldn't live with any of those consequences," Tomás says. "There was only one choice."

They turned the boat around. The young man held the knife to the girl for the several hours it took to make the trip. When they reached the harbor, amazingly unseen by Cuban sea patrols, the young man scrambled for solid ground. Waiting for them at the port was a group of men who asked the captain if they could buy his boat. They, too, were headed for America. He sold the boat, and Tomás watched as the men sailed away, without the cover of darkness.

"A week later, I learned that they reached Miami," Tomás says, closing his eyes for a moment to shut off the movie that had been replaying in his mind. He dunks his head underwater and wipes his eyes, opening them again at the surface as the Tomás I know, calm, smiling, if a bit more sullen. "I won't die here. Sooner or later, I'm leaving this place."

When I turn back to face the shore, Elena is standing on the beach, waving to us. Luisito is halfway out to me when I see him.

"*Oye*, Carlitos," he yells out, "your cousin is here!"

I look back at Elena, and she is standing by two men who begin waving. Even from this distance I recognize Ricardo, that face that screams of my blood, and I wave back with both arms.

Out of the water, my cotton Dockers are dripping wet, and I have not even toweled myself off, but Ricardo does not care. He grabs me, and we embrace like old friends.

What's new, 'mi primote'?

We retrace each other's faces, smiling, recalling features that are both new and familiar to us.

"I want to introduce you to another one of your cousins," Ricardo says, "my son, Julio."

Julio has a baby face with kind eyes, and his short brown hair is spiky in the middle with blondish highlights. He is already his father's height but slender with curves of baby fat, and his skin is perfectly bronzed. His eyes shine with the light and hope and energy of youth. It is a light that seems to have gone out in some older Cubans here, replaced by a smoldering torch of resignation. Julio looks like he's trying to keep serious as he reaches out his right hand to shake mine, but his mouth cracks into a grin, then a smile, then all teeth, and we hug.

"*Hola, primote!*" he says, clapping my back like his father, and it seems as if he's trying to keep from bursting with laughter and joy. "*Primo*, you don't know how much my dad talks about getting to know his dad's family," he says, and those kind eyes begin to fill. He lowers his head to wipe his eyes as his father gives him a reassuring hug.

We sit on the powdery white sand and talk, talk like we don't know where to begin.

"My dad has told me all about *los Frías*. They're four brothers, right? No? Nine brothers and sisters! *Concho*, what a huge family, *qué familión!*" Julio can't contain himself. He wants to know everything.

"We're a little family. Just me and my sister," he says.

"But we love each other a lot and take care of each other," Ricardo says, rubbing his son's shoulder.

"*Primote*, tell me, tell me about my family," Julio says. I look at his father, who is staring with the same expectant gaze, and a flood of childhood memories comes back to me. In that moment, I realize what they have missed. My cousins and I are tight like brothers and sisters. We played football on the weekends as kids. Slept over at one another's houses and played video games into the night. Our children are growing up together, going to birthday parties, pool parties. Even today, we try to play poker once a month just as an excuse to get together. We are family. We are loved. Ricardo and his children have missed out on it all.

I look at my other cousins, and they peek over every few minutes, smiling.

Where do I start? I take a deep breath.

Well, you have three brothers, I say to Ricardo. *Dios,* he has brothers! *And you,* I say, turning to Julio, *have three uncles.* As I say it, I know why the boy looks so familiar. My Tío Ramón has three sons in the United States, and the oldest, Ray, has a boy who looks just like Julio. Julio looks just like my cousin Marcus. *Our* cousin Marcus. How do you catch someone up on thirty years of lives lived, explain friendships that are strengthened by blood? I do my best and name the family members and their children and their children's children. Their eyes widen as if gold coins are falling from the sky and they don't have enough hands to catch them all. I try to pace myself, to drop the coins more slowly. There is just not enough time.

"I tried to call my father once," Ricardo says, "but things didn't go so well."

Julio looks at his father, and I try to imagine the courage it must have taken to make that call. One of the other uncles picked up the phone, he says, and responded, "And what do you want?" My family, in an effort to protect one another, to protect a family secret, can be reptilian cold. How could those be the first words a man hears while searching for the father he has never met? I want to try to defend them to him. But I cannot.

"I don't want anything. I was just hoping to talk to my father,"

Ricardo told him. He ended up speaking to my Tía Teresa, the oldest and the matriarch of the family. "She was very nice and spoke to me very kindly. She said she would encourage my father to call me. But I never heard from him. And I never tried to call again."

Before we know it, the sun begins to melt into the ocean, and we say our good-byes.

"The hours aren't enough for us, *primo*," Ricardo says as we clasp each other's hands, shaking them, again and again, like we do not want to let go. My cousin Luis comes over—"Let's take a few pictures of this beautiful scenery," he says—and he snaps several photos of Ricardo, Julio, and me with our backs to the ocean that separates us from the rest of the Frías family.

"If only my daughter could have been here to meet you. When I told her about yesterday, and about coming here today, you could tell her heart was breaking because she couldn't be here," Ricardo says. "Try, *primote*, to see her when you get back to Havana. Promise me. It would mean so much to her."

'*Claro*,' *of course I'll go see her. Consider it done, 'primo.'*

Ricardo gets e-mail at his office, and I promise we will be in touch. Still, I want to do more, and I give him the e-mail addresses of his brothers. I don't know what their father has told them in private about Ricardo, but I know that if I had a brother out there—or a sister—I would want to know. I see Ricardo's eyes turn red as he looks at his brothers' names and then at me. Julio hugs him this time.

"Tell them about me," Ricardo says, his hands on my shoulders, his eyes welling as he looks into mine. "And tell my father that I don't hold any ill will toward him. I hope he's happy and healthy. And I hope that, one day, we'll be able to meet in person."

Ricardo and Julio wave good-bye, and I watch them walk down the beach in the fading sun until they disappear among the other specks of people on the beach. I return to a spot on the sand next to my cousins, and Elena puts her arm around me. We watch the sun descend below the horizon until only a tangerine sky and wispy lavender clouds remain. The few people still bathing in the ocean are silhouetted against a violet sea. The tide has risen, and

small waves begin their soft crush against the shore, rivulets climbing the sand and licking my toes.

I grab a handful of powdery sand, rub it between my palms, and
feel it slip back onto the beach, taking with it a piece of me. I leave
it here to keep the hidden piece of my mother's heart company.

A day at the beach has left us famished. Our group heads back up
several blocks to the main drag, where Jorge says there is a little
Italian place where foreigners and local Cubans are allowed to eat
together.

The restaurant is painted yellow with cottage-style windows
and a white plaster statue of a Roman-looking goddess out front.
When Jorge opens the front door, a blast of air-conditioning raises
the hairs on my legs from my still-damp shorts.

"*Ay*, how delicious," Andrea says, and I wonder if she means the
cooled air or the scent of hot food.

Small parties are eating quietly at several tables near the windows while the staff push together three tables at the center of the
restaurant to accommodate our party of eleven. When a waitress
brings menus, I am not surprised. Pizza. Mushroom pizza, roasted
garlic pizza, ham-and-pineapple pizza. Pizza, pizza, pizza. But of
course, no one seems to mind. It is hot and fresh, and we are starving. I notice several of my cousins eyeing the prices and whisper
to them to order whatever they want. For three days, I've had their
coffee and eaten their rations, and it is the very least I can do. Call
it a sin of pride. But, yeah, I'm happy that, for one day, I can help
them eat their fill.

"Pizza with lobster, how delicious," I overhear Andrea telling
her husband, Joaquín. She admits that although she's in her thirties
and lives in an island nation, in a city near the water, she has never
even seen a lobster up close. We all order our personal pies, and
the waitress pours our sodas into wineglasses. Tomás cuts Isabel's
pizza into squares at the other end of the table, and the young
lovers feed each other bites. I order a ham pizza with extra cheese
to go, for Tía Sofía and Pipo. We ask for refills of our sodas, and

the buzz of laughter and conversation flows from our table. And I forget for a second that we are in Cuba.

We finish off with rich, hot Cuban coffee, which we use to toast—*a la familia!*—and when I look around the table, I find expressions that are new to me. Looks of contentment, satiety, and I wonder when the last time was that they had these expressions. I drink the rest of my hot coffee quickly to quell the emotion rising in my throat. All my family, here, together.

Outside the restaurant, though, as the air-conditioning fades into a humidity that sticks to my tight, salt-covered skin, we are soon faced with reality. We have to get back to Cárdenas. But it is past ten, and the buses have stopped running. All of the workers in Disneyland are back in their disheveled homes, out of sight of the casual tourist. The Lada seats only four, five tops, and Jorge insists I ride back with him. We pile in the kids, Isabel and Luisito.

We'll just make two trips.

"Don't worry, Carlitos, *resolvemos*, we'll work it out," Elena says.

Tomás and Joaquín will keep the others company as they look for a ride from someone with a private car.

Hitchhiking? No, there's got to be a better way.

Don't worry, they say, shrugging it all off, confused by my concern. This is their way. They'll just flag down an old American jalopy for a couple of Convertibles.

I ride back to Cárdenas in the front seat with my Tía Sofía's pizza warming my lap. When we get to her house, the door is open, and the fluorescent light spills into the darkened street.

"*Mira*, look at how *tostadito*, how tan, you are!" my Tía says as I kiss her forehead. "*Y qué*, how did you like Varadero?" she asks, just like her son Jorge, with a look that says she knows the answer to the question.

'*Maravilloso, Tía.*' Marvelous.

DAY NINE

Moonlight shines down onto the tiny house, down, down into the courtyard where Tomás takes his showers, past the wall that isn't there, to find the bedroom that sleep has not.

The night feels cool, or maybe I've just become accustomed to the weather here in four short days. The fan above my head whirs dutifully. The bed is a soft cloud. And if there are mosquitoes tonight, I do not notice them. Perhaps they no longer see me as an exotic source of food. Whatever the case, I should be asleep.

Instead, I stare at a ceiling illuminated by the reflected moon and know that soon it will be bright with sunlight. Morning will break, and the day will begin. My last day in Cárdenas. My chest is made of lead, and no matter how hard I try, I cannot seem to breathe deeply enough as I lie under a thin bedsheet, motionless. I swallow hard to push down the knot in my throat, but it only tightens. And I know it's not the moon or the weather, the bed or the bugs. I know that with morning comes an inescapable truth: I may never see my family again.

I lie awake, focusing on the wooden shutters and watching as the colors in the room, awash in the cool blue of night, warm with the rising sun. My sheets, swirls of gray and lavender in darkness, recover their flush of orange and green. My skin goes from deathly gray to sun-kissed bronze. The world comes to life, and like it or not, so must I.

The house is quiet when I get out of bed and dress with my last few articles of clean clothes. I rifle through my backpack, which I haven't used since I arrived in Cárdenas, and find the money belt. I hold it in my hands and sigh. Back on it goes.

I sit on the edge of the bed as I repack and come across a plastic bag from the duty-free store in Cancún. Inside is the pack of five toy cars I bought in case I met some little boy whose day I could brighten. It's then that I hear water running in another part of the house. The rest of the family is rousing, and I hear the murmur of a little voice. Isabel will be returning to this bed that she shares with her parents tonight, and I wish, how I wish, that these five little cars were five beautiful dolls.

Knock, knock, knock. The shadow of a little person is on the other side of the louvered bedroom door. When I open it, Isabel is standing there with her fists on her hips, looking at me sideways, a yellow ribbon at the end of her long braid that matches her yellow T-shirt and yellow shorts with a white stripe. Yellow, the color of the day. Isabel's lips are pressed together. She curls her little index finger, wordlessly calling me to bend down so she can give me my morning hug and kiss, and I smell her baby cologne.

"*Buenos días,* Carlitos," she says.

I have a gift for you, 'un regalito,' but I don't know if you're going to like it.

Isabel bites her lip and tucks her hands behind her back. I dig out the set of cars from my bag and hold them to my chest for a second, showing her. These are not girls' toys, I know, and I watch her for a reaction. She takes the unopened box and holds it close to her face, peering into the window where each of the cars is packaged, her eyes studying every detail through the plastic. I hold my breath, waiting for some response. She looks up at me and smiles.

"Can you open it for me, Carlitos, *por favor?*" she says.

We sit on the bed, and I carefully remove each car. She hands me one car, grabs one in each of her hands, and we race them, side by side, crashing them into each other over the rugged terrain of bedsheets, making screeching and *vrooming* noises. She places one lime green car with a chrome engine poking out of the hood flat against the cold tile floor and flings it, "Vrooom!" and it sails across the room. She claps and squeals, and I doubt she knows how much I will miss that little cackle.

I leave my bags packed at Elena's, and the three of us take our morning walk to Tía Sofía's, Isabel with her hands cupped to her chest, cradling her new toys. The door to my aunt's house is propped open, as always, the softest breeze creeping in. Tía Sofía is in her favorite chair, and Andrea is bent over her, running a comb through her silvery gray, towel-dried hair. I squat down to Tía Sofía, take her Ivory-clean hand in mine, and kiss it.

"So today is the day you leave us," she says in her soft, squeaky voice that this morning resonates like a perfect note pulled on a violin, and I can only nod because her words choke me. She pats the side of my face and leaves her hand on my cheek for a moment, and I close my eyes.

"Look what's waiting for you over there," she says, motioning me to turn around.

Spread over the dining room table are flaking yellowed documents and dozens of black-and-white photographs, arranged like a storyboard. On the floor next to the table is a cardboard box the size of a nightstand, so packed with papers and photos that the flaps do not close. While we were in Varadero yesterday, my Tía says, she asked my cousin Ernesto to dig out this box that is a repository for their memories, a window into their past. *My* past. It is part treasure chest, part archaeological find. And I can imagine how Louis Leakey felt the moment he dusted sand off the hidden remains of ancient man.

I sit in front of this collage of memories, flipping through pictures I have never seen of my mother as a teenager, a slender young girl alive in photos that are more than fifty years old. I carefully handle the old photographs at the edges, as if handling them too aggressively will cause them to crumble into dust.

My Tía Sofía lifts herself from her chair with her walker and begins her dedicated shuffle the few feet to the table. I get up to help her, but she shakes her head—"Don't worry, *mi niño*,"—finally making her way to a chair at the head of the table. She lowers herself gingerly, and we sit next to each other with our history spread before us.

"Anybody home?" Jorge calls from the front door, walking in with his brothers and Luisito. Isabel jumps up from the coffee table where she is racing her cars and runs to Jorge. He grunts as he lifts her onto his waist.

"*Niña*, are you made of lead?" he asks her, poking at her baby fat as she squirms.

"Ah, you pulled out the box!" Luis says.

"I almost broke my back dragging that thing out here," Ernesto says.

Andrea puts the coffee on, and its sweet, dark aroma sets the stage as we all sit around the dining room table, shifting photos, reconstructing a jigsaw puzzle of youth.

"*Mira*, look at this one," my aunt says, handing me a picture of my mother with her three nephews hanging all over her. This one was taken at that park near her apartment in Havana, when the boys would go visit, she says. Ernestico is kneeling by her lap, with a wide, closed-mouth grin and his ears sticking out like satellite dishes. Luis has his leg up on the bench, smiling. Jorge, standing stiff as a statue, with a hint of a smile, is next to her. "The little man, *el hombresito*," my Tía says, remembering the boy who is now a grandfather, Jorge showing her that same smile.

"Remember this, *Mami*?" Ernesto says, handing my aunt another picture. She turns it so I can see it. It is a photo of the brothers as teenagers, posing with my cousin Diani, who lives in the United States, but visited Cuba years ago. All of them are in their bathing suits, ready to head off to Varadero.

"We had such a good time," Ernesto says. "Remember how she complained when we had to leave the beach? We loved having her here, showing her around."

She is smiling in the photo, with her arms around her cousins, her large, calm eyes and bright smile exuding what it meant to meet the family she had never known. In this picture, Diani is fourteen, and Ernesto speaks as if she left just last week, recalling all the details of her visit. This year, she turned forty-one.

I keep digging through the box and find photos of three boys I do not recognize.

"Those were my brothers," my aunt says.

Brothers? You had… my Mamá had other brothers?

The only one of her brothers I had ever known was my late Tío Julio. It wasn't until years later that I learned there was an older brother, the oldest child, who was killed in a hunting accident when he was just eighteen. He was shot accidentally by a cousin— cousins who were best of friends and always together, my aunt says. But afterward, the relationships between the families were never the same.

There is another photo here, one of a lovely toddler with a serious pout and blond locks, wearing a sailor suit. Tía Sofía struggles to remember his name. We pass the photo around, everyone remarking on the child's striking visage. This brother died of disease shortly after this picture was taken, my Tía Sofía says. A third son, pictured in a hazy baby photo, died in infancy. That was years before my mother, the baby of the family, was born.

"*Mamá* lived the rest of her life worried about the health of her children," Tía Sofía says, gazing at the beautiful golden-haired child, who never grew to take a photo as a boy.

I never met my grandmother. She died shortly after arriving in the United States, well before I was born. I have only ever seen one picture of her, and it is so worn and she so far from the lens that my mind has not had enough input to create a mental image. I have always heard she was sickly, the emphysema that led to her death just the final health complication.

"*Mami* was very quiet, very prayerful," my aunt remembers. And I can imagine why. She sprinkled dirt over the caskets of three of her babies, including her firstborn child. And when she left Cuba, she left behind her oldest daughter and three grandchildren. I glance again at the photo of my three cousins as boys, and then at a photo of my Tía Sofía in a wedding dress, standing next to Pipo, her groom. Of those pictures, only memories remain as I look at the faces around this table. And I imagine that, in her mind, my grandmother must have said a prayer of Last Rites for them as well.

Tía, why didn't you leave with the rest of them? Why did you stay behind?

An ever-glowing light in my Tía's eyes begins to flicker, a storm rolling in from the sea. It is the first time I have seen her wear anything other than an easy smile.

"We were ready to leave," she says, "but things got complicated."

After missing out on the small-scale boatlift at Camarioca because they had no one to pick them up in the United States, the family decided it was time to leave, she says. They all applied for exit visas—my grandparents, my mother, my aunts and cousins—and waited for their day to arrive. Within months, she says, everyone got their visas, the government's permission to leave, except for my Tía Sofía's family. Pipo told the others not to wait, said that their visas would certainly arrive, sooner or later. They could not wait to leave together or they might never leave.

And so the rest left for Miami from the Varadero airport on a Flight of Freedom in 1966, my aunt says. Families dividing. Lives headed in uncertain directions. I picture my mother in an airplane for the first time, sitting in the window seat next to my Tía Tata, as they pull into the sky. And as she looks out, the sparkling turquoise water and blinding white sand of her favorite beach, where she would stroll and bathe until her ivory skin took a golden tone, is blurry through tears. It is her last sight, her lasting memory, a watery Fatherland disappearing over the horizon.

"I'll always remember when we told Ernestico that Tata—Tata was his godmother—had left for the United States," my Tía says. "No, *coño*, my *madrina* didn't leave me! No, no, no, *coño!* I'm leaving with her!" she remembers him saying, all of them laughing at first at the memory of a cursing-mad little boy, then falling silent at the memory of a cursing-mad little boy. Losing our Tata, our favorite aunt, seems to have that effect on all the children in her family.

My Tía Sofía's family kept waiting for their visas, my aunt says, continuing her story as we study more pictures. For two years, their door was pelted with rotting tomatoes, they were insulted in the street, called *gusanos* for wanting to "abandon the revolution." The local CDR saw to it that everyone on their block knew where the *gusanos* lived, she says.

"Those were two very difficult years for us, but we were hopeful that eventually we would be reunited with our family," she says, her voice soft and low.

Finally, they received the date for their exit interview, when soldiers would come to their house, take inventory of all their belongings—from bed frames to lightbulbs—ensuring that all their debts were paid, and take possession of the house and everything in it. They would lock the door behind them, leaving my family only with the clothes on their backs. But the real problem was the date of the interview. It was several months off, and by then, Jorge, the oldest of my Tía Sofía's sons, would have turned fifteen. He would be of military age and prohibited from leaving. If they left, it would have to be without their oldest son. If they didn't leave, two years later Luis would reach military age and, soon after, Ernesto.

"What was I supposed to do?" my Tía says, looking at her boys around the table. Forty years later, they are still here. "There was no decision to make."

"*Desgraciado!*" Luis would yell at his oldest brother, telling him he had disgraced their family. "It's because of you that we can't leave!" They were a child's words then, and Jorge was already a young man. But when my aunt tells the story, Jorge's eyes betray that the truth was a burden.

I wonder if my mother knew then, when she said good-bye to her family in Cárdenas before continuing on to the airport, that it would be the last time she ever held her young nephews close. That the next time she saw her sister would be not years but decades later. That they would spend their twilight years apart. She could not have been prepared for the life that awaited her. She could not have known she would bury her father and mother, her brother and sister, until only she remained—she and her only living sister separated by ninety miles and ideology. Would she have said good-bye? Would she have stayed behind?

As we continue looking through pictures, Jorge and Luis leave to have the car checked out before the long drive back to Havana this afternoon. The Lada has been running hot, Jorge says, and he would rather his friend, the mechanic who rented us the car, give it a clean bill of health. The rest of us remain at the dining room table, entranced.

I keep digging through the box and find a stack of documents, beige with age and mottled with brown spots, each about the size of a napkin, neatly folded, looking to have been that way for decades. I unfold them delicately, releasing the smell of aged ink, careful not to complete the tears along the seams.

They are certificates that refer to "La Señorita Iraida" and on the back have lists of percentages next to different subjects. My mother's grade school report cards are all here, in black and white, dating to 1947. They do more than document her school years. For the first time, I can picture her a teenage girl, going from class to class, acing some, struggling at others.

Her "freshman" report card shows she started off with a bang. She had a 96 or better in every subject, Spelling, Grammar, Geography, Bookkeeping, and 105 percent in Handwriting. ("What I remember so clearly about your mother was her beautiful penmanship," Emma had said when we met with her.) And then there was English, where she had an 83. The next year, she struggled with it again, earning only a 74 percent. But she shows her mettle in her third and final year, when English is the only class in which she scores a perfect 100.

She wasn't going to let it beat her, huh?

How she must have studied to conquer the one class that had tested her during her entire high school career. I come across another set of grades from her time at the Professional School of Commerce of Cárdenas. Here's an 81 percent in English I. Again, 100 percent in Handwriting. But what's this? A 60 in Bookkeeping, 1 percent above a failing grade? The job she did at the jewelry store she and my father owned for twenty-two years?

"Looks like she just squeaked by on that one," Ernesto jokes.

We're going to have to talk about this when I get home, young lady, I think to myself.

"Take them home," my Tía says, "so you can remind her of the kind of student she was."

I had hoped to be able to bring something special back for my mother, something she never expected. A picture of the crest from her old school, the symbol of Las Madres Escolapias. Earlier this year, the ruby of the graduation ring she wore for fifty-three years cracked, and the golden crest embedded in the stone was lost. I wanted to have a jeweler remake it from a photo. Now, on every page, I see a stamped seal of her school. My Tía Sofía bought that ring for my mother with the money she made from teaching. A woman who appreciated education, Tía Sofía wanted to give her that lasting gift.

"Did you show him the letter?" Ernesto asks.

My aunt pushes a yellowed envelope across the table to me. It is typewritten and addressed to Tía Sofía. "Open it," she says.

I read aloud the one-page letter my Tía was sent by the Cuban government in 1965 when she was a teacher in the school system. Days after applying for an exit visa to "abandon" the country after the "triumph of the revolution," as it is still called, she had been "dishonorably released from her duties," the letter states. She had "betrayed" the children who were to be indoctrinated in the morals of the new revolution.

Teaching was her life. She taught first in a rural country school, with several grades all lumped into one room, then, later, the third grade at the defunct school we saw on the way to Emma's house two days ago. When she saw the textbooks, the syllabus she would have to teach under the new government, she registered to leave.

"They were rewriting history," she says. "One of my students, whom I had the previous year, said, '*Maestra*, I liked it better the other way. If it's all right, I'll just go ahead and remember it that way.'" She laughs. "A few weeks later, his family left 'for the outside.'"

That was not the kind of teacher she would become. She loved teaching, yet when the government offered her another teaching job, she refused it and never worked again.

"I couldn't be more proud of that letter," she tells me, smiling widely.

"Ernestico, show him the things Emma brought yesterday," she says. While we were in Varadero, Emma, whom my aunt hadn't seen in years, stopped by with a letter for my mother. Ernesto hands me an unsealed envelope, about the size of a greeting card. On the outside in red ink is written, "To Iraida from Emma." I can't lie. The nosy reporter in me begs to open the letter, to read what my mother's childhood friend wants her to know after all these years. But I have spent the afternoon filling myself with the knowledge of my mother's past, with my history, and I figure some things should remain private. Along with the letter is a small red booklet and a black-and-white photograph that Emma wanted to lend me.

In the photo, over a layered dress of ruffled white tulle that covers her feet, my mother is wearing a crisp, white graduation gown that nearly reaches her knees and a cap with the tassel turned to the left. She has on just a little makeup, shadow over her eyes and lipstick that makes her mouth luminescent, and, on her left hand, her graduation ring. Emma, my mother's graduation sponsor, wearing white pumps and a simple dress just above her ankles, is handing my mother her rolled-up diploma.

"I think we still have that diploma here," Ernesto says and walks to a buffet cabinet against the wall. He pulls open the bottom drawer and removes several diplomas that are rolled up together. But as I try to unroll the papers, they resist my pull and threaten to crack. They have been fused in this position by time and humidity. I cannot fully unroll them, can do no more than read the names on the first two certificates, my Tía Sofía's and my Tía Tata's, before they begin to creak. I think about what my mother would say to see these, to see her own sheepskin fifty-three years later, but I worry they won't survive the trip. And I'm more than a little surprised to feel that they are safer right where they are. When I slide them back into the drawer, I know I am simply putting them away again, leaving buried a treasure that, someday, my mother and I will find a way to unroll together.

I open the red leather-bound booklet Emma brought and turn to the page she had marked off. Students at my mother's school used these autograph books the way high school students have their yearbooks signed by their friends. On this page, my mother has written a poem to her friend:

"Emmita"

For a brunette, you'd give a penny
For black hair, un millón
For a blond with blue eyes,
All of your corazón

Your friend,
Iraida

I read the poem again, out loud, and can imagine my mother trying to get the beat just right. This was my mother, playful, young, romantic. Just a kid with her whole life ahead of her, a girl with dreams of finding her own prince charming, her own ideal of Emma's boy with blond hair and blue eyes. A young woman with a degree in 1957, when such things were rare even in the United States. This was my mother, a rising star of promise and hope, forced to begin anew in a strange world.

Without a word, my Tía Sofía hands me a business card–size manila envelope. There is a lump inside. I feel the hard mass and shoot my aunt a look that says, "What are you up to, woman?" She fires back with her eyes, "Open and find out."

I spill into my hand what looks like a signet ring with a seal atop. It is blackened and looks more like it has been carved out of coal than silver or gold or bronze. I can make out words above and below an emblem. *Escolapias. Graduada.* And the symbol in the middle must be the emblem I am looking for. A date on the side reads 1949, and inside, my mother's initials are engraved. It is her eighth-grade graduation ring. She must have put this away when she received her high school ring, and it has been waiting here for her ever since.

"Take that to your mother," my aunt tells me. "Let's see what she says when she sees her old ring."

Rubbing it between my thumb and forefinger, feeling the ridges of the date hidden beneath a black patina that has taken fifty-seven years to form, I imagine that my mother never gave this ring a second thought when she left.

She would have been thirty-one years old.

My Tía Sofía cocks her head to look at me.

When she left. She would have been my exact age.

I look back down at the ring, continue rubbing it.

I know what terrifies me. I know that, any minute, Jorge is going to come through that door to take me away, away from my family. Away from my Tía Sofía. Away from this house and this street. Away from this city and this world. And I'm not going to think about this ring or that diploma or those report cards. I'm going to be my mother, riding in that car on the way to the Varadero airport forty years ago, sobbing so that no one can understand what she is saying, so that the scenery is a watery blur.

I have always thought of my mother simply as young at heart because she likes two-door coupes, outfits that won't make her look like *una viejita*, and dyeing her short, curled hair a reasonable auburn rather than letting it go white. I never considered that the girl from Cárdenas who stepped on a plane for the first time in 1966 remains inside her, hidden in a place she keeps secret, emerging only when her guard slips. I know she visits the girl when we're not around. I have walked in on her during those moments, when she's ironing or praying and her eyes are red with emotion. You ask her what's the matter, and she answers simply, "*Nada*, just thinking about many, many things."

I know that's why she offers so few stories about her past. And why all of them, funny or sad, always end in tears. Visiting her memories means waking the girl who still tans on the beach with her nephews and goes to church bazaars with her friends to see if she can catch sight of the boy she has a crush on. The girl lives in her, forever.

Tía Sofía puts her hand on my cheek, and I press against it as she pats my head, calming the heat that rises in my chest, in my throat, in my eyes. I squeeze the ring between my fingers. I have what I came looking for.

It is midafternoon, and we are still examining photos when Jorge calls. His friend says the Lada has a cooling problem, and Jorge barely made it to the mechanic's before it overheated. He is working on the car but isn't sure he trusts it for a three-hour trip. He has spoken to Santiago about driving me back to Havana in the Blue Bird, but I would have to be dropped off at his house in Matanzas. That's about as far as they trust the Lada to travel.

"Carlitos, I think I'm going to have to say good-bye now," Jorge says. He is already near the house of the friend he stays with when he visits Cuba, so rather than test the Lada with an extra trip, Luis is going to drop him off now, then swing by to take me to Santiago's house.

"*Primo*, I feel lucky that we could be here together," Jorge says.

I'm glad you were here, 'primo.' To tell you the truth, I felt like I was home.

"Now you can tell your mother you've seen her hometown. You've swum at her beach. You've met her old friends. You visited her school. *Vaya*, you can tell her you got to know *her* Cárdenas," he says.

'Gracias.' For everything. You were a great tour guide.

I promise to call when I reach Havana, and he promises to call when he returns to the United States next week.

I guess I'll see you 'allá'—on the other side.

"I'll see you at home."

Luisito is rocking in a chair by the door when I pull another rocker next to his. He has been moping ever since he missed the buddy who came looking for him this morning to play baseball down at one of the fields.

"I try to play every chance I get. When school starts, I get busy and I only get to play on the weekends," he says as we rock to keep the breeze moving. There are just a couple of weeks left before school starts, and he's going to miss being here at his *Mima's* house. He spends almost every day here during the summer and even keeps his baseball equipment here.

It must be hard leaving for school.

"At least I'm lucky. I go to one of the good schools," he says. He rethinks his answer. "Well, it's one of the least bad ones."

Two years ago, Luisito entered one of Cuba's few "pre-universities," a sort of college prep boarding school where teenagers begin to study technical careers. It is forty-five minutes away in Matanzas.

He is *becado*, he says, meaning his grades allow him to go to this better school. Otherwise, Luisito would be attending a school in the country. There, the toilets back up. Mosquitoes frolic and multiply in the dense grass. Beds are decades old and playgrounds for biting bedbugs.

"I have friends from *primario*, elementary school, who have to go to the country school," he says, shaking his head. "It's not good."

Gangs of boys run the schools, he says. Children knife other children. Girls go home pregnant.

As it is, he must pack all of his own clothing, bedsheets, food, even bottles of water for the week. One of his classes is taught by nothing more than a television and a videotape. A teacher comes in the room to turn it on and leaves. Obviously, there's no such thing as raising your hand to ask a question.

"I don't want to end up at one of the country schools, so I work to keep my grades up so I can stay there," he says. I think of Elián, who will be attending his school of choice, right in his hometown, and that line from George Orwell's *Animal Farm* plays in my head: "All animals are equal, but some animals are more equal than others."

The lessons from books are not as difficult as the ones Luisito learns from his older classmates. He has already been approached about joining one of the communist guilds. It is the first step in a lifetime of attending government-ordered rallies and taking tests to prove you are up with the latest dogmas of the state.

"My *Papá* taught me how to handle it," he says. When he is approached by a student who has already bought in, his father told him to reply: "I'm just a boy. I don't think I'm mature enough to represent the revolution."

It must be hard to keep your mind on school.

He shrugs his shoulders.

"That's life."

Luisito is fighting a battle. One he will not win. His father's strategy might buy him two or three years. But eventually, if he wants to have a career, he must sign on. His father hasn't told him this part. He will be a communist one day, on paper if not in spirit. But every day until then, he will learn how to fight it.

"We all have to live a double life, have two faces," my cousin Luis had told me. He was actually drafted to go to war in Angola, but Jorge had a doctor friend certify that his brother had a condition with his back that made him a liability in battle.

Still, with the uncertainty surrounding Castro's illness, he has been doing guard duty and "being mobilized." What does that mean? He and others whose day it is to do guard duty sit in an outpost and go over military tactics about how they would react if *los americanos* attack this particular part of town. "Playing soldier," he called it. From the time they are boys, younger than Luisito, they are taught that someone is out to get them.

Amid all of it, Luisito finds time to play baseball with his friends after school, with the twine innards of an old ball and whatever stick they can find. Here at home, he says, other boys have bats, and they can get a real game together. He silently scrapes his foot against the ground as he rocks, lost in thought.

Is that baseball field far from here?

"You can walk there," he says, without looking up. "But they finish playing early, before it gets hot. I'm sure they're gone already."

Do you have a glove here?

He stops rocking. "And what a glove, *mi hermano!*" he says, jumping up. We walk to the back of the living room, where an old black trunk with rusted brass buckles is pushed up against the wall. He opens it with a loud *creak* and pulls out a black Ken Griffey, Jr., glove that Jorge brought him from the United States two years ago. It is supple and broken in, and when he puts it on, it fits the contours of his fingers snugly, perfectly.

What position do you play?

"I used to play the outfield," he says, punching his fist into the pocket of the glove with a *thwack*. "But since I got so tall, they moved me to first base."

Do you have more than one glove?

He digs into the trunk and pulls out another, whose laces have come loose, one that is floppy and worn from years of use, white and faded like it has been living underground.

Well, get a ball and let's go have a catch.

"Okay, cool, *bárbaro! Mima,* we're going outside to play," he yells, and I can't tell which one of us is more excited. I want to see him handle his Griffey, but he insists I take the good glove. "No, Carlitos, you don't know this glove. Only I know how to handle this devil."

We step out into the street, where the blazing Caribbean sun has dried and cracked the sewage in the gutters. We begin popping the glove, and my shoulder feels like the elastic from an old pair of underwear. We start only a few feet apart at first, just chucking the ball back and forth, then running and throwing, like Derek Jeter—his favorite player—scrambling to get the runner at first. A few people come out of their homes and watch us. We play and sweat and laugh at my lousy throws. I yell, *"Carro!"* and he holds the ball whenever an old Chevy or a horse and buggy come rambling down the street, and I am careful not to let the ball skip into the dusty filth at the edge of the road.

For a time, I forget where I am. Forget that I'm thirty-one and my arm will be sore as hell tomorrow. Forget that Luisito is a kid whose existence must be based on living two lives.

At this moment, he is the rookie first baseman from Cárdenas. And I, the old veteran from Miami. We are just two ballplayers on a street having a catch.

Tía Sofía and I sit across from each other at the kitchen table, sorting through a pile of black beans that will be her supper as we wait for Luis to arrive and take me away.

The beans slide across the table with a hiss into two piles. One will go in the trash, the other will make up the soup that is her daily staple. This bean is split; out it goes. This one crumbles to dust in my hands. This one is shriveled but still edible. This, this is a rock! It's the best she can get, buying her rations at a store that sells to those who can pay only in national pesos. She will cook them on her standard-issue burner, which barely heats the beans enough to soften them, and that will be her dinner, chewy black beans and rice. I watch her fine, bony fingers separate the beans quickly, as if she barely needs to think about it, and her atrophied arms dutifully slide the beans to their places.

As we sit at the two-person, green-and-white table between the hole that is a window and an open door, which leads to the courtyard, a light breeze blows in. And several seconds pass before I notice that the tickle on my ankle is not the wind. I jerk my leg back quickly, then look down to see a black-and-white kitten that hardly flinches. It blinks slowly when it looks up at me and meows softly, faintly.

"*Misu*, you've come looking for your supper?" my aunt says. "Pipo, your little friend is here, and I think she's asking for food."

"I already put food out for her, but she's not eating," Pipo says, coming into the kitchen from the courtyard. He holds up a small plastic dish. Chewy black beans and rice. The kitten, as small and gaunt as a ferret, meows in a whisper as she moves toward Pipo, and I see the ribs ripple beneath her fur. She rubs her wilting body against his leg, and Pipo bends down to pet her gently.

"I don't know what's wrong with her," he says. "It's as if she doesn't have the will to eat."

"Well, be careful that the neighbor doesn't catch her *mansita*, so tamed," she tells Pipo.

Does the neighbor not like cats?

She and Pipo look at each other, and Tía Sofía gives a slight snicker as she turns back to sorting beans.

"The problem is that he likes them too much," Pipo says.

"You two are terrible," Elena tells them, putting on the afternoon coffee. "That poor man."

During the "Special Period," after the withdrawal of the Soviet Union, food was scarce everywhere in Cuba, Elena says. For a time, people thought it would finally be the end of communism on the island. The neighbor, Pipo says, set up traps around his yard to catch the cats that roamed the neighborhood. He would skin, butcher, and eat them.

No, Pipo, I don't believe you.

"You would hear those cats screaming and screaming, then, *boom!* silence. Carlitos, things got really bad here," he says.

"That poor man just did what he thought he had to do," Elena says, pouring us cups of coffee.

'Resolvió.'

"The only problem is we started having an issue with rats, because now there were no cats to keep them under control," Pipo says.

I look back at the kitten, who seems alive only at her contact with Pipo, rubbing back and forth between his ankles, now purring. My Tía Sofía hands the sorted beans to Elena, who puts them in a pot of water for my aunt's supper. Jorge, before he left, had a doctor friend write a prescription saying she needed beef as part of her diet. She gets it a couple of times a month. Technically, it is a lie. In truth, I look at her and wonder how much thinner, how much more frail she might be without it.

I've come to know the engine noise of the Lada, and when I hear it stop out front, I know it is time.

Elena and Isabel walk me back around the corner to get my bags at their house, where Tomás is resting on the couch in their hallway of a living room. He stands up and shakes my hand firmly, like you'd expect from the human pit bull, then claps me in a strong hug. And I thank him for everything, for opening his home, for giving up his bed, for . . . everything.

"Any day now, we'll see each other again—over there," he says. And I believe him.

As I reach for my bag, I feel a little hand tug at my shorts. It is Isabel, and she has something for me.

"Here, Carlitos," she says, handing me two stuffed little bears, one with a British flag on its chest, the other, smaller, wearing a Canadian flag on its bottom. "These are for my cousins, Elise and Amelia. The big one is for Elise because she's bigger. The little one is for Amelia because she's little."

I hold both bears in one palm, unable to speak. I look at Elena, at Tomás, and they nod their heads, like they know.

"That's very nice, *Mamita*," Elena tells her, stroking her head. I try to tell Isabel to keep them here so she can play with her cousins when they come to visit. I do not want to take her toys for my children, who live in the land of plenty. Her little smile disappears. She looks, instead, like she's starting to feel hurt, like she doesn't understand not sharing the things she has, and I say quickly, *Oh, wow, 'Mamita,' these are beautiful! The girls are going to love them.* She smiles again. I drop my backpack and pick her up, hug her tight, tight, tight, the bears in my hand. Baby cologne. Russian Violets. A giggly little chortle.

"Carlitos, when you come next time, will you bring my cousins so we can all play together?"

It's just that simple for her: "When you come next time . . ." I have given myself permission to come this once, to oppose the beliefs of my father, my mother, my family, and visit Cuba through a loophole in their credo. But as I look into Isabel's eyes while she waits for an answer, I give her the only one she deserves.

One day, 'Mamita.'

One day.

She won't let me take her picture.

"C'mon, *Mima*, let him take one picture," Elena implores my Tía Sofía.

Simply taking the camera from my pocket makes her cringe into her rocking chair, her arm covering her face.

"Don't you dare—*no te atrevas!* I'll never forgive you!" she yells, more animated than ever.

It's been like this for four days. And when I look back through the pictures in my camera, I realize I have not taken a single photograph inside my Tía's house. Today, I ask her one more time. I kneel next to her rocking chair, take her hand, and hold it.

Please, my Tía, so I can remember you. So your sister can see you.

She places her hand against my cheek and sighs.

"Remember me how I was," she says—with her hair coiffed, her nails done, and standing strong on her own two feet after her last visit to the United States.

Luis takes my bags to the car. And I feel it. I know it is coming, rising, burning. I fight it off to focus on all the faces that greeted me that first night, to hug them, to thank them. I look them in the eye, photographing them with my mind, framing them against the patchy cobalt blue paint on the walls.

But when I come to my Tía Sofía, it is like the first night all over again.

The heat in my throat rises, and I cannot stop it and do not want to. I cannot speak. Only cry. We have picked up right where we left off that night, and it occurs to me I never really stopped. I have been crying on the inside. I smell her Ivory-clean skin, feel the sinew and bone beneath her cool house gown, and my arms lack the strength to hug her as I should. I am losing her. She is losing me. Losing my mother, all over again.

I stare at her as I get into the car. Stare and wave and smile and crumble as we drive away, as the car splashes through puddles of sewage and swerves to avoid potholes and horse manure and children running barefoot between the teetering houses.

The entire drive back to Havana, I sit quietly in the passenger seat of the Blue Bird. Santiago is giving a family of hard-core communists a ride to the airport and told me to say very little, to say I'm his cousin from Havana if they ask.

I stare out the window and watch evergreen scenery fly by. I pretend to sleep at times, as the breeze bats my face. I close my eyes and can still see her standing there, like a picture.

I am remembering my Tía Sofía just as she is.

DAY TEN

Push and pull. Float and fall. I spend the night aloft between two worlds.

I feel them strongly now. They hold me to the bed. They keep me in my clothes, dusty and sweaty from the drive through the countryside.

They haunt and wail and laugh and moan as I watch rain fall for the first time since I came to Cuba. A gray sky is a silver screen for defiant memories.

I can only lie in my hotel room, in the dark, and look through the stained-glass windows up to a weeping sky.

And there they play. Too short to be stories, too real to be dreams.

Images.

Memories.

Memories that flash with the lightning above, the icy blue lightning that cuts through the sky with crackling delight and illuminates the stained glass, red and gold shapes playing against the walls as the storm rolls on.

The images play, end to end, without order or apology.

Raw sewage and bare feet.

Shriveled beans and shriveled hands.

White sand and turquoise bathwater.

Russian Violets and Ivory soap.

A strange cousin and a familiar smile.

A starving kitten and a weak aunt.

Chewy black beans and rice in a plastic bowl.

I want to hide from them, but they find me here, unable to move. Unwilling. They wash over me, terrify me, these memories that will not fade.

Ten days in Hell.

Ten days in Heaven.

The taxi tiptoes over puddles, slowing to ford flooded streets as we head west toward Marianao, a blanket of rain becoming a veil. Although it is past one in the afternoon, the sky remains gray, obscuring the sun. We deviate from the familiar route because parts of the city have been flooded by overnight rains. An old American car is stranded on the side of the road, and its driver trudges through knee-deep water swirling with an oily rainbow. He steers with one hand, pushing with the other as a friend puts his weight behind the car. A trickle of people take to the sidewalks, covering their heads with newspapers to endure a fine mist that permeates as they try to go about their daily routine.

I was supposed to be at Alina's house by now. But all over the city, torrential rains and poorly draining streets have forced a change of plans.

Diesel engines growl, horns honk, apartment after tall apartment juts into the sky as my mind tries to acclimate itself back to city life. The soft classical *danzón* that had been playing in my head has been turned up too loud, becoming a jumble of fine noise. I close my eyes and sit silently in the cab, trying to hush the cacophony.

I focus on Alina, remember the rasp of her smoky voice, and it cuts smoothly through the noise and the gray Havana sky. And I know I will miss it when night falls and I say good-bye to her for the last time.

When we turn up the Royal Causeway, I open my eyes. Familiar sights seem to be pulling us forward, toward La Plaza de Marianao, and when I see it, blue and white over the horizon, it is like the lighthouse at the mouth of my home port.

"*Muchacho*, what happened to you? Did the bedsheets stick to you? Mario has already called me twice wondering where you were," Alina says as we hug at her door, the cab waiting, and her voice and her tone are just as if I've walked into an aunt's house back home.

My father's cousin here, Mario, won the sweepstakes over who would cook dinner for me on my last visit to Marianao. Alina's house is too small, he told her. Rosita's house, too loaded with politics, I said. But his, we decided, was just right. It was up to me to pick them both up and take them to his house for lunch.

Sorry, 'perdóname,' Alina. This rain, it just wouldn't let up.

"That's what I told him, to calm down, that the storms probably delayed you," she says, still holding my hand, patting it to assure me she defended me adequately. Her nails are impeccably manicured for the event, painted a shimmering rose with white tips. Her short, golden brown hair is neatly combed. She is wearing her special earrings, the gold studs my uncle sent her, and the gold band on her ring finger that I do not ask her to explain.

We make quite the pair, I, dressed as best I could for the event in my honor, in a black polo and khaki slacks, and she in a black-and-gray striped shirt with a Mickey Mouse embroidered in the center. As the cab waits out front, I call Rosita to tell her we are on our way.

"Oh, you're at Alina's house again, Carlos. *Mira*, I'm going to start to get jealous. Every time you come to Marianao, you go see her first," she says in a soft, paced voice, and I can almost see her standing with her hands on her hips. "Well, come on over, I'm eager to see you again so I can know that our first visit wasn't all a dream."

Her wit and her tone make me smile, and I wonder if it was that personality the uncles prized when they hired her. She wins you over, in a second and for a lifetime. And I realize how important it is for them to stay in touch with her. She is their lasting link to this place, to a time when they were young and on top of the world, and when she visits, she brings with her the memories of their youth. It hurts me to imagine what my uncles will think when

I tell them what I now know about her, about the man she married, about the path they've chosen.

Rosita is waiting outside when we arrive. I tell the driver to keep the car running. I step out, and she approaches me with arms open, clip-clopping in her small heels, dressed in a silky, sleeveless, polyester pink blouse, newer looking slacks, and her blond hair perfectly coiffed. She hugs me and pats me on the back quickly. It's then that I see him.

Behind her, a man stands expressionless. He is short, about her size, and bald with a severe countenance: a long, pointed nose and deep-set eyes that give him the look of a small hawk. As I hug Rosita, he looks at me the way boxers stare at each other when they enter the ring. Unaffected by their opponents. Unflinching. Rosita introduces me to her husband, Raúl.

"*Mucho gusto,*" I manage to say. I reach out to shake his hand, and as if surprised, he quickly offers his.

"*Hola. Sí, mucho gusto,*" he says and forces his lips into a grin.

We match glances and fall silent. I look from his face to the floor to the black-and-white sign on the glass door that I missed during my first visit: *Comité de Defensa de la Revolución.* The pleasantries end there.

"*Bueno,* we should get going. I know Mario is waiting for us," Rosita says.

"We won't be too late," she says to her husband.

I nod good-bye to Raúl—*Hasta luego*—and hope that *luego* never comes.

The rain has stopped, and a painted blue sky with vanilla clouds replaces the gray. The air is thick as the ground begins to warm and steam the pooled water. Our cab takes familiar turns, slowing to avoid water-filled potholes along the way. We pass the Royal Causeway, La Plaza, Alina's house. Rosita sits up front, Alina next to me in the back, her hand on my knee as they ask me about my visit with my mother's family and my time in Cuba, of which only one full day remains.

We follow the route that would take us to the house my father lived in as a young man until the driver stops where Alina tells him. She leads us between a pair of peach-colored houses with fencing on either side as if we are headed toward the yard at a prison. The long house to our left appears to have been divided in two, and Alina stops at a door in the back and knocks.

"Mario, it's Alina! *Oye*, we made it at last," she says.

A slender, caramel-skinned woman who looks to be in her late thirties opens the door, and she and Alina hug immediately.

"*Mi niña*, how are you?" Alina says, hugging Mario's younger daughter, Lucía, as we step inside to find we are the last of our small party to arrive.

"At last, at last!" says a slender man who looks to be in his late fifties with Lucía's complexion, his short, wavy hair a nest of salt and pepper. He walks with measured paces out of the kitchen, wiping his hands with a towel.

"I was starting to think I was going to have to eat all this food myself," he says, winking at me.

"*Ay*, Mario, leave the boy alone. It was the storms, just like I told you," Alina says, leading me by the arm as I come to meet my father's first cousin.

The famous cousin Mario. 'Papi' always talks about you.

"Am I *famoso* over there?" Mario says as he shakes my hand firmly, then pulls me in for a hug. His body, his arms feel thin, bony, as I pat him on the back. "If I'm famous, it's because of your *Papá*. He has never forgotten about me."

Mario introduces me to his other daughter, Lídia, who looks like a copy of his younger daughter, and his wife, María, a heavy-set woman with vitiligo. The seven of us squeeze into the small living room that adjoins the even smaller kitchen. A round table that looks too small for all of us has been set up in the middle of the room for our feast. Lídia props open the door and turns on a fan to circulate the vapor-thick air that makes us sweat instantly.

"Carlos, did you lose electricity at your hotel?" Mario asks in his raspy voice. "Well, we did here. It happens when the big storms come through. It happens so often we don't say we have blackouts, *apagones*, we have light ups, *alumbrones*.

"Well, *mira*, I've been working on these tamales too hard to keep them waiting any longer. Why don't the three of you sit down, and I'll serve you myself," he says.

He and his family waited as long as they could for us, he says, before they went ahead and had lunch. I know I should have been here sooner. And I might have if not for the storm outside as well as the one within. But Mario's good spirits and the scent of steamed white rice and seasoned meat say all is forgiven. It is well past two, and just the suggestion of food makes my stomach moan.

Mario brings out a plate piled high with tamales, cornmeal cakes with pork in the center, wrapped in corn-husk leaves and boiled until they are hot, al dente packages of delight. He took the day off work to spend the morning making the tamales. He plunks down two on my plate, way more than I think I can eat, heaps on a couple spoonfuls of rice, and covers those with thick, soupy black beans. The *tamal* is perfectly cooked, tender without being mushy, and the pork in the center—which he bought from La Plaza—is savory in all the right ways. Between bites, the three of us shower Mario with equal parts of the praise his tamales are showing our stomachs.

"And I have one more surprise," he says, walking slowly to the kitchen and returning with an icy beer, a Cuban-made pilsner in a red can. He cracks it open for me, and I ask for a glass to share with Alina.

We sit in a semicircle facing the others so we can eat while Mario tells us about his days, his life. He has a license to sell jewelry at a little stand near La Plaza. He does a little better than break even—he must pay the same license fee whether he sells a lot or a little—but at least it's a job out of the hot sun, a job he can do without taxing his health. He has had to take more and more time off. When I ask him how he's feeling, he says he's had problems with his stomach. He's been to several doctors, but the discomfort continues. He shows me a packet of medication he keeps in the refrigerator and says it's very good but very expensive. Still, he has some contacts through the black market where he can buy sample amounts. Actually, it was one of his doctors who told him the medicine wasn't available for Cubans. The doctor gave him the prescription and the name of an underground contact who could sell it to him. For all his over-the-counter needs, he sends letters to my father.

"Your *Papá* sends me everything I ask him for. This is the best stuff," he says, patting a bottle of Pepto-Bismol. He shows me bottles of Tylenol and says it, too, helps him when the pain in his abdomen flares up. "He has been a saint for me and my family."

A young man who looks to be in his late twenties, early thirties, comes through the door. He nods hello, and I can tell from his slurred speech as he talks with his sister, his slack mouth and vacant look, that he has some sort of mental disorder. Lucía walks him through the kitchen into a room in the back.

That's your son, Mario?

"How did you know *that* was my son?" he asks, perhaps to see whether my answer will match what he expects me to say.

Growing up, I remember my father sending off packages wrapped in brown paper to this maternal cousin in Cuba, who had "a son with mental problems." I had never asked what condition his son had or what medication my father sent. But my father was dutiful to his cousin, whom he has known since they were boys. I can tell immediately from Mario's reaction that he has had to defend his son from public taunts, and I quickly try to reassure him.

'Papi' mentions you a lot, and I've heard him mention in the past that you have a son. So, I just assumed.

"*Sí*, that's *mi niño*, my little boy. He lives here, with us. He's a good boy, *un buen muchacho*," Mario says, smiling, adding nothing more.

The tamales begin to swell in my belly, and Rosita, Alina, and I can't say enough to Mario about his prowess with pork and cornmeal. Lídia picks up the plates and heads to the kitchen to put on some coffee. Now I understand why my father says no meal is complete without *un cafecito*, the "degreaser" for your insides. And I find I have come to rely on its sweet, aromatic nectar to complete my meals as well as my sense of well-being.

"*Bueno*, Carlos, tell me: Did you meet Ricardo?" Alina asks, as we all sit with our coffee cups.

'*Sí,*' *can you believe we were in Cárdenas at the same time?*

"Do you mean Ramón's son?" Mario asks.

"*Ay,* Carlos, tell me what he said," Rosita says.

The room leans in, and I can tell they all know how the story left off when my uncle departed for the United States in the 1960s. Now, they want to know how the story ends. I tell them about our meeting in Cárdenas, the way Ricardo's eyes filled with tears as we sat in Tomás and Elena's house. About our meeting at Varadero the next day, meeting his son, Julio. How Ricardo reacted when he found out he has brothers, that he's one of fifteen cousins. That his father told my wife I should find him.

"Carlos, can you imagine what that meant to him?" Alina says. "He must have been so happy."

They discuss between them how much Ricardo looks like my uncle, and I can only agree after our meeting. He is as I would picture my uncle in his forties. But he also has an air of our grandmother Teresa, I say, and I think Ricardo would be stunned himself if he ever saw a photo of her. This is not the end to our relationship, I tell them. Only the beginning.

"It's just that all these Frías men were fire, *candela,*" Alina says, and I know she is heading back down a well-traveled path. She returns to the stories of the innumerable women my father and uncles dated, and Rosita, watching them every day at the cafés, stands as witness to their actions. She, herself, before marrying Raúl, was engaged, even had her dress purchased and the ballroom selected when she found out her fiancé had been unfaithful. She broke things off, as much as it pained her, and never gave him a chance to work his way back into her heart.

The room falls silent when Alina turns to me, crosses her arms, and puts one hand under her chin.

"Carlos, you never had a little indiscretion with your wife, *un tarrito?* Tell me the truth."

I am silent for a moment, surprised.

No, Alina. I would never do anything like that to her.

"Carlos, you don't even believe that yourself," she says, crossing her arms in the other direction.

I have come to realize that these affairs are a matter of routine here, in the past and in the present. Several of the men I've met have surprised me with confessions that they have been unfaithful. In some ways, it's no different than back home, except these affairs seem to carry no gravitas. If anything, the wives, not the husbands, carry the guilt of the act. For the men, it is embarrassing as a bad habit, not as a cardinal betrayal.

I try to explain that, in my mind, being unfaithful to your wife is a symbol of weakness and disrespect, a mark on your character. They all nod as I explain my personal beliefs, puritanical or idealistic as they may be, but they are mine. If this journey has done nothing else, it has solidified my beliefs, especially after meeting Ricardo, feeling the flesh and blood of someone not affected but *shaped* by a broken home.

"Well, at least I know *I* never had to worry about that," says Mario's wife, María, after a long silence, fanning the sweat that beads on her forehead.

"This one," she says, pointing a thumb at Mario without looking at him, "was too ugly for any other women to want him."

Her phone rings and rings with no answer.

Over the course of the afternoon, I try calling Ricardo's daughter with no success. Even as I sit at Mario's house, laughing and joking and unearthing the history of my family, the falling sun seems to be ticking. My mind wanders from their conversations to Ricardo. I remember looking into his eyes, full with emotion, and promising him I would see his daughter, Magaly, before I left Cuba. But the sun slips lower, and so does my chance to make good on that pledge. Finally, a young man picks up the phone at the house of Magaly's boyfriend. He says she stepped out, but he takes a message, and I give him my cell number. Hours pass, but my phone never rings.

"Nothing yet?" Alina asks as I come back inside after another fruitless call.

I promised him.

Alina pats my hand.

I wonder if Magaly is holding the number in her hands, tracing my name and the digits, debating whether she can make this call. This call to a stranger. To a stranger who is family. To the stranger who is her father's only link to the family he does not know. Will she want to meet this Cuban cousin who is not Cuban?

We begin having to squint at each other as the day turns to dusk, and Lucía turns on the fluorescent light in the kitchen. It is getting late, and Rosita should be getting home, she says. Alina calls friends of hers who have a car to see if they can pick us up and take us all home. While we are having our last cup of coffee, my phone begins to ring. All conversation stops, and everyone turns to me.

Magaly's voice is sweet but proper. And my excited rambling about meeting her father, my voice escalating in pitch from my nerves, only serves to accentuate her flawless diction and calm demeanor. When he told me that she was in her early twenties—and, moreover, that she had stayed at her boyfriend's instead of joining the family for their vacation—I expected a disinterested youth with her own priorities. But in her carefully chosen words, I know she, too, feels the tension of first contact. She is like me, a generation removed from the decisions of her forefathers. She is like me, a nervous kid meeting a ghost.

She says that, yes, she would like very much for us to meet and gives me directions to the house. Alina says she has been there before, and it's a very short drive, and Rosita adds that it is very close to her house. When we hang up, I find I am even more nervous about meeting Magaly than I was about meeting Ricardo.

"Carlos, why don't you let us go with you?" Alina says.

"*Ay, sí,* Carlos, we should all go together," Rosita adds. "It would be good for us to get to know her because we can stay in touch with them and tell them more about *los Frías.*"

Three chirps from a car horn tell us Alina's friends have arrived. I hug and kiss Mario's daughters, his wife. When I come to Mario,

I help him get up from his chair. But on his feet, he is a much stronger man, and he claps me a strong hug.

The famous cousin Mario. His family is leaving again. And again, he is staying behind.

"I hope you liked the meal," he says.

Mario, you are truly a chef.

"Tell Fernando that it gave me such pleasure to meet his son," he says. "Tell him that we can never forget everything he has done for me and my family. And that I didn't let you leave without filling your belly to say *gracias*."

Alina, Rosita, and I walk the narrow path between the caged houses to find a faded red Lada parked out front, a man and a woman sitting up front. The driver, a man, steps out of the car, kisses Alina on the cheek, and opens the rear doors for us. Nelson and Antonia were running errands in this part of town, Alina says, but they live near central Havana. So after they drop everyone off, they can take me back to the hotel. As we sit tight in the back and the Lada zips ahead through the darkened streets, Alina tells me that Nelson is a nurse and his wife, Antonia, a doctor. When they aren't working, they use their car as a taxi—illegally, of course—to take in a little money on the side so they can make ends meet. They both have been dispatched overseas, they say, as we turn up the Royal Causeway, and that earned them the right to buy this car when they returned.

"This was the biggest reason why we decided to take the assignment," Antonia says. "With a car, things can get a little easier."

We head in the general direction of Rosita's house, and in the moments we are quiet, I can feel my pulse begin to quicken. Although it is still warm and humid from the afternoon rains, my hands are cold and clammy.

Antonia guides Nelson with prompts from the directions I wrote down, and we turn onto a wide street with a statue in the median. Nelson inches the car along, looking at house numbers through his open window under pale lights, and the breeze in my face settles my stomach. He stops suddenly at a path between houses, and Alina says it is right through there. Although I don't know how long we will stay, Nelson and Antonia say they will wait in the car.

I help Alina and Rosita out, and each of them puts a hand around one of my arms. We walk together, between the buildings, to a set of one-story apartments. Yellowish green fluorescent lights peek through the bars on the windows of different apartments as we walk past. Alina stops in front of a door with iron bars and the interior door left open for the breeze. I look at her, swallow, and knock on the edge of the gate.

'Hola, buenas noches.'

Fluorescent lights flicker in the back room, and I hear shuffling shoes before a face appears behind the iron bars.

Magaly?

The room is dark, and it's only after she unlocks the door and light falls on her face that I get my first good look at my cousin.

"*Pasen, pasen.* Please come in," she says, stepping back into the small room to let us through. She is petite, about five foot three, and because her jet-black hair is pulled into a bun, it accentuates the round, sweet, smiling face that seems borrowed from her mother. Her eyebrows are manicured, arched. She is wearing a pink, strappy cotton dress with blue and green flowers, her lips painted a subtle rose. She, too, has dressed up for our meeting.

I hug her immediately, and she hugs me back but with apprehension. And I can feel in our embrace that she does not know what should happen next. I hold her hands and pull back to see her. She studies my face, and I know what Ricardo must have felt as I searched him for clues just a few days ago. She needs to hear it, I know. And I need to say it, simply.

I'm Carlos. I swallow hard. *I'm your cousin.*

Her eyes burst with tears. She wipes them away, but more flow. She hugs me again, and Rosita and Alina both put their hands on our backs as the four of us succumb to the emotion that keeps us silent but for our sobs. For what feels like several minutes, we cannot speak, only hold one another. When we manage to sit down, we all sit close. Magaly and I continue looking into each other's face, laughing, crying. And I know this is a moment she thought would never come.

"His father's family, it has been such a phantom in his life," she says finally, still wiping her cheeks.

After Ricardo and I met in Cárdenas, he called her and couldn't stop talking about our meeting. Her brother, Julio, did the same the following day. Ricardo could hear the pain in her voice at missing the opportunity. She tells us she wished she could have gone with her family to visit the uncles and aunts she grew up with in Matanzas. But she had to stay behind because of school. She is studying accounting and had to prepare for exams.

"All we've ever wanted is to know. To know more," she says, her eyes an endless fountain of emotion. "And now, because of you, we do."

Rosita, Alina, and I all sprinkle her with stories, careful not to overwhelm her, careful not to touch wounds that are too raw. I feel immediately protective of her, like she is my lost little sister. She is not like the young girls I see around Cuba, babies pushing babies in strollers. She and her brother, both young but full of ambition and determination, give me hope, hope for my family, hope for this country, hope for whatever happens next.

I give her any details she asks for and show her pictures of my wife and daughters, and she oohs and aahs at how beautiful the girls are and finds the similarities to their parents. All the anger that could have flowed, all the resentment and disappointment that could have spilled, never did. Not from Ricardo, not from Julio, not from Magaly.

Yes, these are the forgotten ones. But whatever happened between my Tío Ramón and this girl's grandmother, whatever the circumstances, is someone else's lifetime, someone else's decisions. The boy left behind—the boy who is almost fifty—with half a family and only half the story decided long ago that his children would be full and complete. Whatever their truth, I know that Ricardo has not passed the baggage of his parents on to his children. Magaly and Julio are born free.

"You don't know how happy you've made him," Magaly says. "All his life, we would ask him about his father's family, and he never knew what to tell us. And yet, he was never bitter, never an angry person. He has always been a good father and worked hard to give us a good life. We are a little family, but we love each other a lot, *mucho, mucho.*"

Rosita asks if she has ever seen a picture of her grandfather. Magaly shakes her head, and Rosita promises she will bring one over. She thinks she has a picture of him from his youth but is certain she has a recent one from her trips to the United States.

"I can always get another one, but I think you and your father should have that picture," she says.

Still wiping her eyes, Magaly stands up, clears her throat, and says, "Well, let's see. Who wants coffee?" She rushes off to the kitchen, and in a few minutes, I can hear the gurgle and hiss of the espresso maker followed by that intoxicating scent. Once again, the coffee is therapy. It's the only thing Cubans have that they can offer so freely.

Plus, I think it calms her to make it as much as it soothes me to drink it.

Alina and I sit quietly in the backseat of the Lada as it pulls away from Rosita's house.

"What's that?" Alina says, watching me handle a scrap of paper.

Rosita's daughter. I wave the paper. *She gave me her number in case I want to call her when I get back to Miami.*

As I tuck it into my pocket, I immediately decide I will. I need to know why she did it, why, after seeing what happened to my family firsthand, Rosita decided she could live as the wife of a dyed-in-the-wool communist. Her daughter may not have all the answers. But I need to ask. I need to try to understand.

Nelson turns the Lada down the back street where La Plaza de Marianao stands as a dark, silent sentry. I feel Alina's hand on mine as we approach her house, until we are stopped and all that remains is what remains: Good-bye.

The car keeps running as I open the door, help Alina out, and walk with her, arm in arm, to her front door. I wait for her to unlock the iron bars with the key that hangs around her neck, open her door, and turn on the incandescent bulb of the patio, which lights her face in natural tones.

I kiss her on the cheek, and when we hug, she holds on, holds on as if to make the moment last just a little longer. She puts her tiny hands in mine and breathes hard.

"Don't forget about us," she pleads in a whisper.

She is beginning to cry.

"Don't forget about us."

She holds my hands tighter.

I won't forget, I start to say.

We are both crying now, crying on her doorstep. It is 1969, and she is saying good-bye all over again.

I ride off in the Lada, and she is waving with one hand, covering her mouth with the other. The car turns, she is there, and then she is gone. It turns again. La Plaza is there, and then it is gone. The Gran Teatro across the street. The Royal Causeway. Alina, standing on her porch, waving good-bye. They are all there, and then they are gone. Gone for good. Gone forever.

As his car took these very turns thirty-seven years ago, did my father consider he might never see this place again before he died? I wonder if I will. Or maybe this is all that remains.

The images.

The memories.

The good-byes.

My eyes stay full all the way back to the hotel, and I am not much conversation for Alina's friends. I can think only of her. I wonder if my cousin Felipe will be upset somehow that I have gotten so close to a woman who is still very much in love with his father. Who wears the earrings he sent her. A gold band on her ring finger. And carries a memory of him that time has not corrupted.

I decide he would like her anyway. You can't help it. She is the historian for our family here, the lighthouse beacon that has helped me find my way. And who will, one day, I hope, help all my family find their way back home.

I won't forget you, Alina.

DAY ELEVEN

Breathe and move.
Do not stop.
Do not think.
Breathe and move.

I finish my final assignment for the newspaper and put it away in my mind. And just as quickly, I turn to one last task. It is good. It is necessary. And it keeps me from sinking beneath the knowledge that today is all that remains.

As the cab moves through the city, I cannot deny that my eyes, for better or worse, have grown accustomed to this place.

For a time, we drive a road I know leads to Marianao. That street, there, with the statue of the horse that my cousin Jorge used to climb as a boy, leads to the apartment where my mother used to live. In less than two weeks, the scenery has gone from foreign to familiar. Only when we turn down a new road does it all douse me again in a wave that is so determined to drown me.

It's then I notice the misshapen trees lining the streets, the old American jalopies sputtering blackness, the collage of cracks and flaking paint on every building, the covered military trucks shuttling olive-clad soldiers to points beyond, the rivulets of sewage that creep down the sides of the road, children climbing piles of concrete rubble where a building used to be, the boy wearing only shorts, sleeping on a square of cardboard on the stoop of a shuttered building, the babies in Lycra pushing babies in diapers.

It is always there, like the carcass of an animal lying beside a road you drive every day, decaying, disintegrating ever so slightly with each sunset, until one morning, you don't even notice when it has ground into oblivion.

I don't know how much more I can absorb. I think I just want to go home.

One more visit.

One more errand.

And then I can hide. I can go to my hotel, close my eyes, and await my final sunrise in Cuba.

In a park across from a pair of high-rises, I call Maria Laura again.

As happened this morning, a woman answers the phone and asks me to hold. The line seems to go dead for several seconds, and then Maria Laura picks up.

"Carlos, where are you now?" she says.

Here, across the street, in the park. Blue shirt, beige pants.

I step out from under the shade of a tree so she can see me from her balcony.

"Carlos!"

The voice comes from the phone and the sky. I look up and see a woman in a red top reaching over a railing to wave, a brown ponytail wagging behind her. I wave back. She says she's on the ninth floor, but the elevators, unfortunately, haven't been working for months. So I climb the tight, marble staircase, dingy beneath layers of grime, resting on the fifth floor before making it all the way to the top. At the end of the hall, behind a locked gate of iron bars, a draft that cools the sweat on my neck blows through the open door. Maria Laura unlocks the gate and hugs me with a few quick pats on the back, letting me inside.

The apartment seems well-maintained, with off-white walls that look to have been painted in the last few years, and the gray-and-white diamond-patterned terrazzo floor swept and mopped. We walk beyond a glass-topped dining room table with six chairs into a comfortable living room with a couch and an oversize chair.

"What a surprise it was to hear my cousin Ileana's name," Maria Laura says. "Now, tell me again who you're married to."

I'm married to Ileana's daughter, Christy. Ah, and that reminds me . . .

I reach into my wallet and hand her money my mother-in-law asked me to drop off for Maria Laura, and another sum that should go to their family in the country. She has a trip planned there next week, Maria Laura says, and will take it then.

"I can't believe my cousin has a daughter who's married—oh, she has *three* children, just like me! I can't tell you how much I've missed her over the years. How time passes . . ." she says, shaking her head, resting her face in her hand. "I think so much about her."

This apartment, Maria Laura says, used to belong to my wife's grandmother, Estela. I say "used to," but Maria Laura speaks as if it still does. Estela purchased it when it was built in the 1950s with a loan from the U.S. Federal Housing Authority, underscoring how close these countries used to be. When Estela and her family left, in 1961, Maria Laura's family remained here.

"We've taken good care of it for her," she says, remembering how she and her husband painted the walls a few years back when Maria Laura's godmother, who also lives in Miami, came to visit.

"Look, this is Estela's," she says, showing me a sculpted vase of pink glass. "I had a foreigner offer me a hundred dollars for it. But I would never sell it," she says, wiping it with a cloth. "It reminds me too much of her.

"And look at this," she says, gently putting the vase back on the center of the table and posing next to a shrine to St. Barbara. This also belonged—belongs—to Estela. Maria Laura's husband has kept it up over the years, repainting the little statue and its castlelike grotto with whatever color paints they could find, most recently red, white, and blue. It hangs by the window, where it has been for more than fifty years.

Maria Laura is younger than my mother-in-law. She says when she was a toddler, she used to curl up and fall asleep between Ileana's legs. There was always someone visiting, sharing a room in this two-bedroom, one-bath apartment. And she always found the spot next to the older cousin she idolized.

The phone rings, and Maria Laura takes a call from her children, who say they are just around the corner on their way from work. Hurry home, she tells them. She has a surprise, she says, winking at me. When she hangs up, I ask her who the woman is who answers the phone when I call. She says the phone line belongs to the upstairs neighbor. Since home phones are rare in Cuba, her husband rigged this extension, and the neighbor rings down whenever a call comes for Maria Laura's family.

"Here, we make do, *resolvemos*," she says.

I'm starting to learn . . .

The sound of footsteps blows in through the open front door, and Maria Laura jumps up to introduce me to her children.

"Look, *muchachos*, this is Carlos. He's *familia* from Miami!" she says. "He's a *primo*, a cousin!"

And just like that I'm in, inducted with a word, in a moment and forever.

When I see her daughter, Normita, I'm sure my mouth hangs open for a few seconds. She is the image of my wife's grandmother, from the fair skin and blue-green eyes to the waves of golden blond hair. She is petite, with slender arms, and looks even thinner in a tank top with a flowery pink design and tight, flared-leg jeans. If her mother hadn't told me she was in her twenties, I would have guessed she had just celebrated her *Quinces*.

Wow, the Spanish genes are strong in this family!

"Hola," she pants, giving me a peck on the cheek before crashing on the couch, her eyes half-closed, breathing heavily, her arms limp at her sides. She holds up a hand as if to say, "Give me a minute," and it takes longer than that before she can look at me again. Maria Laura speaks for her. She says Normita has asthma, and when the air is thick with pollution in the summer, it gets worse.

Enrique is Normita's twin in constitution if not coloration. Her brother is wiry, and his chiseled features are highlighted by spiky black hair against caramel skin. He wears his goatee cropped and his sideburns long, like an American kid, and from the red cutoff T-shirt with the Yankees logo covering his entire chest, you'd guess he's from the Bronx.

"How are jou?" he says in accented English, laughing.

"And this is my 'adopted' son," Maria Laura says, rubbing Normita's longtime boyfriend, Ismael, on the belly, and he hugs her back, smiling. When we shake hands, we are at eye level. He is taller than all of them, older, in his late twenties, his receding hair trimmed into a neat buzz cut and his goatee short like Enrique's.

"*Oye*, how is the programming going?" Ismael asks Enrique.

"It's almost done. I should be finished today," he answers.

What do you mean, 'programming'?

"Go, go, show him," Maria Laura says.

"These *muchachos* are brains, *cerebros*, with anything that has to do with technology," Maria Laura says. "Go, show him. I'll start working on dinner."

She takes two steps, then stops and turns back to me. "Carlos, you are staying for dinner, aren't you? You have to stay. I'm going to make my special fried rice for you."

"It's her specialty," Normita adds quickly, her breath returned to her. "Mmm, I could eat my *Mamá*'s fried rice every day."

I was planning on just leaving the money and getting back to the hotel so I could pack for my 8:00 A.M. flight. But I've stumbled on an unopened treasure chest that belongs to my wife. I can't resist looking inside and, maybe, bringing her back a few precious jewels.

You hit me where it hurts, Maria Laura. I love fried rice.

"Good. You kids take him to the room, and I'll start dinner," she says.

"Follow me, *primo*," Enrique says and leads me through the balcony to one of the two bedrooms.

Metal venetian blinds are drawn over the one window, which has been patched around the edges with concrete. But the late afternoon sun shines directly through the open door to light the room where Maria Laura's three grown children sleep. Two of the three twin beds are made up with cartoon sheets, one pink with bears riding a hot-air balloon, another blue with puppies chasing a ball. It might be like any other kids' bedroom in Cuba, if not for the pair of brand-new Dell computers at one end of the room.

On a desk against a wall is a black desktop, a seventeen-inch flat-screen monitor connected to a pair of CPUs. Next to it, on a smaller desk, a new-looking laptop with the screen open flashes pictures of Ismael and Normita as its screen saver. The computers are newer than any of the terminals at the Internet cafés set up for tourists or in post offices for local Cubans. They look like they have just been purchased from a U.S. retailer.

What is all this?

"This is our escape," Ismael says, sitting down at the laptop, Enrique at the desktop.

All of this, Enrique explains, is courtesy of his and Ismael's jobs. They both work for the government in Cuba's technology sector and are able to legally have this equipment. Encouraged to have it, he says, so they can work on projects from home. But the biggest benefit, Enrique says, is unrestricted access to the world. The real world. They connect to the Internet through a method the government has not approved for the general public, specifically because they have not found a way to restrict access.

The four of us huddle around the computer as Enrique connects. Automatically, the computer signs in to an instant-messaging program. Immediately, two dozen "friends" come up on his screen. Within a few seconds, a little *pop!* sounds when someone sends him a message. It is a girl—most of the friends on his messenger are. They type back and forth, sending each other messages in real time. She lives in Panama, Enrique says, and they have been messaging and e-mailing for months. With this method, he meets people his age all over the world, kids, just like him, who tell him what life is really like off the island. They even have a Webcam, he says, so they can see each other while they chat.

"That's my girlfriend," Enrique says with a sideways grin after sending her another line.

"That girl is crazy, *está loca*," Normita says. "Do you know she actually proposed to him online?"

Enrique opens a file on his desktop and pulls up several pictures of the girl, a cute blonde who is nineteen.

"She wants me to go visit her in Panama. I'm thinking about it," he says.

Enrique, you have to be careful, man. You don't know who's really on the other side of that connection.

He chats with her for a few minutes and tells her he'll be back later because his cousin from Miami is here. Long story. He'll tell her all about it. He scoots his chair over and lets me surf. We huddle behind the monitor, and we are off. We view CNN, *The Palm Beach Post*, even *The Miami Herald*, one of many sites blocked at the Internet cafés.

I navigate my way to a Web site where my wife has pictures posted and introduce them, for the first time, to their cousins in the United States: Christy and our two girls. The connection is slow, deliberate, but delicious.

"*Mami*, come see this!" Normita yells, and Maria Laura hurries from the kitchen, wiping her hands. She sits at the edge of the bed closest to the computer, next to Normita, as I take them through our pictures, our memories. Birthdays. Trips to Disney World. Family get-togethers. They gasp when they see a picture of my older daughter, Elise, with her blue eyes, light hair, and fair skin.

"Normita, that could be your daughter," Maria Laura says.

In one picture, Elise is pouting. Here, she's laughing hysterically. In most pictures, Amelia has that shy, distrustful expression that makes her look cherubic and positively edible. And Christy is hugging them, kissing them, and you can feel it even sitting here. How I miss all my girls.

I show them pictures of my mother-in-law, Ileana, with my wife.

"*Dios*, is that my cousin?" Maria Laura says, moving closer to the screen. "But they look like twins. I can't believe how young my *prima* looks! *Oye*, she really takes care of herself, *se conserva*."

While we browse through pictures, Enrique and Ismael are looking at a pair of files on the laptop. Enrique explains he is writing software for a guy running an underground Internet café from his house. Enrique charged him twenty Convertibles for the work, then found out that the guy planned to put the program onto four computers.

"If I had known that, I could have charged him more. A licensing fee, right?" he says.

*Right. That's very . . . capitalistic of you. Your Mamá is right. You two
are brains.*

"*Resolvemos,*" Enrique says, winking.

Ismael shows me a hard drive full of downloaded contraband
while Maria Laura and Normita scan through more online photo
albums. There is music: Green Day, Metallica, Coldplay. There
are movies: *Shrek, The Lost City,* Andy Garcia's recent documentary
about the torments of Castro's revolution. Television shows: *Lost* and
House—"Those two are my favorites," Ismael says. He follows the
shows, and watching them only helps him better his English. He
opens a photo-editing program and shows me pictures of Paris from
a trip he took there with two other technology students as part of a
government-sponsored training. In one photo, he has superimposed
himself and Normita standing on the top floor of the Eiffel Tower.

"It looks just like we were there, doesn't it?" she says.

"One day," Ismael says, pulling her close.

In another photo-editing feat, he has perfectly placed Normita's
face on Britney Spears' body.

"Normita Spears. Didn't you know? We're cousins," she jokes.

The outside world slips in. And as I look at my new, young cousins reaching out from beyond this bedroom, where the wooden
windows have rotted and fallen out, in a high-rise building where
the elevator doesn't run, in a country where phone service is a
privilege, I see their eyes alive with a light from within. They still
believe in hope and possibility.

I have to call Christy.

The cousins turn to me.

She has to meet you. All of you.

The cell phone nearly slips from my clammy hands as I dial my
wife. We speak hurriedly, conscious of the quickly elapsing minutes, wary of being cut off in midsentence.

*My love, you're not going to believe this! I'm surfing the Internet. Chatting
online. In Cuba. With your cousins!*

She tells me she is at my mother-in-law's house right now, and
I tell her to get online from their computer and download the program so we can chat.

"Mom wants to know if you've seen Maria Laura," she says, quickly.

She's here.

I look at my mother-in-law's baby cousin.

Maria Laura's sitting right next to me.

"*Lind*, this is so exciting!"

A chirp on my phone tells me it will cut off in sixty seconds, and we rush our good-bye.

Enrique sends a message to a friend of his—another girl—who lives in Miami, and she calls my wife out of the blue: "Hi, you don't know me, but I'm friends with one of your cousins from Cuba. If you get online, your husband would like to chat with you." She talks my wife through the process, and in less than thirty minutes, we hear our first *pop!*

Hey, you made it! I type.

"At last. I'm here with Mom," she responds.

We type and enter, and the words immediately splash, back and forth, hers in red, mine in blue, on a little window in one corner of the screen. We sit as translators, Christy typing for my mother-in-law, I for Maria Laura and the cousins.

"*Primo*, let's hook up the Webcam!" Enrique says. We won't be able to see them because they don't have a camera. But Ileana can see the home she left behind forty-four years ago, and Christy will see cousins she never even imagined.

Enrique adjusts the camera so that I am captured within a separate little window on our computer screen, typing away, cartoon-covered beds in the background, the same image my wife can see.

He carries the Webcam to the balcony, stretching the cord as far as it will go, and swivels the little camera slowly so that Ileana can see the actual moving picture of Havana, cars motoring by, children playing baseball in the park as the last bits of light fall on the street where she grew up.

He turns it back and slowly moves it around the room where Ileana slept. There I am at the keyboard. There is Maria Laura, and she waves frantically, blowing kisses to the camera. There are Normita and Ismael, and they are all waving.

My wife is meeting her cousins for the first time. And Ileana is back in her bedroom in Cuba for the first time since she was nine.

As the camera zooms past the closet door, Maria Laura mentions there used to be cartoons painted there.

At the same moment, a little *pop!* comes from the computer.

"Mom says there used to be a Mickey Mouse painted on that door," reads the message my wife has typed.

Wow, this is amazing.

We are in Cuba. But we are not in Cuba.

Maria Laura runs to the other room and returns a few minutes later with a handful of black-and-white photos. I prop them up in front of the camera. My mother-in-law is seeing pictures of the aunt who helped raise her and Maria Laura. She died in Cuba, and Ileana never saw her again.

"Mom is crying," my wife types.

I turn around to see Normita's arm around her mother as Maria Laura caresses the picture.

"So is Maria Laura," I respond.

For more than an hour, we type for our family, transcribing everything from Normita's resemblance to my wife's grandmother to catching Ileana and Maria Laura up on the family. At times, Maria Laura types directly to her cousin. At others, Normita to my wife. Christy and I get a crash course in typing Spanish—pressing Alt 1-6-4 yields an ñ, by the way—and we bridge the gap of nearly five decades and the ubiquitous ninety miles.

Maria Laura, popping in and out of the kitchen, comes in to say dinner is ready. We leave the program running and promise to meet again after supper.

The glass-topped dining room table is covered by a white tablecloth with pink stripes, and on it, Maria Laura has served a feast: Two enormous bowls of fried rice with chicken and pork—no beef, of course—a dish that was passed down from my wife's Chinese-Cuban grandfather to Maria Laura's father to her. The steam rises into our nostrils with savory delight. She has bought beer and soft drinks and made fresh *tostones* to go with a deep bowl of garlic-and-lime-marinated yucca.

The table is packed with food in a way I have not seen in my days here, and I remember my Tía Sofía sorting black beans on a table that has never seen, nor could ever hold, this much food.

This is why people from all over the island try to find ways to move into Havana, illegally if necessary, since the government has placed a moratorium on relocating to the city. Here, they are not forgotten. They share their crowded city with diplomats and tourists and a handful of foreign journalists, and because of that, the locals have access to food and a level of services they can only dream of in other parts of Cuba. Here, young people like Ismael and Enrique can find government jobs, Ismael making about 500 pesos a month, more than the average doctor. And even though there are five people living in this two-bedroom apartment in a dilapidated high-rise, they all pull in one direction and help lift one another up to a better way of life.

It's then that Maria Laura's oldest, Pablo, finally arrives home with her husband, Raciel. Maria Laura pop-kisses her husband on the lips and gives Pablo a squeeze and a peck on the cheek. Pablo is thin, like his siblings, but age wears on him, deep lines down his cheeks and crow's-feet sprawling from the corners of his eyes, making him look much older than his late twenties. Raciel is ruddy with salt-and-pepper hair, about as tall as his sons and a little thicker from age, but not heavy.

"Pablito, did you have any luck today?" Maria Laura asks as we all sit down to eat. They insist I sit at the head of the table, Raciel at the other end.

"No," he says, between spoonfuls of tender fried rice. "I think it's just going to be like this until things get straightened out."

He has spent the day trying to find work, he tells me, but things are especially hard since he was arrested for having a few gallons of gasoline stored in a car he was driving. The Cuban government calls that hoarding, and he spent eighteen days in prison in another province before he was allowed to meet with a lawyer or family. He is free on bond, but until his case is resolved, no one will hire him. He continues to work on the side for a mechanic.

"I almost died in those eighteen days," Maria Laura says, resting her hand on her son's arm.

They pepper me with the realities of life here, releasing a bit of frustration with each story. I lean forward as they speak, so they will not have to raise their voices. The walls here have ears, we know, and they begin to speculate about what will happen next—after Castro, who has become a phantom, unseen in nearly a month. His name continues to appear in the newspaper, but the groundhog has yet to emerge from his den.

"Here, no one knows anything," Enrique whispers.

"A lot of people think he's already dead," Raciel adds. "They're just not telling the public so they can slowly transition."

"What are they saying over there?" Ismael asks.

Just like this. Speculating. But no one knows anything, either.

"I think you guys in the U.S. will know something before any of us," Enrique says.

Tired of a topic with no answers, Normita wants to know about life in the United States. As we eat, she introduces one topic after another with the words "Let me ask you something."

"Let me ask you something . . . is it true if you go to a hospital in the United States, they'll just let you die if you don't have insurance?"

". . . is it true they'll give you money to go to school?"

". . . if I wanted to, could I be a flight attendant in the United States? I've always dreamed of that."

No, they won't let you die, I say. They'll save your life and then they'll bill you. . . . Yes, you can get scholarships and financial aid to go to college. . . . And yes, if you really want it, you can be anything you want to be. Anything.

"We hear so many stories, we don't know what to believe," Raciel says.

"So, the lion is not as fierce as they paint it, huh?" Ismael adds.

The entire family has put in for the lottery—*el bombo*, they call it—every year since 1998 for the right to emigrate to the United

States. They have been turned down every year, but they always reapply. Maria Laura tells the story of when she was set to leave through the 1980 Mariel boatlift. She had given away all her belongings, "even my underwear," she says. Ileana's brother drove his boat to the port to pick her up, but was allowed to take only one family member, and the government filled the rest of the boat with people he had never met. Maria Laura went back home with only the clothes on her back and soon started a family.

They are convinced that one day their approval will come, even though it has been nine rounds of annual heartbreak. Meanwhile, they make ends meet where they can, working, like all Cubans, in the gray market. Maria Laura works in a bakery and keeps a little bit of flour, a little bit of sugar to bake cakes on the side.

"You should see her cakes," Normita says. "They are works of art. Let me ask you something . . . do you think people would pay good money for a nice cake like that in the U.S.?"

I'm sure they would.

Her husband, Raciel, technically doesn't have a job, but he does ironwork. He replaced all the wooden windows of this apartment, which had been eaten by termites over the years, with metal ones. It's all illegal. The Cuban government will grant permits for private businesses but can arbitrarily say, "Sorry, there are too many permits already for ironwork." The government ensures its cut from everyone's wages by assigning inspectors, who have to be bribed. Even if Maria Laura's husband could get a permit for ironwork, you can't just buy supplies in a store like you would at Home Depot. The supplies must be bought illegally, and how would you explain that to the inspector?

"The system won't let you fend for yourself," Raciel says. "They make you rely on them for everything. And they *give* you nothing."

It's not exactly the kind of dinner conversation we would have in the United States. But it's the way of the world in Cuba, where rations of eleven ounces of chicken a month can't feed a hungry mouth.

With dinner just over, the cousins are already up from the table, back at the computer, signed in and typing with my wife. Pablo is a technophobe, but he smiles and waves and tells me what to write, that he wishes her all the best and hopes they can meet one day. He watches us as we type, the cousins, all of us together, tethered by an invisible electronic connection that binds us with every press of every key.

It is past eleven, and we have been online for more than an hour. I watch Normita's face in the Webcam screen, concentrating as she writes back and forth with my wife, sometimes blowing kisses, sometimes wiping her eyes, other times laughing at private jokes between her and the cousin she's only just met.

"You look tired, my *Lind*," Christy writes as I take my seat to say good-bye.

I look at the image on the screen. My face is shiny, my hair mussed, and there are dark circles under my eyes, which I am forcing open. Our cousins are sitting behind me, holding their heads up in their hands, their eyes also fighting to stay open as I type. But none of us wants to stop.

"What is she saying now?" Normita says through a yawn.

She says it's getting late.

And we all know it's true. Each of the cousins takes a turn typing good-bye to my wife, even Pablo, pecking away at the keys, "like a rooster eating kernels of corn," he jokes. But we have exchanged information, phone numbers, e-mail addresses. This is not good-bye. It is only the beginning.

And I know my wife and I have a Webcam to buy when I get home.

DAY TWELVE

A rattle and a hum. A rattle and a hum.

Ringing and flashing lights break the serenity of sleep. My cell phone vibrates off the nightstand and crashes onto the Cuban tile floor at exactly 5:00 A.M. I stare into the darkness and know that it is time. Time to go home.

The phone dances on the floor for a few seconds before I can sit up in bed. I lean over and fumble around in the dark to turn off the alarm before lying back down with it to my chest. I can feel the spot just below the phone, the place where my heart should be, buzzing with anxiety. I close my eyes, knowing that sleep won't come again, and I take deep breaths.

Count. Breathe.

One. Two. Three . . . Ten. It is beating, threatening to race again, but at least my heart is ready to do what I need it to. Steady enough for me to get up. Sturdy enough for me to leave Cuba. Maybe forever. It picks up beats again at the thought, and maybe it's too soon to let it in on the whole truth. If it is not broken, I know it is definitely not the same.

Larry King is interviewing someone I've never heard of in the background as I fold eleven days' worth of dirty clothes neatly so they will fit back into my bag. The television volume is low, and the pale yellow glow from the lamp on my nightstand is just enough to finish the work.

Only these two little eight-inch notebooks remain to pack. Blue. Cartoon characters on the covers. They are creased down the middle from being folded in half and stuffed into my back pocket. I sit on the edge of the bed, close to the lamp, and flip carefully through the crinkly and wavy pages. Some are streaked with a mixture of sweat and dust from my hands. Ink has run on other pages in places where flecks of rain or tears met the page, smearing the words ever so slightly. An asterisk here. A word underlined twice there.

The handwriting changes with my mood. On this page, my words are a messy scribble, letters floating above and below the lines as I managed to write only "CDR" and "husband the president" at Rosita's house. Here, the letters are pressed together in a hurried script, with no punctuation to speak of for page after page, a rambling stream of consciousness that erupted while I lay in bed at Tomás and Elena's house. Each page brings back a memory, a story. "I wish I could pick you up, pick you all up in my arms and carry you away from here," I wrote on the final page from my last day in Cárdenas.

These little books are filled with more than just memories and images and colors. They are crammed with facts. Names. Addresses. Telephone numbers. And in a moment, I can hear José, bellhop-cum-confidant, repeating his words after driving me to Marianao: "What you're carrying in that little notebook is *dinamita*—dynamite. That little book stays with *you*." And I know there is one more hurdle to pass. My notebooks still have to make it out of Cuba with me. And if they are confiscated, *Dios*, if they are confiscated . . . I don't know what will happen. I can always write from memory. The marks this place has left on me can never be removed. But those who have trusted me with their stories would lose their shield.

I grab a pen and begin scratching and scratching out names, frantically. I change telephone numbers, give new names to family members on the spot and hope I will remember them all. But what do I do with whole phrases of criticism, references to the cities I've visited? What to do with my mother's report cards? The rubbing of my grandfather's headstone? My solution seems so simplistic, childish, naïve. What I have cannot be camouflaged. What has been said, unmistakable. My fear for days was about getting into the country. I never considered what it might require of me to get out. Either these notes make it out with me or they cost everyone I have come in contact with more than I dare myself to imagine.

I yank my clothes out of my bag and search the edges for a place to stash my notebooks. I unzip an interior pocket to the lining of my suitcase and carefully lay the notebooks flat before closing it and piling my clothes on top. If an X-ray machine finds these, will my solution make them look even more suspicious? I can't think about it. I sit at the edge of the bed, packed, dressed. And unable to move.

I can feel a heat rising and beads of sweat gathering on my forehead. I wash my face with cold water, staring back at myself in the bathroom mirror, waiting for the answer to magically appear on my face. And then I hear the music playing from the television. Rock. I sit back on the bed and listen as Bon Jovi plays, taking Larry King's show to a close.

I went as far as I could, I tried to find a new face
There isn't one of these lines that I would erase
I lived a million miles of memories on that road . . .
Take it in. Take it with you when you go
Who says you can't go home?

I listen to the entire song and can feel my heart quiet. The band from New Jersey might as well be from Havana. I grab my bags, turn off the television, and take one last deep breath before closing the door. It's time to go home.

Orange streetlamps wash Havana in a stark contrast of light and dark as the cab zips through the city unhindered before dawn.

I sit in the back with the window open, the sights whisk by

with the wind and embed themselves in my memory. The neon lights of El Floridita are only dark outlines on the shadowy building. Faceless men unload bushels of corn at a storefront market. Craggy high-rises, pockmarked cement façades highlighted by the unearthly orange glow, lean over the road, standing guard as we pass. The cab rumbles west over the uneven streets as the high-rises become low, squat homes, giving way to dense, black countryside with the sound of jet engines blaring overhead, flashing lights disappearing in a moment against a gradually lightening sky.

Even before dawn, José Martí International Airport is buzzing. Lines are growing along ticket counters, stretching toward the wall of glass that forms the entire second story of the concourse. While I wait to pay the twenty-five-dollar exit tax, I turn to look out and over the landscape as the golden light of morning cascades across a sea of green and outlines the mirage of the city on the horizon. There, Alina is waking to the sounds of La Plaza. Ricardo is rubbing his eyes, putting his glasses on. Andrea is helping my Tía Sofía undress for her morning bath under cupfuls of lukewarm water. I go on, and they go on. And we go on without each other.

As I wait, a woman in an airline uniform approaches passengers, asking if anyone has Cuban Convertibles they want to exchange for dollars. She is holding a small wad of her own money, exchanging as she goes.

"They're worthless anywhere else," she says nonchalantly when she reaches me.

I open my wallet and remove the remaining fifty-one Convertibles. I trade her my two colorful twenties and a ten for a greenback with the picture of Ulysses S. Grant. I hold it up to the light to check for the watermark and put it into my wallet, next to a single Convertible, the president face-to-face with the crest of Cuba.

I wait in a line behind a locked door to the security screening area as an immigration agent checks our passports and buzzes us through, one every few minutes. The closer I get to that solid wooden door, the more I wonder what is on the other side. I hold on tightly to the handle of my roll-aboard and try not to think too hard about the notebooks inside, as if just imagining them will reveal their presence.

The door buzzes another person through. I am next. I walk into the cubicle and hand my passport and Cuban visa to an agent in an olive military uniform. She is older, her dark hair stark against her angular, pale face as her eyes move from the passport to me. Wordlessly, she holds up the passport and peeks out from behind to examine my face. I try to look around, to seem bored and disarmed as blood pulses through the arteries in my neck.

As a matter of routine, and without a word, the agent stamps the visa and keeps it, leaving no record in my U.S. passport of my entry into Cuba. Without looking at me further, she buzzes the door. I swallow hard and step through.

On the other side, between me and the gates to points beyond, is one conveyor belt with three guards in military uniforms shepherding bags through an X-ray machine. I try not to imagine what the notebooks will look like on a screen that I cannot see. I put my bags on the belt, and they are off, passing me and the passenger in front of me, heading to an open black mouth ahead of us. I glance every few seconds at a screener who is moving the bags back and forth under the X-ray machine, as if studying the contents of something inside.

The metal detector chirps loudly and brings me back to the line. The passenger in front of me reaches into his pockets, then shrugs his shoulders as he is taken to be screened further with a wand. I watch the conveyor belt for my bags. They have not come through. The screener is waving the wand over the passenger in front of me, and the longer they take, the longer my bags seem to wait inside the X-ray machine.

Just send them through. Just send them through! my mind yells.

The machine spits out my bags, and I peek at the screener for any signs. The passenger in front of me moves on. My bags sit at the end of the conveyor belt. The screener with the wand waves me through the metal detector. I hold my breath and cross. No chirp.

I force a smile, quickly grab my bags and head down the hallway
to the gates, the blood still pumping loudly in my temples.

I recognize them.

Not their faces but their nature. All around the gate, waiting
to board a flight to Cancún are *Yumas*. Humans. Free Cubans returning to the land that has made them persons, via the Mexican border. Few of them are hindered with any baggage. Most
are slumped in chrome chairs, fanning themselves from the lack
of air-conditioning, waiting to board. How different they were on
the way here. They were just like the thousands of Cubans who
make this journey every day, their arms overwhelmed with bags
of clothing, toys, medicine, all the things their families here crave
and can get only with help from the outside.

They take this trip through a third country, knowing it's both
illegal and necessary. The risk when family is at stake is no risk at
all. I look down at my bag filled with dirty laundry I could easily
have replaced with mere money, clothes that could have gotten
years of use from Tomás or Luis or his son, and a hot rush of shame
burns me from within.

A woman's voice over the public address system says the Jetway
is damaged, and we will have to board our flight on the tarmac.
Passengers all around me gather their few bags, and the glass doors
to the outside open, letting in a fresh blast of hot air, redolent in
jet fuel. We march, single file, with our bags at our sides, guided
by ground workers in olive fatigues. White and silver, and with a
soft whining of its engines, the plane awaits, a stairway leading up
to the cabin. Stairs that will lift my feet from Cuban soil, possibly
forever. Passengers queue up, there's an uncomfortable bumping
as we await our turns, the plane growing closer with each unstoppable step. I come to the edge of the stairs. People shuffle ahead
of me. Someone has dropped a bag, I think. And it's just the time I
need to focus, to say good-bye.

A stiff breeze, heavy with the vapor of the sea, blows my hair,
and I turn to face it. A golden sun warms me. A cloudless sky the

color of the waters at Varadero is the canvas. I breathe deep, pull in the air until my lungs stretch and hurt, until they can take in no more, and I exhale. I look down, and there is room to step. Right foot. Then left. And then, the ground is gone.

Passengers follow me up the stairs, up, up into the plane, and with every step, every inch of distance between me and Cuba increasing, I feel a painful tug, like a living spider's web tearing from its anchors. Over the years I have spent as a sportswriter, I have heard athletes talk about scar tissue tearing away after surgery, the painful but necessary damage that must happen for true healing to begin. And I think, now, I understand.

I was broken when I came here. I needed Cuba to make me whole. And this tearing—this blinding, excruciating tearing that forces my eyes to swim as I sit with my head against the window, watching the evergreen landscape blur as the plane speeds down the runway—is part of this process. We must hurt before we can heal. It tears, tears away as we climb higher and higher. Tears away as mounting clouds shroud the red earth in a dressing of mist. One cloud. Two clouds. A thousand. Tears, until the sight of Cuba fades into a horizon where sky meets sea and only my mind remembers what the pain is like.

After the pain comes the numbness. Numbness as the plane lands in Mexico. As another takes off for Miami. Numb as the perfect grid of the city appears beneath a carpet of billowy, white clouds. As I pass through immigration. Numb through the airport.

Numb, until the healing can begin. Until the voice of my wife, my muse, is clear on the other end of the phone. Until I can see our Jeep come closer as it pulls up at the curb and stops in front of me. Numb, until her smile tells me I'm home.

HOME

She looks like a bride in her sparkling white dress, taking turns dancing with her father and grandfathers across the parquet floor.

The song "Butterfly Kisses" threatens tears that could ruin the makeup she is allowed to wear for the first time. Her eyes, though, are bright, alive beneath freshly shaped eyebrows. My cousin Kristie is a woman today. She is fifteen.

This is a special day for her. These *Quinces*, a long-standing tradition, mark the coming of age in Cuban culture. All of our family is here, more than fifty of us from as far away as Tampa, seated at white-linen-covered tables in a Rusty Pelican ballroom to help her celebrate. We watch her float around the dance floor in a strapless gown and glistening tiara that make the girl look like a woman.

It is a special day for me, too.

I am seeing my family, all gathered for the first time since I returned six days ago from visiting our homeland.

Light applause greets one grandfather as the other cuts in. And I remember sitting in a Cuban home just a week ago, paint peeling off the walls, recalcitrant springs popping up through a lumpy sofa whose pattern hasn't been popular since the 1960s, and looking through the photo album of a girl—no, a young woman—posing for her *Quinces*.

That girl was made up, too, her smooth black hair impeccably styled. In one photo, she was wearing a rented emerald green evening gown. In another, a white dress a cousin in the United States sent from her own *Quinces* years ago. She posed in an elegant, Victorian-looking living room, which a family in the once-luxurious neighborhood of El Vedado had fixed up to rent out for just such occasions.

Even with such need, they still cling to this custom.

Kristie is dancing with her father now. His hand rests gently on her bare shoulder, and I look at my girls, wondering whether they will want to follow in this tradition when the day comes. I lock eyes with Kristie's father, whose look says it all: "It was just yesterday I was carrying my baby around on my shoulders."

I watched them float across the dance floor, and it was a moment of peace. Because the questions from my family had not stopped since I came through the door.

My wife and I are the last to arrive. We climb a grand, dark wood staircase together to a ballroom that overlooks Biscayne Bay, holding our daughter Elise's hand. She wears a crisp A-line dress with cherries along the hem and insists on walking. Amelia, a red bow in her hair, wrinkles her blue-and-white linen dress as she clings to my chest, sleep still in her eyes from napping in the car. At the top of the stairs, my father and two of my uncles are waiting. They turn to watch us take our last few steps, wide smiles on their faces.

By now, they have all seen my pictures, more than two hundred of them. My wife put them up online, and I captioned them so my cousins could show their fathers and mothers what has become of the places they once knew. Their house in Marianao. Their businesses in La Plaza. The jail cells at La Cabaña. Their father's grave in Havana. All the people and places they have not seen or heard about in nearly four decades.

"Get ready," Christy says under her breath, and I try to hide a smile.

Questions begin the second I reach the top of the stairs.

"So you did it. You went to Cuba," my Tío Ciro says, clapping me on the back, shaking me.

"*Muchacho*, do you know what a risk you took?" he says, looking more serious.

I try to explain that I kept my head low, stayed well out of the way of anyone in a uniform.

"No, no, no. You have to promise me you won't go back. You don't know what those *comunistas* are capable of. No, promise me you won't go back."

Tío, I can't promise you that. If the newspaper sends me again . . .

"You tell them that once is enough," he says, moving his hands like an umpire after a runner slides home safely. "You have family here to think of. *Vaya*, if you go again, you and I are going to have a problem. I'm just going to tell people that I don't have a nephew named Carlitos anymore."

My Tío Ciro is a master of overstatement, and I can tell he is making a point from the upward curves at the edge of his lips. But I understand what he means. He was worried for his nephew.

My Tío Rafael, my godfather, the oldest and tallest of the brothers, is waiting his turn, his fedora, as always, perfectly set on his head. He grabs me in a tight hug, and I can smell the strong cologne that is his signature. He hasn't seen the pictures yet and wants to know about La Plaza, if the restaurant is still there. And their house, what does their house look like? Who owns it now? he wants to know. The pictures have spared me talking about what I saw, and I am thankful for that. But under their questioning, I do not know if my uncles are ready to hear in words what the pictures suggest, that what they remember of their homeland is devastated.

My father puts one arm around me.

"*Muchachos*," he says to his brothers, cutting in and leading us into the party. "He went everywhere. And he saw everything."

We find our seats across from the dance floor, and as I walk out to the lobby to bring back drinks, I see my Tío Ramón returning from the bar. He is smiling widely and grabs me in a tight embrace.

"Did you meet Ricardo?" he asks me, in a low, casual voice about the son he's never met. "Does he look well? What kind of a person is he?"

They are the same questions his son in Cuba asked me. He wants to know. They all want to know: What is happening on the other side of the Florida Straits?

He's a great person, Tío.

I tell my uncle about Ricardo, about being in Cárdenas at the same time, our meeting at Varadero. I tell him about Ricardo's children—Ramón's *grandchildren*—who are so studious, so well-mannered, so interested in knowing everything, anything.

More than anything, Tío, I think he would like to hear from you.

"*Ca!*" I hear someone call out.

My cousin Felipe walks toward us from the ballroom, where slow-dance music is playing.

What's up, 'cabrón'?

My Tío Ramón returns to the party.

"Hey, I was talking with my dad, and he has a buried treasure, too," he says. Just the other day, they talked all about it. They drew a map, marked off the paces on the floor, and moved, side by side, as if they were over the very spot where his father also buried a metal can with sentimental treasures from a lifetime ago. He wants to go now. We can go together to dig up both metal cans, he says. One will distract the old drunk who lives there while the other starts digging.

Fine. You dig.

Just as I am about to ask him if he and his father have spoken about Alina, I catch my Tío Felipe out of the corner of my eye. He has circled me a couple of times but hasn't approached me yet. I want to say something to him, tell him how his old girlfriend led me around Marianao like a tour guide and watched over me like a guardian angel. I want to ask him if he knows how she still feels. But two other cousins, Frank and Jesus—Ramón's sons—corral me and invite me to the downstairs bar for a drink.

Jesus buys me a vodka tonic, and we make small talk before Frank says, finally, "Okay, so, tell me about my brother."

Ricardo, the brother they knew nothing about. The brother whose picture they have now seen online. Frank admits he learned about Ricardo from his father years ago but kept it secret. To Jesus and their other brother, Ray, Ricardo is a revelation. I tell them Ricardo gets e-mail, and I promise to send them his address.

"I'll definitely e-mail him," Frank says.

You should call him. Man, you would make his life if you called.

"I don't know. I mean, I don't know how my mom feels about it," Frank says.

"Why would Mom care, Frank? It's not his—his name is Ricardo, right—it's not Ricardo's fault about what happened with Dad. I'll definitely e-mail him," Jesus says.

I ask about their once-oldest brother, Ray. He and his family live in Atlanta and weren't able to make it for Kristie's *Quinces*. Ray is now, technically, a middle child. They look at each other, shake their heads.

"Ray says that's no brother of his," Jesus says.

"That we're the only family he knows," Frank adds.

I have brought many things back with me. Not all of them pleasant. And as we finish our drinks and head back upstairs, I know that my trip is going to force some in my family to deal with issues they thought time and distance had buried.

Back at the party, I am sitting at the table, watching a photographer try to pose sixteen children—my girls and their cousins—around the *Quinceañera*. She finally sits on the floor, her white tulle dress spread around her, with Amelia, the youngest of the generation, on her lap. She reminds me of myself as a kid, shy, the youngest of my generation, as the other cousins huddle around her for the photo. It's then that my Tío Felipe finally approaches me.

"So," he says. "You met Alina."

'Sí, Tío.'

"She's a very good person," he says.

I know. She took care of me. Like family.

He nods, wordless, when my Tío Rafael joins us, and so does my father, the three who were jailed together at the prison in La Cabaña. Felipe says he was looking at the pictures of my trip at his daughter's house when my cousin flipped to a picture of me standing by the rows of cells at La Cabaña. He had to leave the room in tears.

Today, at the party, he tells me the story of hearing prisoners screaming as they were being taken away to be executed by firing squad.

"Right there where you were standing," Tío Felipe says, "they would bring us out at three in the morning, make us strip naked, and they would blast us with jets of cold water."

"Just to intimidate us," my father says.

"Animals," Tío Rafael whispers, almost to himself.

"And there were female guards, standing up on the walls, right there where you took the picture, laughing at us," Felipe adds.

He begins telling the story of political prisoners who were moved to "the special cells" underground, where the walls wept with rainwater in the darkness and prisoners emerged six weeks later, their skin white, their eyes rounded in dark circles, and their bones pushing through their skin.

"Like Martians," Felipe manages to say, his eyes bright red and watery, and he has to walk away again, his voice cracking.

I have seen Cuba, but with every minute home I'm learning there is still much I do not know about the pain that has lain dormant for decades. I have brought back my own impressions. And I find, faced with those who left a broken paradise years ago, that the hardest question to answer is "How did you like Cuba?"

My answer is always the same. Merciful.

I loved meeting my family, getting to know my history, I tell them.

I do not say that Cuba is little more than ruins, a modern-day Machu Picchu still inhabited by the original conquered souls. My family's Cuba exists only in anecdotes.

The more they ask, the less I can say. My experience is like a river curbed by a dam with a tiny crack. A deluge is waiting to rush out. I am waiting to burst. The stories are trapped inside me. All the sorrow, all the joy, all the hugs, *all of it*. I am numb.

How did I like Cuba? Where do I begin?

The music plays on, we take pictures, dine on chicken cordon bleu. At the end of the night, as my wife, my kids, and I wait for our car at the valet station, Amelia hanging on to me again, her dress askew, her curly hair a sweaty nest sweetened by baby perfume, I feel a hand on my shoulder.

It is my Tío Felipe. His eyes are dry, but his voice still unsteady.

"One day, you're going to come to my house, and we're going to talk about everything," he says, swallowing hard, clearing his throat. "Even if I have to cry through it."

⌀

Dominoes crash into one another as my father and the uncles take their usual seats at the table.

The sound is like waves breaking on the beach, the black dots facedown, surging and crashing across a Formica table as the four men sweep their hands over the chips, soothsayers conjuring over their crystal ball. That sound must be like a meditative wave to these men, who have been playing together for the better part of sixty years, since the time, as boys, they would play under the shade of the large, waxy leaves of an avocado tree in Oriente. Now that they are in their seventies and eighties, that sweeping motion is about all the exercise they get.

Usually the fifth brother is odd man out, waiting for his turn and commenting on the game like a sports announcer.

"*Ave María!*" he says after one player has broken the strategy of his partner across the table.

"*Coño*, I can't believe how *malo* you are!"

His colorful commentary is rewarded with a low, grumbling "Quiet, *chico!*" This is a mute game, they remind him.

Today, however, the fifth man takes a break every few minutes.

The sliding glass door at my Tío Felipe's house is opaque with humidity, because the eliminated players have been going in and out of the house to serve themselves plates of rice and sausage and to take a peek at the video playing on my laptop on the kitchen counter.

It is connected to the Internet using my uncle's phone line. I have managed to cue up a video slide show I made for the newspaper, where I narrated the photos of my journey in Spanish and English. They are seeing places and hearing names of landmarks they have not thought about in nearly forty years. My Tío Ramón has earbuds tucked into his ears. The plate of rice and sausage is sitting beside him, getting cold. His eyes go back and forth over the pictures, my voice in his ears, his eyes welling with tears. As the screen goes black, he turns and says, with something of a smile, "*Coño*. That made me cry."

There are moments of silence in the house when the fifth man returns to the patio by the pool. My Tía Teresita, Felipe's wife, is keeping busy around the kitchen, cleaning up after the Neanderthals. As Ramón steps outside, I am caught off guard when she puts down her rag and quickly pulls up a barstool to sit across from me at the counter.

She is always serious-looking, my Tía Teresita, walking and sitting tall, her eyes the color of the shallow ocean, piercing. But she manages to soften the Spaniard in her with dry humor, quick wit, and an occasional but perfectly timed English phrase, like "I don't think so!" Although one of my aunts is a registered nurse and another was once Teacher of the Year for Dade County Schools, my Tío Felipe's wife is the only one I knew who had subscriptions to *Time* and *Newsweek* and bought her son *Popular Mechanics* when he was a boy. She is smart and self-assured. But today, she is not sure where to begin.

"I want to ask you something," she says, folding and refolding her hands, first on her lap, then on the countertop, then back on her lap.

"Do you think . . ." She trails off. She is steeling herself to ask a question her mind hasn't allowed her mouth to form.

"Do you think she's still in love with him? I mean, do you think she *thinks* there's any future between them?"

She is talking about Alina.

Before I went to Cuba, I had heard my family mention her. They joked openly about my Tío Felipe's old girlfriend, but I never imagined the extent to which she was still a part of their lives.

They are separated by more than just time, the space of nearly forty years. My Tío Felipe is married, has two grown children, even three grandchildren. But it's clear there is a sort of debt he feels he owes. Over the years, he has sent money to Alina. My uncle and aunt also owned a jewelry store and sent little trinkets to her, a simple bracelet, a thin necklace, even the pair of flower-shaped gold studs that Alina has worn daily for the past fifteen years.

Tía Teresita did more than was required of her. She went shopping for clothes for Alina herself. She bought panties and bras for the woman who could be her rival. I try to picture my aunt, the fair-skinned Gallega, taller at about five foot six, plump but not heavy, sifting through the underwear section at Marshall's, shopping for my uncle's old girlfriend, waifishly thin, with olive skin and bobbed golden hair, which was once jet-black and reached her waist.

They corresponded for years, Alina hearing about my uncle's entire life, from when they opened their jewelry store to when his children were born. That was, until the letter came.

Several years ago, Teresita tells me, she opened what looked like one of their usual letters from Cuba. In it, Alina wrote with a passion and outpouring of loss, of love, of emotion like Teresita had never read. It shook her.

"Some of the things she wrote are *muy fuerte*—very strong," she says, shaking her head.

Teresita has kept *that* letter.

Talking to my cousin Felipe a few days ago, I confided my conspiracy theory. That Tío Felipe might indeed have a daughter in Cuba, Magda, Alina's niece whom she has cared for as her own since the girl's mother died in childbirth. I tell my cousin to go back online and look at the photo of the girl in the red tank top. Maybe I'm crazy, I tell him, but she looked to me to be the image of his sister, Lily. He didn't see the resemblance as I did. But over a family dinner the following weekend, Lily asked my uncle, "So, *Papi*, Carlitos says you might have a daughter over there."

Leave it to Lil, the master of tact.

However it came about, it led to the conversation. My uncle swore that he does not have any other children, because any child of his "would eat at my table alongside me," he told them flatly, no matter who the mother was. And he also swore he never had intimate relations with Alina. He left her a virgin, he told them.

And I better understand, why, after all these years, Alina still pines for him. In her eyes, he is perfect, their relationship untarnished, simply one that "could never be."

"Do you think she believes one day they'll be together again?" Tía Teresita asks me once more, her eyes searching for an answer.

I tell her what I know to be true. On November 5, 1969, when Felipe left Marianao—left Cuba, forever—something remained frozen in time for Alina. Memories. Hope. Perfection.

For Alina, life ceased to exist the following morning. Every day since has served only to romanticize the life she lost. She was at the center of everything in the city of Marianao. From the front porch of her house, she could hear the salsa music and smell the fragrance of fried steak and plantains wafting from the restaurant my father and his brothers owned in La Plaza. She can still see my grandfather standing at the cash register of the restaurant, where they would wave to each other throughout the day. On the weekends, my Tío Felipe would pick up Alina and take her for a ride through the city, her long black hair flowing out of the passenger's window.

She was young, beautiful, full of life, and ensnared in love's tender grip.

Forty years later, she is still there, in that apartment. Now, it faces what is the trash room of La Plaza, the smell of fetid meats and overripe fruit mixing with the din of merchants selling their wares in the open market. But when she stands on her porch, she can close her eyes and vividly reclaim her past, rebuilding it piece by piece. Like so many Cubans of her generation still in Cuba, she is living a life that was—and could have been.

I tell my Tía Teresita not to worry. I explain that, for a brief moment, she had the misfortune of walking in on Alina's waking dream—a sleep from which she cannot be stirred.

⌒

Elise is in school and Amelia napping when my wife begins to type. She pecks a quick hello, and it leaves the computer with a little *pop!*

CHRISTY: HEY, COUSIN!
ENRIQUE: COUSIIIIIIIIIIIIIN!!
CHRISTY: HOLA. HOW ARE YOU?
ENRIQUE: BETTER, NOW THAT I CAN TALK WITH YOU.

Enrique is at work, but he can instant-message for a bit. If he is in the middle of programming software, he will tell her to hold tight and message her later. Usually, he makes time, though. They both do.

This is part of our world now. At night, when both girls are in bed, we sit down to chat with our new cousins in Cuba over the Internet. They are my wife's cousins, in truth, but they have adopted me since I helped them make contact.

When it's my turn to chat with Enrique, I make the mistake of calling him my *socio*, my friend.

ENRIQUE: WE'RE NOT SOCIOS. WE'RE COUSINS, RIGHT?
WE'RE FAMILY.
ME: RIGHT. OF COURSE.

We're family now.
We know we are also privileged. Not everyone gets this access.

We don't know when or if the government will change its mind and crack down. So, we don't take it for granted.

My wife and I hear about their daily lives. She counsels Enrique about the girl from Panama who swears she's serious about marrying him. I talk to Ismael about music and movies. My wife and Normita get lost in "girl talk."

Five days after I return, we learn a cousin of my wife's is going to Cuba. We scramble to buy something for each member of our newfound family.

So we buy a bottle of Perry Ellis perfume for Normita; for Enrique, a jersey of his favorite World Cup team, Germany; a bottle of the same Dolce & Gabbana cologne I use for Ismael; and for Pablo, an MP3 player so he can keep up with his tech-savvy siblings.

We sign on and wait anxiously to hear that they have received their gifts. Normita, Enrique, and Ismael all love theirs, they write.

CHRISTY: AND PABLO?

There is a pause of a few seconds.

NORMITA: THE LITTLE MUSIC PLAYER DIDN'T MAKE IT.

The Cuban government confiscated it at Customs. Pablo has no gift. We imagine the gifts being distributed and only Pablo left to watch other faces light up. We are numb. Pablo takes it in stride.

The next day, they send us a digital picture of a plastic bag Pablo taped to the refrigerator. Below the bag is a note that reads: "This fund is for poor Pablito, who had his MP3 player confiscated." His dad put a nickel in it as he left for work.

Some topics we all take more seriously. Normita writes to my wife about her health issues. The government won't prescribe an inhaler for her asthma, they say, because they are not available. If she has an attack, her family must rush her to the hospital, where she shares a communal nebulizer. When my daughter Elise went to the doctor for bronchitis last week, he asked if our family has a history of asthma. A month ago, we would have said no. Now, we know better. We know better about a lot of things.

As our daughters sleep, we sit at the computer and type, our written Spanish improving with every conversation. It is past ten, and Christy is recapping our day for our cousins living across the great divide. I sit next to her on the couch, watching television and keeping her company as she exchanges messages with Normita.

"No," Christy says. "No, no, no! No way."

She is sitting with her hands slack as Normita types.

What is it?

"You have to read this," she says.

With each little *pop!* Normita unfolds the story of her recent visit to the doctor. She had been feeling a pain in her lower abdomen and decided to walk in one afternoon. After examining her, the nurse told her the problem is with her intrauterine device, her birth control. It has embedded itself into her uterine wall, and she will need surgery to remove it.

Except Normita never had an IUD put in.

Normita: I told her no, no, I would know if I had something like that done.

But very clearly, the nurse told her, looking at her chart, on such-and-such a day she went in to have the procedure done. Then it started to make sense. When she was just nineteen, three years ago, she got pregnant. She was unmarried, and already five of them were living in their little two-bedroom, one-bath apartment.

"I wasn't ready to be a mother, God forgive me," Normita types as we read, not needing to respond.

She went in to have an abortion and was told she had to come back the next day for a checkup. When she returned, they told her she was having some unusual bleeding, and they had to perform a brief procedure. She went under general anesthesia. By the time she woke up, doctors had placed an IUD inside of her, without her consent, without her knowledge. She asked the nurse who authorized this procedure.

NORMITA: SHE JUST TOLD ME IT CAME "FROM UP TOP."

My wife and I look at each other as words continue to *pop!* onto the screen.

Population control: They're chemically sterilizing women.

"Without their knowledge," Christy says.

Normita writes that she is nervous. She must have a procedure to remove the IUD later this month. My wife and I try to console her, telling her it will be all right. Sometimes we laugh in these late-night sessions with our cousins. Some nights, we stop typing to cry.

Our cousins have not been online all day.

Soon, it is days.

We leave the computer running around the clock, waiting for their names to become highlighted on our screen, indicating they are online. But it never happens. We send instant messages that are not answered, e-mails that go without reply. Six months into our new relationship with our cousins, it goes unnaturally quiet.

"I'm going to call them," Christy says. And with the girls in bed, we dial directly to Maria Laura's home.

"Normita!" Christy yells, the phone on speaker.

There is a delay.

"*Prima,* is that you?"

"*Sí. Hola? Sí.* Damn this delay. Normita, why haven't you been online?"

"*Ay, chica,* they've taken it away from us," Normita says.

Normita says all over the island the government has been clamping down on Internet connections. Employees such as Enrique and Ismael who were legally allowed to have the Internet at home have had those rights revoked. They are being monitored closely at work, and instant-messaging programs are being purged from computers. Our connection is lost.

Nights are quiet now. We still sit in the home office out of habit, waiting to see our family's name *pop!* back again. But there are only occasional e-mails from Normita. Now, she has to go to an Internet café to send her notes at a cost of two Convertibles—about two weeks' salary—an hour. But she saves up, and sometimes she will call my wife on her cell, a surprising and wonderful call in the middle of the day, and ask if she can be online at a set time when they can sit and chat and pretend, for a few minutes, that something precious has not been lost.

A few days after our connection is broken, I get an e-mail from Enrique:

We here love you guys a lot, and we will never forget you, despite the little communication we have now.

We always talk about you guys and the wonderful family we have just ninety miles away.

I hope we can stay in touch, even if it's just through e-mail. Count on me for anything you might need. In me, you have more than a cousin. Here, you have a brother.

Enrique

⌒

A hurricane is coming. Or so we are told.

The aluminum panels go up on all the windows, and now it's

time for me to stuff everything on the patio into a cluttered garage. As a slow, steady drizzle falls, I lug three of Elise's bikes toward the garage. There's a Barbie tricycle, a Barbie Big Wheel, and a Barbie scooter—all for one kid who never rides any of them.

I can't help but think of Isabel, my cousin Jorge's five-year-old granddaughter. And I am back in Cuba in my mind.

She is my shadow, my *compañerita*, my companion for three days in Cárdenas, sitting on my lap and posing for pictures by every monument. I wonder if she still plays with the little toy cars I left her. They certainly can't compare with the beautiful Barbie Big Wheel that sits unused on my screened-in porch. I wonder if she is looking at the picture of my wife, my girls, and me at my Tía Sofía's house, wishing we could all play together. I wonder if she misses her toys, the little bears she sent to my daughters, my daughters who have so much.

The early rains of tropical storm Ernesto soak through my shirt and bring me back to Pembroke Pines, where the toys are now all picked up. Are we spoiling them rotten, I wonder, my children who have so many toys, who never lack for anything, from private school to new clothes?

As I head to the shower, I peek into Elise's room and find her and Amelia playing with several dolls, including the two bears.

'Mamita,' who gave you those little bears?

"My *primita* in Cuba," she says, dancing one of the bears over to another doll without looking up.

"*Papi*, I want to see my little cousin in Cuba," she says suddenly, as I turn to leave.

Me, too, 'Mamita.' Me, too.

⌒

She is trying very hard to defend her father.

"A lot of people in Cuba are blind," Maira says, attempting to explain why her father, Raúl, after all these years, is still a president of the Committee for the Defense of the Revolution. And why her mother, Rosita, has never said anything to my family about it.

I need to have this conversation. I need to understand how Rosita, a person my family trusted so completely, married a man so dedicated to Castro's revolution that he would agree to lead a neighborhood watch group. Rosita had seen my father and his brothers lose their businesses, go to jail, and finally, have to live in exile for disagreeing with the political system. She had worked for them from the time she was sixteen, her first real job. And now she was married to the president of a local CDR.

"*Ay, mijo,* a lot of people in Cuba go around believing in something because they have never seen anything else," Maira says.

She is speaking from her home in Miami. She *has* seen something else. She put in for the lottery to leave Cuba in 1998 and never looked back. Today, she is married, works in a bakery, and has an infant daughter. And she has heard all about me. Rosita called her and told her about my visit.

I try to remain pleasant, leaving out the detail of how I got sick to my stomach after learning that, if her mother were not so loyal to my family, her father would have been obligated to turn me in to authorities for being a journalist in Cuba. Several of my uncles were incensed to learn her husband was so involved with the communist party. Some have vowed never to let her into their homes again.

But, Maira, why didn't Rosita say anything?

"I think she's embarrassed. It's not something to be proud of," she says.

Rosita has explained to Maira that, before she was born, her father had been a real believer in the revolution. He had trusted that it would lead to a better way of life—up until the 1990s, after the Russians pulled out of Cuba and even food was scarce.

"That's when my father started seeing what it was all about," she says.

And then, after his daughter left, he visited her in the United States. In 2002 he spent several weeks here, where "he saw with his own eyes how things really are," Maira says. "That's why I say that people who have never left Cuba are blind. They are not allowed to see anything else."

I feel for Rosita. She was genuinely concerned for my well-being when I visited, and she would be truly heartbroken if she learned she had let my family down. She didn't turn me in, and her husband turned a blind eye. For their part, Maira's parents tell her they won't consider leaving Cuba. But her father has been trying for years to unload the CDR presidency onto a willing neighbor. He has yet to find a taker.

"He's going crazy trying to get rid of it," Maira says.

I hope that counts for something.

The next time I meet with my uncles, they are playing dominoes at my Tío Ciro's house, and I tell them about my conversation with Rosita's daughter.

"I won't give her another cent, not one red cent!" my Tío Ciro bellows. "And wait until I see her next time, you wait and hear all the things I'm going to tell her."

Tío, she protected me. She could have turned me in. You haven't lived there, Tío. You and I can't imagine what they've had to do to live, to survive.

He seems unconvinced, but he is silent, thinking. The brothers go back to their dominoes, and not another word is spoken about Rosita.

⌀

Only one person ever uses this e-mail account. But I keep it anyway. I don't want to change a single thing that would lead to losing my connection to Ricardo.

I check it daily, and still, I can't keep myself from smiling when I receive a message from my cousin in Cuba.

"Cousin, you can't imagine how happy I am (how happy we all are)," he writes. "My brother, Frank, wrote to me and sent me a picture of all of my nieces and nephews, and another with him, my old man, and [Frank's] youngest daughter. I won't live long enough to repay you all the joy you are giving me and mine. . . ."

Ricardo's e-mail connection remains active in his office. And, fortunately, we are able to keep in touch at least once a week. I e-mail him and his children, Magaly and Julio. One Friday afternoon, I get a message from Magaly saying she will be with her family and friends on Saturday because they will be celebrating her twenty-second birthday. And I know that same day we will be at a birthday party for my cousin Frank's youngest daughter, Isabella.

Ricardo and his brother have children celebrating birthdays on the same day.

I have to stop and weave to keep from being run over by the line of children dashing from the living room to Isabella's bedroom. There is constant noise, constant laughter from the dozen or so other children who are here to celebrate her birthday. We, their parents, just try to stay out of the way.

Frank and I sit in his computer room as the locomotive of girls dressed as princesses steams by the open door. He is showing me a downloaded clip of a comedy show when I notice the phone blinking on his work space and remember Ricardo.

You know what today is?

He looks up from the keyboard.

Magaly is turning twenty-two today.

"You're kidding? Today?"

Actually, I was thinking about calling her. And I was thinking, maybe, we could both talk to her.

"Now?" He looks around, as if searching for something with which to steady himself. "Right now?"

Yeah, man, right now! C'mon, you know what that would mean to her?

But I know what it means to him. What it meant to me before I visited Cuba: This is forbidden territory. Cuba is a place we talk about, dream about. But my visit has made it real for me, for us. And I can no longer allow us to believe it is a place that exists only in a fairy tale.

"Man, I don't know," he says, rubbing his face. "We can just call direct? Right now? With all these people here?"

C'mon, bro. Today's her birthday! We're all here for Isabella's birthday. This isn't a coincidence, this is meant to be!

He lets a smile creep across his face.

"All right," he says. "Close the door."

The phone rings differently, like a soft honk, as the call goes through. Frank stares at me expectantly while I wait for Ricardo to pick up his cell.

'¡Primo!' It's your cousin Carlos!

I told him I was going to surprise Magaly today with a phone call. But he doesn't know the surprise I have for them both. I hear his voice for the first time in months. It is raspy, deep, familiar. It is still true: There is no denying this man is my family. He puts me on with Magaly, and I congratulate her.

I'm sorry I couldn't send you anything for your birthday. But I do have someone I want you to talk to.

I hand Frank the phone, and he reaches for it tentatively with a half smile. His eyes dart up only long enough for me to read his thoughts: Here we go.

"*Hola,* Magaly. This is your Tío Frank . . ."

I can't contain a chuckle, a spasm of giddiness, and I start to leave the room to let them speak. I bump into my cousin Jesus at the door and tell him we are talking with Cuba, with Magaly, it is her birthday, Ricardo is there—it all comes out as a jumbled mess.

"We have to get Dad," Jesus says, his eyes wide, a smile twisted in disbelief.

He returns with my Tío Ramón, and I close the door to give them their privacy, pacing the living room like an expectant father. After about twenty minutes, Tío Ramón emerges with his eyes bright, a smile etched on his face. He looks lost, as if he has just seen a celebrity. He sees me in the living room, walks over, and shakes my hand.

"I just spoke with my son," he says.

It takes several seconds before I can match the voice on my cell phone with the one I heard when we spoke on her birthday. And I don't know how I manage to stay on the road at her news.

"*Primo*, it's Magaly. I'm here!"

Here? You're . . . Oh my God, 'prima,' you're here!

Magaly is here. In Miami. I know she has been planning her escape through Mexico for months. And yet, when it all happens overnight, the ninety miles that stood between us don't seem so far. My voice instantly goes up an octave. I can tell from her voice that she is smiling, and we cannot stop laughing.

Has she spoken with her Tío Frank yet? What about her *Abuelo*, my Tío Ramón? No, she says. I'm the first person she called, even though Tío Ramón and the uncles pitched in to help pay for her breakaway. She's staying with her grandmother and aunt who came here several years ago. Where, she's not sure, but it's near something called the "Orange Bowl."

"*Papi*, that's my *primita*?" Elise says from the backseat over the singing of my middle daughter, Amelia, and the baby, Catalina, who is cooing and playing with a toy on her car seat.

"*Ay*, are those the girls? I can't wait to see them!" Magaly says.

I can't wait for you to meet them. 'Bienvenida, prima.'

Welcome.

She is one of us now.

～

A nun we know, one who presided over my Catholic elementary school, recently came back from a trip to Cuba. As she always does, she left a package of medicine for my father's cousin Mario in Marianao.

But this time, she didn't bring a letter in return. Only bad news: Mario has stomach cancer. And he doesn't have long to live.

Mario is my father's last connection to his family in Cuba. Yes, there are other distant cousins in distant provinces, but none that he has kept in contact with. Mario knows my family's history, and I realize he has one relative in Cuba that he has never met: Ricardo. I write an e-mail to Ricardo, who lives less than a mile from Mario, and tell him to visit Alina, so she can take him to meet our cousin one afternoon.

Two weeks go by before I receive a note from Ricardo. Mario is gravely ill. The cancer has metastasized. It is only a matter of time.

"Alina introduced us, and we spent a long while talking. His impression was the same as yours: How much I looked like my father!" Ricardo writes. "He spoke to me a lot about your father. And I took the opportunity to speak a lot about you."

Twelve days later, I get another note from Ricardo.

Mario died on a Wednesday.

He had his wife and children at his side when he passed, when "the life finally slipped from his fingers," Ricardo wrote. "It seems that *Dios* did not want to lengthen his suffering or his family's."

❧

The Marlins are losing again.

My father and I sit in my living room, illuminated only by the light of the television, watching our baseball team struggle to score runs.

My father is focused on the game.

I am focused on my sister.

He knows that I know. Know that I have a sister. A sister in Cuba. A daughter he has never spoken of. Christy had the conversation with him, the one I should have had before I left. The one we should have had years ago. She broke the ice. But I am left to jump into the icy water.

I have been back for nearly two weeks, and still I can't seem to broach the subject, and neither can he. There never seems to be a right time, a right place. Either my mother is in the room or my girls are running around us. Other times, I simply can't form the words and breathe out at the same time to make the noise we call speech. I guess I don't know how to talk about this with my father.

He leans forward to watch this at bat. I face the screen, leaning back on my couch, but my eyes trace his face, looking for a soft place to fall into this conversation. But there seem to be only hard landings.

"Look at the pitch he swings at!" he says, shaking his head.

I nod. Breathe deep. And we sit together in silence for several seconds.

'Papi.'

"Hmm?" He is watching the screen.

I want to ask you something.

"Uh-huh . . ."

About your daughter.

He continues facing the screen. Bluish light falls on his expressionless face.

About my sister.

The buzz of crowd noise fills the long pause between us.

"Just leave that alone," he says finally.

The batter grounds into a double play and jogs back to the dugout. We sit wordlessly, facing the screen, two feet apart, but the distance between us seems to grow. I wonder if either one of us is following this game.

'Papi,' I'm not judging you. I turn to face him. *I just want to know about her. I have a sister out there. I just want to know.*

He sits upright—*too* upright—and plays with his fingers, still watching the television as the game goes to commercial.

"It was a long time ago," he says, glancing at me for only a second. "I was just a boy, *un niño.* The two of us, we were both *niños.*"

He met Maribel Sánchez when he was just twenty, working in a *bodega* in Oriente, he says. She got pregnant and had the baby.

"Ana Ester," he says. "That was her name."

A few years later, he moved across the country to Havana to follow his brother Ciro, he says. The game comes back on. The Bad Guys are batting. I don't notice the score.

Did you ever see her again?

"Once," he says, facing the television, gently wringing his hands. "She came to Marianao, all grown up. But I never saw her after that. When I was in prison, *Papá* came to see me. He said he was thinking of acknowledging her as his own. I said, *'Viejo,* that's your decision.' But as for me . . ."

He grimaces and shrugs his shoulders. We sit in silence, a silence filled with the buzz of thousands of faceless fans. And I know that, today, I can't ask him any more.

⟶

She is turning the ring over in her hand.

The black tarnish has been polished from the surface, and the solid silver glistens with the year of her eighth-grade graduation. Clearly embossed on the seal of the signet ring are the words "Escolapias. Graduada." Graduate.

"Imagine this ring back in my hands after all these years," my mother says. She tries it on, moving it from finger to finger, until it finally slips halfway up her pinkie.

Tía Sofía wanted you to have it. So you can remember.

She puts it back into a clear plastic box, where it sits, undisturbed, like an exhibit in a museum. Her report cards from a million years ago are also spread out before her like unfolded memories. She has taped together a pair of them where they had worn and split in the fifty-plus years since they were printed.

"This nun"—she points to a signature on the back of one report card—"used to tell my mother when I was a girl that I had electricity, *electricidad*," she says in her best Galician imitation.

She has opened the letter from Emma, her friend from a lifetime ago, her graduation godmother. The letter is folded, words written in red ink, tucked into the envelope.

"She wants me to write to her," she says. "But where to begin?"

How to bridge the lifetime that has passed between them, she means.

She piles the report cards together with the letter, places the boxed ring on top, and stores them in a cabinet where she keeps everything from her nail polish to her checkbook, the things she refers to daily. They are proof. Proof of a life that was hers. Of a life that exists only in the trinkets of her youth.

"You know, when you step onto the plane, you're not in Cuba anymore," she says, her eyes soft and reddening.

I see the girl again. The girl in her who never left. She is here, with us for a moment, as the tears push forward. My mother blinks, wipes her eyes. And she is gone again.

⌒

My father is kneading ground beef with onions, green peppers, and seasonings, adding a splash of red wine vinegar to the cold sauté pan, and letting what will soon become *picadillo* marinate.

He works quietly as Elise and Amelia sleep on his couch just a few feet away, tired from playing at Abu and Abuelita's house all morning.

"Your mother lucked out today," he whispers, checking the yucca that is soaking in a pot with salt water and adding salt and vinegar to a chopped tomato salad. "Today, I'm the chef, *el cocinero*."

Eleven months have passed. Eleven. And in these quiet moments, I wonder when the time will be right. The time to mention his daughter to him again. I am thinking of her constantly. Can't stop. Thinking of her at Christmas. Thinking of her at New Year's. Thinking of her when I e-mail Ricardo. Thinking of her when my wife e-mails her cousins. Thinking of her as I write this book. Thinking. But not asking.

In the months that have passed, I only have more questions. I want to know why. Why he didn't her recognize her legally? Why he never communicated with her again? Why I had never heard of her? Why, sixty years later, he could manage only a strained conversation when I brought her out of the past?

Most mornings, I write in an unused office in my parents' two-story, four-bedroom home, my childhood home, which is too large now for my empty-nesting parents. I see my father just about every day. And every day, I struggle to find the courage to ask him again. Until today, July 10, 2007, when I can't seem to write another word because the weight of the unexplored, the questions that have not been asked keep me from pushing another key.

I munch on a buttered roll, taking a break from writing as he finishes prepping the meal.

"How's the book coming?" he says, wiping his hands on a towel.

Good. Really good.

The girls are asleep. My mother is out. I take another bite and swallow.

But there's one more interview I have to do.

He looks up at me.

I have to interview you.

While my girls sleep, my father and I slip out of the house and onto the back porch. He cracks open a small can of Budweiser and hands me a twist-off—"Here, because you're younger than me." A heat wave is crashing against South Florida, and the moment we open the door, a puff of hot air escorts us into the backyard. But something about the shape of this corner patio, shaded by surrounding fruit trees, forces a draft, and a breeze that defies the July heat moves the air over us.

My father and I sit close, he on a beige nylon hammock, and I next to him, in a chair. I take the blue notebook from my back pocket, the one with the cartoon soccer player on the cover, and I begin to interview my father at last on the only subject that remains.

Dad, I'm writing about a lot of things. About a lot of people, a lot of lives. And there's one person I want to write about. But I only want to do it if it's all right with you.

He is swinging slowly, sitting up.

I want to ask you about your daughter again.

I call her "your daughter" and not "my sister," because it helps me maintain a bit of distance. I can be the interviewer, and he can be my source. And this way, I hope, he can tell the story without fear of revealing himself to his son.

He takes a deep breath and kicks off with his feet, swinging again. "All right," he says.

Tell me about that time in your life. Tell me who you were.

He begins to rub his hands.

In the farming town of Veguita, his father, Pancho Frías, had bought a small farm with a two-thousand-dollar loan from his cousin. He had rented land for years but was determined to have something to hand down to his eleven children. Over the years, my father says, his father paid the loan back dutifully, but in hard times, my grandfather began to fall behind. A thousand dollars remained to be paid. It got to the point where this man, this cousin who was already wealthy, threatened—no, promised—to foreclose on the loan and take the family land.

"We had one little milk cow for the family, and that cow gave us what we needed to live," my father says.

He begins not rubbing but kneading his hands, as if he is trying to wipe something indelible from them.

"Poor *Papá*," he says and sucks his teeth. He rubs, rubs, rubs his hands. "He went into the city to sell that little cow—"

He stops. His eyes fill behind his gold wire-rimmed glasses, and he begins to sob, openly, unabashedly, the memory of his father still fresh, and he, still that boy living on his father's farm. I put my hand on his knee. I am the interviewer, and only that distance keeps me from crumbling at the sight of my father weeping as I have never seen him do. He pats my hand, wipes his eyes.

"It's just that the memory of how hard he worked for us, how much he struggled, gets me emotional, *me emociona*," he says, forcing himself to speak through his own sobs. His voice becomes a whisper.

"He came back from town after three days . . . pulling our little cow behind him . . . We were all waiting for him." He stops, sobs. Continues. "He told us, 'I'm no good for anything. I couldn't even sell the cow.' "

My father lifts his glasses and wipes his face with both hands, covering it for a moment.

"When he got home, Felipe and Dania"—my father's brother and sister—"were waiting for him. They had each bought *un pedacito*, a lottery ticket. And while he was gone, they had both won."

Felipe and Dania each won five hundred dollars. The farm was saved. And their little milk cow returned to her stable.

When my father was twenty, he says, he got an opportunity to leave the farm. A man married to his first cousin opened a *bodega* in the town of Manzanillo. Pancho Frías encouraged his son to go, to find his own path, even though my father was his "right arm, *su brazo derecho*," and never to be afraid to come home if things didn't work out.

"But I had made a promise to myself," my father says. "I told myself I *was* going to be a businessman. And no matter what, I was never going to go backwards. Never. I was not going back to the farm. It didn't matter if I had to sleep on a dirt floor and go hungry."

And so he set off, with three changes of clothes, on the train to Manzanillo, a seaside town on the very western end of Oriente. On his first day there, he met up with his cousin Rafael, and together they visited two other cousins who also lived in town. While they were visiting one of those homes, my father's cousin told Rafael, "You'd better get going home before it gets dark, because we don't have anywhere for you to sleep."

"She said it loud enough so I could hear it. So I knew not to ask to stay there," my father explains. As he and Rafael walked across the town square while dusk became night, Rafael asked him where he planned to sleep.

"*Olvídate*, forget about that, Rafael. I'll just curl up right here in the park until I can find a place. Don't worry about me."

Rafael insisted he shouldn't sleep in the park but didn't offer to let him stay at his house. My father never would have asked. Rafael did, however, hand my father the key to a kiosk he had in the nearby plaza where he sold oranges by day.

My father unlocked the fruit stand and found several burlap sacks on the dirt floor. He pushed them into a pile and slept inches above the ground on the first night of his new life. At 5:00 A.M., the workers came in to open the stand, giving him his wake-up call. Eventually, he says, he fashioned a hammock out of the burlap sacks. That was his home for three months.

I watch my father tell the story, now reclined in a beige nylon hammock under the shade of a mango tree, swinging softly with the summer breeze, wearing a white cotton under-shirt to keep cool. He is wearing khaki shorts and sneakers, just like me.

When the cousin started grumbling that he was staying too long, my father moved in with an old man who had built a wooden shack onto his one-room home, where he lived with his two grown sons. My father was making only thirty pesos a month as a bicycle delivery boy at the *bodega* (although he had never ridden a bicycle before), and eating one square meal a day that cost him fifteen pesos a month at a nearby *fonda*. So he took his burlap hammock with him and, for eight pesos a month, moved into the house where he had to step around his sleeping roommates at night to use the outhouse. Sometimes, the old man didn't make it out of bed in time to use the bath-room, and my father would bail the floor with water in the mornings. He endured it all, holding to his own promise rather than go back to the farm.

Is that when you met Maribel?

Yes, he says. He rode past her house every day on the way to work. She came to visit from the Oriente city of Bayamo, which was farther east than his childhood home. She was a tall, shapely *mulata*, pretty, with kind eyes. They struck up a romance and went out several times. A few months went by, though, and he didn't see her.

"One day, she showed up at the *bodega*, with a *barriga*, a preg-nancy belly out to here," he says, sitting up from the hammock. "I immediately acknowledged her, 'Yes, the baby's mine. But what can *I* do for you?' I was barely able to take care of myself."

Because Maribel went back and forth to Bayamo, she passed right in front of the Frías farm in Veguita. "You could see the train station from my house," my father says, looking off as if he can still see it from his hammock. Maribel brought the girl to see her grandparents several times on her way to Manzanillo. My Tía Dania, the youngest of the eleven children, who would have been about ten years old, tells a story of seeing the girl, two or three at the time, looking through a window of the little farmhouse as rain fell on the coconut trees and yelling to my grandmother, "*Mima, Mima,* the coconuts are getting wet!"

For three years, my father continued working at the *bodega* in Manzanillo and living in the back room until his brother Ciro, who found enough work in Havana that he needed help with his delivery service, called my father to join him. He went off, and in the years that followed, all that Fidel Castro said was not possible for someone from the country became possible. My father and his brothers became businessmen. His sisters became college graduates in Havana. And my grandparents eventually joined them, leaving behind the farm, the countryside—and the little girl.

I thought you told me you saw her again.

"Not until years later," my father says, swinging slowly in the hammock, staring up at the porch ceiling.

In the spring of 1965, after Castro's revolution, while my father was working the counter at El Restaurante Oriental in La Plaza, a tall, beautiful girl escorted by a man in an olive military uniform asked him for Fernando Frías.

"I'm Fernando," he told her.

She hesitated for a moment.

"I'm Ana Ester," she replied. "I'm your daughter."

Ana Ester was eighteen and tall, "like your Tía Teresa," my father says, referring to the oldest of his siblings, a woman who, even at eighty-two, is nearly five foot ten, statuesque. The young woman wore a beige dress, pleated at the waist. And her dark curly hair, "like your brother's," contrasted with her hazel eyes and light caramel skin, "like yours," my father says. The man with her was her uncle. She asked for nothing. She had come just to meet him. Together, they drove to the family home in Marianao, where Ana Ester spent the day with her grandparents, *my* grandparents, and our father. As night fell, my father drove them to the bus station for the trip back to far-off Oriente. They hugged, kissed on the cheek. He told her to call him if she ever needed anything and promised they would see each other again.

A few months later, he and two of his brothers were arrested for trying to leave the island and sentenced to two years in La Cabaña. The very afternoon my grandparents got word that my father had been arrested, there was a knock at the door of their home in Marianao. My Tía Dania opened it to find a tall, caramel-skinned girl with her curvaceous figure hidden beneath olive green fatigues and her curly black hair tucked under a soldier's cap, olive with the red star of the revolution. She wore black combat boots and a pistol as a sidearm. Ana Ester had come looking to visit my father. My aunt broke the news to her, and she went away, stunned, with barely a word.

At one point, my grandfather came to visit my father at La Cabaña and told him he was thinking about acknowledging Ana Ester as his own and giving her the Frías name.

"That's why I told *Papá* to do whatever he thought was best. What good was my name going to do her?" my father says now.

He is swaying silently, and I have stopped writing. There is just one more question I need to ask. And yet, it is the hardest to form into sound. I whisper it.

Do you regret it?

He turns to look me in the eye as a row of papaya and coconut trees frame his serious expression.

"Of course. It was the foolishness of youth. I could have claimed her as mine. It's something I should have done," he says, as if enunciating a thought he has whispered to himself for years. "Today, here and now, I would have done things differently. It's something that weighs on me."

We are both silent for a few minutes, and I sip the last drops out of my beer.

'Papi,' if I ever get the chance to go back to Cuba, I think I'd like to try to find Ana Ester.

He swings, swings, nods.

"I'd be all right with that," he says.

Girlish laughter resounds. We look up to see my daughters pressing their faces to the sliding glass door. My father and I wave to them and laugh.

I tuck the blue notebook into my back pocket one last time.

"*Gracias, Papo,*" he says, as we head back inside. I put my head on his shoulder.

No, 'Viejo.' Thank you.

⌒

We are having *café con leche,* milk with Cuban coffee, and toasty, buttered Cuban bread at my parents' house. My mother is saying something about the roof that is about to fall in at my Tía Sofía's. She wants to ask my cousin Jorge how much it will cost to fix, so she can send money to help pay for it. She sits silently for a moment and looks up from her coffee.

"You know, if I had known . . ." she says, pausing. "If I had known I would never see my family again, I don't know if I could have made the decision to leave."

She stirs her drink silently as my father begins his trip down memory lane. It's a treacherous path, from the restaurants at La Plaza to the cells at La Cabaña. He is not crying, not emotional. It is just a truth for him. A truth I now know.

"No one can tell you stories anymore," my mother says, finishing her *café con leche.* "You've seen Cuba. Now, you know how things are."

They are speaking to me differently now. Not like the day I told my father I was going to Cuba during Castro's illness and he later blurted out to my wife, "How can the newspaper dare to send a boy into a situation like that?"

A boy.

I know them more deeply now. I understand them in a way I never have. And they look at me like I, too, know a deeper truth.

Author's Note

Alina is not Alina.

And Jorge is not Jorge.

Sofía is my Tía, but she is not Sofía.

It is not a riddle, but a sad fact: I can't tell you everything about my family.

I wish you could see them. I wish I could use their real names, publish their faces in pictures, instead of fearing for their lives if they are discovered to have spoken with me, their family, a foreigner, a writer. So I had to change their names. Sometimes, I changed the color of a house or the make of a car or the name of a street. I changed them because living in a totalitarian government, despite Raúl Castro's recent concessions, means speaking with one voice. The voice of Fidel Castro. But Castro would never say that my aunt is too thin. That parents, not politics, should help shape Isabel's young mind. That jailing my father was the real crime.

But in Cuba, there are many voices, voices that the government would rather not be heard. So I am forced to disguise them.

Yet I hope that if you meet any of them one day, you will recognize them clearly from their stories.

ACKNOWLEDGMENTS

I never believed I could write this book.
A book.

Any book.

I considered it something like landing on the moon. It was Christine Martínez de Castro Frías who made me believe. She, my wife who I kept up at night with my bouts of insecurity, who wouldn't read the manuscript until it was complete so I wouldn't question myself. She was ever so confident in my ability that my self-doubt infuriated her. She managed to be my rock, my twin moon, as she always has been, while holding down the dueling job of working mother of three. She says she, herself, could never write a book. But I disagree. I think she can do anything.

Yes, my 'Lind,' you told me so.

As much as I relied on Christy's patience and support as I put this book together, one person helped shape it as much as any character in it. Bill Greer, my editor at *The Palm Beach Post* and in these pages, sat me on the proverbial therapist's couch and made me explore every memory, every feeling, every sight, and every sound. And if the words sing at any point, it is because his keen ear discerned the melody.

I have to thank my bosses at *The Post*, who not only blessed this project but made it possible. There are excerpts from my five-day series in the paper sprinkled throughout, and that made the writing

Acknowledgments

easier. I will never live long enough to thank our editor in chief, John Bartosek; managing editor, Bill Rose; deputy managing editor, Tim Burke; and my sports editor, Nick Moschella, sufficiently for thinking of me when they decided to send teams into Cuba. It was these men who made telling the story of my life possible, and for that, I am eternally grateful.

My friend Liz Balmaseda, as beautiful a writer as I will ever be lucky enough to know, shoved this story in front of her editor at Atria, the ever-patient Johanna Castillo, and my very capable agents, "the Erics," Rover in Miami and Lupfer in New York. They took me on and made a dream a reality. So, too, did my friend John Manasso, who showed me the dedication and guts it takes to make writing a book go from a passing thought to black and white.

If my parents are proud today, my "other" parents, *mis suegros*, are beaming just as brightly. Never has anyone believed so surely in something as my mother-in-law, Ileana Martínez de Castro, has in me. And never has anyone provided me food and toilet paper so dutifully as my father-in-law, Orlando. (That bit of encouragement along the way didn't hurt, either, Old Man.)

If you learned just one thing in these pages, it is that my family is intensely private, incredibly close, and airing dirty laundry is not in our vernacular. So thank you to my *tías* and *tíos*: Teresa Suarez; Rafael and Antonia Frías; Georgelina and Julio Portales; Ramón and Gladys Frías; Ciro and Edita Frías; Felipe and Teresita Frías; Aida and Nene Vega; and Dania and Mario Pendas. And to my *primos*, my adoptive brothers and sisters who breathed life into those nights at Abuela Teresa's house: Ray, Jesus, and Frank; Flip and Lil; Ciro and Edylin; and the "Tampa cousins": Kiki; Robert and Eileen; and Soli, Danita and Mayitín. Thank you for your patience and strength in absorbing facts that, I know, were difficult to bear. But our past is our past, and it makes us who we are.

That's why *Mami* and I were so hard on you, Elise, Amelia, and Catalina, about speaking to us in Spanish. This is your history. This is who you are. And your language is part of that connection.

No te entiendo nada. ¡Háblame en español! I can't understand a word you're saying. Speak to me in Spanish!

Acknowledgments

And I thank my parents, Fernando and Iraida, for their bravery, not just forty years ago but in every day they fought for a new life here, for themselves, for me. They are the heroes who make writing about them such a treat and such a responsibility all the same. Thanks, *Mami*, for offering to lend me money to publish this book even as I tried to tell you *they* were paying *me* to write it. Unconditional support: That's a mother's love. My mother, my number one fan.

I told my father he was crazy when he kept insisting years ago that I should write about his life. I guess I was wrong.

'*Tú lo sabias, Viejo.*'

You knew it, all along.

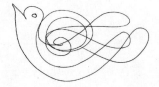